Cultivating Cosmopolitanism for Intercultural Communication

This book engages the notion of cosmopolitanism as it applies to intercultural communication, which itself has been undergoing a turn in its focus from postpositivistic research towards critical/interpretive and postcolonial perspectives, particularly as globalization informs more of the current and future research in the area. It emphasizes the postcolonial perspective in order to raise critical consciousness about the complexities of intercultural communication in a globalizing world, situating cosmopolitanism—the notion of global citizenship—as a multilayered lens for research. Cosmopolitanism as a theoretical repertoire provides nuanced descriptions of what it means to be and communicate as a global citizen, how to critically study interconnectedness within and across cultures, and how to embrace differences without glossing over them. Moving intercultural communication studies towards the global in complex and nuanced ways, this book highlights crucial links between globalization, transnationalism, postcolonialism, cosmopolitanism, social justice and intercultural communication, and will help in the creation of classroom spaces devoted to exploring these links. It also engages the links between theory and praxis in order to move towards intercultural communication pedagogy and research that simultaneously celebrates and interrogates issues of cultural difference with the aim of creating continuity rather than chasms. In sum, this book orients intercultural communication scholarship firmly towards the critical and postcolonial, while still allowing the incorporation of traditional intercultural communication concepts, thereby preparing students, scholars, educators and interculturalists to communicate ethically in a world that is simultaneously global and local.

Miriam Sobré-Denton is assistant professor in the Department of Speech Communication at Southern Illinois University—Carbondale, USA.

Nilanjana Bardhan is associate professor in the Department of Speech Communication at Southern Illinois University—Carbondale, USA.

Routledge Studies in Rhetoric and Communication

Cultivating Cosmopolitanism for Intercultural Communication

Communicating as Global Citizens

Miriam Sobré-Denton
and Nilanjana Bardhan

Routledge
Taylor & Francis Group

NEW YORK   LONDON

First published 2013
by Routledge
711 Third Avenue, New York, NY 10017

Simultaneously published in the UK
by Routledge
2 Park Square, Milton Park, Abingdon, Oxon OX14 4RN

*Routledge is an imprint of the Taylor & Francis Group,
an informa business*

© 2013 Taylor & Francis

The right of Miriam Sobré-Denton and Nilanjana Bardhan to be identified
as authors of this work has been asserted by them in accordance with
sections 77 and 78 of the Copyright, Designs and Patents Act 1988.

Library of Congress Cataloging-in-Publication Data
Sobré-Denton, Miriam, 1976–
    Cultivating cosmopolitanism for intercultural communication :
communicating as global citizens / by Miriam Sobré-Denton & Nilanjana
Bardhan.
        pages cm. — (Routledge studies in rhetoric and communication ; 15)
    Includes bibliographical references and index.
    1. Intercultural communication.   2. Cosmopolitanism.   3. Culture and
communication.   4. Culture and globalization.   I. Title.
    GN345.6.S63 2013
    303.48'2—dc23
    2013000839

ISBN13: 978-0-415-65610-8 (hbk)
ISBN13: 978-0-203-07815-0 (ebk)

Typeset in Sabon
by IBT Global.

SUSTAINABLE FORESTRY INITIATIVE
Certified Sourcing
www.sfiprogram.org
SFI-01234
SFI label applies to the text stock

Printed and bound in the United States of America
by IBT Global.

Preservation of one's own culture does not require contempt or disrespect for other cultures.

Cesar Chavez

Imagination is more important than knowledge. Knowledge is limited. Imagination encircles the world.

Albert Einstein

We cannot trample upon the humanity of others without devaluing our own.

Chinua Achebe

Contents

Foreword

From the inception of the formal disciplinary study of intercultural communication (a response to real and practical problems of intercultural challenges and projects), scholars have searched in different ways with different epistemologies and methodologies to understand and identify attitudes, behaviors and practices that facilitate human interactions across cultural boundaries, including ways of seeing and interacting with culturally different Others (Leeds-Hurwitz, 1990, 2010). For example, there was scholarship in the 1960s and 1970s that promoted the notion of the "universal man" (Walsh, 1973) and "multicultural man" (sic),—a 'new' type of individual who was equally at home in many different cultural contexts (Adler, 1977), and "cosmopolitans" (someone oriented to the world and local community) (Gouldner, 1957, 1958; Lammers, 1974). In addition to these 'types' of 'men,' scholars also identified attitudinal stances that facilitated intercultural interaction, e.g., "overseasmanship" (Cleveland, Mangone, & Adams, 1960) and "world-mindedness" (Sampson & Smith, 1957). These concepts grew out of and reflected the scholarly focus on the experiences of U. S. American business(men) and diplomats engaged in post WWII rebuilding in Europe and Asia, those privileged enough to travel in relative ease to foreign places. They did not reflect the intercultural experiences of cultural groups struggling against oppression and marginalization (Cooks, 2001).

Over the next 40 years, intercultural communication studies proliferated, often attempting to theorize and measure attitudes and behaviors that led to facilitating successful intercultural encounters, including intercultural competence/effectiveness, adaptation, empathy, third culture building, intercultural personhood, to name a few. Theorizing became more sophisticated, and the scholarship more inclusive—a variety of epistemologies, paradigms and methodologies were accepted and promoted. There were important changes, including the move from an atheoretical to a functionalist paradigmatic perspective in the 1980s (Moon, 1996), the important move to more critical/interpretive positions in the 1990s (Halualani, Mendoza, & Drzewiecka, 2009), as well as recent postcolonial approaches (Shome & Hegde, 2002).

Where are we now? From my vantage point after almost 40 years in the discipline, it seems to me that we have made great progress from those early days of the "universal man" and the "cosmopolitan." Intercultural communication scholarship is more inclusive—in theory, values and methods. Critical and postcolonial scholars encourage us to conceptualize culture as fluid and dynamic rather than as static 'nation-state' entities, and to consider the important role of history and political, social and economic power imbalances and the intercultural experiences of those struggling against oppression and marginalization (Nakayama & Halualani, 2010).

However, the nature of intercultural encounters has changed dramatically in the last 50 years, and "people from around the globe with different cultural, racial, national, economic, and linguistic backgrounds are coming into contact with each other; . . . developing relationships and struggling through conflicts; building alliances and activist networks, . . . more intensely, and with greater impact today than ever before" (Sorrells, 2013, pp. 26–27). This age of postcolonial globality presents several challenges to our scholarship that remain unaddressed. The pendulum has swung from rather naïve beliefs in the possibility of the universal 'man' of the early postpositivists to the more nuanced, contested, context-driven and critical approach. However, critical and postcolonial scholarship often struggles with offering *accessible perspectives* and *pragmatic guidance* for *actually engaging with intercultural others*—across divides of race, class, gender, as well as nationality—and collaborating to contest problematic and oppressive power structures and communicative practices. In addition, there have been few scholars who have addressed the *ethical challenges* that arise in communicative encounters across cultures. In sum, the question facing intercultural communication scholars now is—*how do we live a hopeful, ethical and just intercultural life in an era of postcolonial globality?* This is the broad question that Miriam and Nilanjana address, and in their attempt, they effectively meet the challenges of twenty-first century intercultural communication scholarship.

But first a little background—how did we get from 'cosmopolitan' to 'cosmopolitanism'? Barnett Pearce is credited with (re)introducing the notion to the communication field in the 1980s (Stewart, 2008), and communication scholars have turned once again to cosmopolitanism as a viable philosophical stance that addresses the 'big' questions. The cosmopolitanism of the twenty-first century is much more complex, more dialogic, and more interested in social justice than the 'cosmopolitans' in earlier scholarship. In a recent edited book, *Communication Ethics: Between Cosmopolitanism and Provinciality* (Roberts & Arnett, 2008), communication scholars explore the ethical issues of the tensions identified by Appiah (2006): the tension between the global and the local, i.e., the "obligations we have to others beyond those to whom we are related by kith and kind . . ." and that we also need to "take seriously the value of particular lives, take interest in the practices and beliefs that lend them significance" (p. xv). More specifically, how do we engage in ethical dialogue with Others? After exploring the ethical issues by engaging various philosophies and the consequent implications for communication practices in general, Roberts and Arnett, in their afterword, admit that for some (especially intercultural communication scholars) the question remains: Is cosmopolitanism "simply modernity masquerading under another garb?" and "is humanity a single moral community?" (p. 285). In a way, these questions are the starting point for Miriam and Nilanjana's book. As they extend Roberts and Arnett's (2008) work and approach cosmopolitanism from an intercultural communication vantage point, they systematically and effectively refute the charges that cosmopolitanism is necessarily an elitist, Eurocentric and modernist concept and then set out to show how cosmopolitanism, as a macro framework and ethical vision for the planet, functions as a "philosophical net" that holds together and helps articulate views from a variety of disciplines and voices within conditions of "postcolonial globality," and intertwined with recent scholarship in intercultural communication, can lay a way of understanding how "humans may forge meaningful intercultural connections through everyday mundane interactions" (p. 6).

Miriam and Nilanjana embrace the *ethical* mandate of Appiah's (2006) cosmopolitanism, where human beings, "in all our cultural complexities and not despite them, matter and that this mattering *needs to be an inherent part of how we communicate across cultural differences*—as critical global citizens" (p. 13, italics added). They demonstrate how *difference* is at the core—both of intercultural communication and cosmopolitanism, and show how intercultural communication (influenced by cosmopolitanism) can help us move beyond the traditional view of cultural differences as absolute and negative, and see that difference is something which we all do and can do in new ways, opening up the possibility then of entering into the "in-between with others to work through and negotiate our differences in a manner that promises more hope, empathy and creativity" (p. 43). Thus, drawing from dialogic approaches as well as a dialectic view where difference is not always a negative but a reality charged with "ambiguity, pregnant with possibility and open to dialogue" (p. 47), they unpack the symbiotic relationship of cosmopolitanism and intercultural communication and show that together they yield the rich concept of "cosmopolitan communication."

With these ethical and hopeful foundations clearly established, Miriam and Nilanjana show how critical and postcolonial views of identity (as intersectional, dynamic, negotiated and performative), interwoven with the cosmopolitan notions of dialogic interplay of the Self, Other and the World, and a mode of critical *self-transformation*, pushes us towards a sense of belonging that is thoroughly interdependent with the cultural Other. Through such a sense of Self, cultural Other and belonging, they bring in the notion of intercultural bridgework and emphasize the importance of forming collective alliances across differences through cosmopolitan communication. Working off of Appiah's (2006) call to perform "kindness to strangers" both near and far (because they are us), they explain that it "requires an intelligent form of empathy and an informed moral outlook" to perform such kindness (p. 86). Then they offer us their concept of "cosmopolitan peoplehood." This concept emphasizes cosmopolitan solidarity and critical self-transformation. Miriam and Nilanjana are careful in explaining how their notions of cosmopolitan communication and cosmopolitan peoplehood are not just a reordering of existing intercultural communication concepts and models, and that they offer something different.

After establishing the conceptual framework for critical cosmopolitan communication and peoplehood, the next sections of the book show how this framework can guide and inform intercultural communication research—both as *method* and *phenomenon* of study. This discussion is particularly apt as it answers the call for research processes that transcend paradigm "silos" and embrace dialectical and multi-paradigmatic perspectives (Martin & Nakayama, 1999, 2010).

By offering various interdisciplinary examples of studies engaging cosmopolitanism, Miriam and Nilanjana offer us exactly what is needed now in our research—a conceptual framework that works across and in dialectic multi-paradigmatic perspectives. They then illustrate exactly how this can work by describing Miriam's research-in-progress with Hostelling International—Chicago that utilizes the framework outlined here and the notions of cosmopolitan communication and cosmopolitan peoplehood. In addition, they present seven research examplars, research articles that demonstrate specifically how cosmopolitanism could be integrated both empirically and theoretically into intercultural communication scholarship. Finally, being teachers as well as scholars of intercultural communication, they offer suggestions for a program of cosmopolitan pedagogy for intercultural communication.

Cultivating Cosmopolitanism for Intercultural Communication is a very important work. It is unique and groundbreaking, both paradigmatically and theoretically. Building on current scholarship in intercultural communication, it points to the future of our field by offering a hopeful vision for scholars who seek to understand how we all can live an *ethical and just intercultural life in an era of postcolonial globality.*

Judith N. Martin
December 6, 2012

Acknowledgments

Over the past five years, we have both read deeply on the topic of cosmopolitanism. The more we read, the more we realized how much this literature resonated with our own lived experiences as cultural and human beings who have negotiated borders throughout our lives. These negotiations have been (and continue to be) joyful as well as difficult. Borders have been, for us, spaces we feel personally invested in, spaces where we often find home. Borders are spaces of critique, ethical vision, possibility and hope. Cosmopolitanism, for us, is a cultural philosophy for living and communicating as ethical human beings in a world that is simultaneously local and global and chock-full of borders. We felt it was time to begin building a bridge between intercultural communication and cosmopolitanism, a bridge that we hope will open up more pathways to theorizing and researching what it means to communicate, relate and strive towards social justice as people who share the same planet rather than just inhabit distinct nation-states. Fortunately, we were able to receive help from various amazing individuals during this process. This book would not have been possible without the following contributors, colleagues, friends and advisors.

Special thanks go to Judith Martin for writing the foreword, and to Devika Chawla and Amardo Rodriguez for reviewing the first draft of the manuscript. Special thanks also go to Youna Kim, Melissa Curtin, Eva María González Barea, Jane Jackson, James Petre and Jay Brower for letting us describe and reference their work. Miriam would particularly like to thank her students from her cosmopolitanism class for their contributions: Robert Carlsen, Nathan Columbo, Milica Obretkovich, Carlye Schweska, Jana Simonis, Ryan Trone, Ashley Wahlgren and David Whitfield. She would also like to thank her contacts at Hostelling International (HI) Chicago, particularly Arielle Semmel, Megan Johnson and Kat Morgan, as well as Robert Carlsen and Veronica Gruel, both of whom worked as assistants on the HI project. Nilanjana would like to thank Craig Engstrom for being a supportive and understanding partner, Tee Ford-Ahmed for being a cosmopolitan soul par excellence, Ronald Pelias for his support and encouragement, and Jolanta Drzewiecka for providing challenging and thoughtful critiques. Finally, we thank Charlotte Cline-Smith for working on the index, and we extend our gratitude to our editor, Elizabeth J. Levine, at Taylor and Francis, and to the anonymous reviewers who saw promise in our initial proposal.

Introduction

Another world is possible if . . . (George, 2004)

inequality

Globalization, or more accurately neoliberal globalization, fueled by advances in travel and communication technologies, has compressed time and space to the extent that it is now more possible to imagine the world as one whole entity (Featherstone, 1995; Giddens, 1990; Harvey, 1989). At the same time, despite much technological progress and the effusive promotion of market ideology as the solution for a better planet, our world remains a vastly uneven place. It is a place where some cultures and countries continue to benefit at the expense of others. Within countries, the disparities between the privileged and the marginalized continue to widen.

But what if another world was possible, one where we value difference, shun oppression of the cultural Other, strive for peace, work collectively to protect the earth as a single entity, build intercultural alliances for social and global justice, engage more in difficult intercultural dialogues and believe in the importance of communicating ethically and critically as global citizens? The heartening news is that there is evidence, from the past and the present, that humans around the world are capable of valuing such values and engaging in such praxes. Therefore, we must continue to invest our energies in discussing how we can make this kind of a world the greater reality.

Since globalization is here to stay (actually, it has been with us for a long time), we need to think carefully about what kind of globalization we want for the future and chart out ways to steer its processes in directions that will do more good than harm (Krishna, 2009; Ritzer, 2007). As intercultural communication scholars, we can look for some ways to accomplish this within our own field. Communication is action, and it can transform perceptions and bring about change for the sake of social and global justice. But first we need to ask what it means to communicate ethically and critically across cultural differences as global citizens. In this book, we use cultural cosmopolitanism as an ethical and philosophical framework through which we may envision intercultural communication for a better world.

We have wondered why the communication discipline, specifically intercultural communication, has paid scant attention to the promise of cosmopolitanism and its ethical vision. Have the sharp critiques leveled at cosmopolitanism that are wary of the potential of any seemingly universalizing concept to generate oppressive master narratives convinced us that it is a path not worth pursuing (Commisiong, 2012)? Is cosmopolitanism really as Eurocentric a vision as many argue it is (see Chapter 1)? Or is it because our theorizing of difference has been too negative, oppositional and absolute, and we are unable to veer away from such ways of thinking? We make the case in this book that in its current revised postcolonial and critical form, cosmopolitanism is not a Eurocentric philosophy (masquerading as a universal) that imposes a particular set of ideas that threatens exclusion or attempts to erase national/local particularities. The new cosmopolitanism has a different approach to universals.

As Terry Eagleton writes, "The universal . . . is not some realm of abstract duty set sternly against the particular . . . " (1990, p. 415). Similarly, Seyla Benhabib (2002) argues against extreme reactions against universalism, and proposes instead a pluralistic, ethical and enlightened approach to universalism. Rather than thinking in terms of a universal–particular binary, we prefer to think of cosmopolitanism as an outwardly-directed ethical imperative that weaves together particulars for a moral vision that is planetary in scope. It is an imperative that works at a level higher than the purely particularistic with the vision of building connections and solidarity across cultural differences. As philosopher and leading scholar of cosmopolitanism Kwame Anthony Appiah (2006) writes in his book *Cosmopolitanism: Ethics in a World of Strangers*, those who engage with cosmopolitanism " . . . suppose that all cultures have enough overlap in their vocabulary of values to begin a conversation. But they don't suppose, like some universalists, that we could all come to agreement if only we had the same vocabulary" (p. 57).

Cosmopolitanism helps us get to the heart of some of the central concerns within the field of intercultural communication—culture, difference, power, identity and the need for alliance-building across differences—and it does so by questioning divisive cultural boundaries and nation-state-centric thinking. We live and communicate within nation-states, across nation-states, and within the flows and disjunctures of a larger interconnected world (Appadurai, 1996). The time is ripe for exploring the potential of the cosmopolitan moral vision in intercultural communication within the context of globalization, and that is our endeavor in writing this book.

GLOBALIZATION AND POSTCOLONIALISM

Globalization is centuries old. It has existed in various phases and forms since humans started traveling for the purposes of trade, war, colonization and religious proselytization. There is no single narrative for globalization. While discourses of Western modernity might want to label globalization as progress, the postcolonial view sees globalization as steeped in colonial violence, European (and later U.S.) hegemony, and economic and cultural imperialism. Capitalism, enmeshed with the politics of colonialism, grew alongside Europe's expansion into the rest of the world (Chakrabarty, 2007). These two narratives of globalization exist side-by-side today with the former being dominant, and postcolonialism's political project is to remind us of the continuing effects of centuries of European colonization of territories and knowledge production, as well as resist "the inequalities, exploitation of humans and the environment, and the diminution of political and ethical choices that come in the wake of [neoliberal] globalization" (Krishna, 2009, p. 2). If we connect the two narratives, it would be appropriate to say that today we live in conditions of postcolonial globality (Shome & Hegde, 2002).

The last three decades have seen the immense speeding up of neoliberal globalization. While it is possible to describe globalization from economic, political and cultural perspectives, we are inclined towards Sorrells' (2013) description, which aptly captures an intercultural communication view. According to Sorrells, globalization is a:

> . . . dynamic movement, confluence, and interconnections of peoples, cultures, markets, and relationships of power that are rooted in history and yet are redefined and rearticulated in our current global age. Through advances in technology—and open markets, people from around the globe with different cultural, racial, national, economic, and linguistic backgrounds are coming into contact with each other; consuming each others' cultural foods, products and identities; developing relationships and struggling through conflicts; building alliances and activist networks, and laboring with and for each other more frequently, more intensely, and with greater impact today than ever before. (2013, pp. 26–27).

Sorrells' description also reminds us that we need to problematize how we think about culture and communication within conditions of postcolonial globality.

We can no longer conceptualize culture and communication in static, bounded and nation-state-centric ways. We have to think more in terms of cultural deterritorialization and reterritorialization, hybridity and complex relations between the local and the global. Since the meanings and workings of the nation-state have changed along with heightened globalization, we can no longer simplistically equate country with culture (a predominant tendency in everyday conversations as well as in the social sciences). Culture and cultural ideas and ideologies "travel," to use historian James Clifford's term, with people and through the global mediascape, and cultures keep reconfiguring through interactions within such movements (Appadurai, 1996; Clifford, 1992; Hannerz, 1996). This is a space-based rather than a place-based view of culture and cultural flows. The politics that attempt to fix or freeze culture can be of many types (including strategically essentialist efforts described by postcolonial scholars such as Gayatri Spivak), but any kind of essentialism that harms Others is problematic. In this climate of traveling cultures, we have to become comfortable with the tension between the need to fix and to make sure that culture and identity do not become hegemonic traps (Carrillo Rowe, 2005). Furthermore, culture needs to be seen as being more about difference and how we perform difference in relation to the cultural Other. According to Appadurai (1996):

> Culture is not usefully regarded as a substance but is better regarded as a dimension of phenomena, a dimension that attends to situated and embodied difference. Stressing the dimensionality of culture rather than its substantiality permits our thinking of culture less as a property of individuals and groups and more as a heuristic device that we can use to talk about difference. (pp. 12–13)

Similar arguments about "culture-as-difference" rather than as separate homogenous entities have been made by Bhabha (1996a). This view of culture in relation to difference is one which we subscribe to in the context of postcolonial globality. It is a view that helps us understand that culture is always hard at work through difference within proliferating intercultural spaces which may be actual, virtual or mediated (Shome & Hegde, 2002). An "intercultural space," according to Pearson-Evans and Leahy (2007), is a space:

> . . . where conventional norms and values can no longer be taken for granted, where there is the opportunity, and often the necessity, to challenge unexamined assumptions and existing structures. . . . [such spaces] provide a meeting point for diverse ways of interpreting and being in the world. . . . [and they are spaces where] difference is the norm, with minorities and outsiders taking centre stage, and challenging the status quo and majority beliefs and values. (pp. xv–xvi)

Intercultural spaces are not specialized spaces; they increasingly exist in mundane and everyday ways, and they exhort us to see the importance of becoming critical and ethical global citizens in a cultural and communicative sense.

The notion of citizenship is usually tied to the nation-state or states and provinces within nation-states. This is the political view of citizenship. There is another view, the cultural and social one, which is well-equipped to serve intercultural communication. According to the cultural and social view, global citizenship is deeply linked to social and global justice and is not simply a vague awareness of the world. Those engaging in global citizenship do not partake in any collective decision or communicative act that helps some cultures benefit at the expense of others. They respect and value diversity, are outraged by social and global injustices, attempt to figure out how their own actions (including communication) can make a difference, have an educated understanding of the complex ways in which the world works, and see themselves as meaningfully belonging to that world. Critical and ethical global citizens take responsibility for their actions, are able to navigate the nexus of the local and the global, and engage in action likely to actualize social and global justice goals (Davies, 2006).

According to McIntosh, global citizenship is based in the idea of human "needs" rather than "rights" and involves seeing plurally, intricately understanding power systems and diverse cultural locations, and working from the heart to validate others without losing one's own sense of integrity (cited in Sorrells, 2013). Critical global citizens do not work to 'save' less fortunate cultural Others. They work *with* Others as allies with the willingness to be critically transformed themselves (Andreotti, 2006). Becoming a global citizen does not mean giving up local or national cultural affiliations (see Chapter 8 for details on our view of global citizenship in relation to cosmopolitanism and cosmopolitan pedagogy).

COSMOPOLITANISM

The idea of global citizenship naturally brings us to cosmopolitanism. According to Delanty (2012): "In the broadest sense possible, cosmopolitanism is about the extension of the moral and political horizons of people, societies, organizations and institutions. It implies an attitude of openness as opposed to closure" (p. 2). Over the last two decades, there has been a surge in scholarly debates and publications within the intellectual area of cosmopolitanism. Authors from various disciplines such as anthropology, sociology and political philosophy have demonstrated renewed interest in this concept that promises hope for a world increasingly connected through technology, media and travel, and yet plagued by continuing neocolonial and postcolonial inequities, social and global injustices, terrorism, poverty, ethnic conflicts and wars. There is a growing realization that we live in world where we must find ways to address problems that are global in scope and *cannot be solved by any one country or group of people alone*, e.g., environmental degradation, global warming, world hunger, arms proliferation, terrorism and so on. For this to occur, we must find ways to communicate within expanding intercultural spaces as global citizens who are able to think, communicate and expand their cultural horizons in world-oriented ways while simultaneously maintaining local and national attachments. Here we provide just a brief overview of cosmopolitanism and its usefulness since the first two chapters of the book delve into the details.

Cosmopolitanism, or the notion of belonging to a world larger than our own localities, has been debated by philosophers and scholars for millennia. However, the more recent critical and postcolonial turn within cosmopolitan thought provides an opportunity for fleshing out a vision and role for intercultural communication in the project of interrupting the hegemonic directions of neoliberal globalization. Briefly, for us, cosmopolitanism functions as a philosophical net that holds together and helps articulate views from postcolonial and cultural studies, sociology, anthropology and education, and in so doing enables a cosmopolitan intercultural perspective for communicating within conditions of postcolonial globality. Similar to Appiah (2006), we do not see cosmopolitanism as some "grand accomplishment" but as a way of understanding how humans may forge meaningful intercultural connections through everyday mundane interactions and communication.

Similarly, there is no grand definition of cosmopolitanism. Trying to define cosmopolitanism is like trying to bottle air, and we feel this is actually a good thing. Concretely defining cosmopolitanism would actually be an obstruction in the way of its outward and unfolding vision. It is heuristic to think of cosmopolitanism as a philosophy, an attitude and orientation, and a moral standpoint (Roudometof, 2005) for being, growing and relating with the cultural Other in this ever-changing world: "Cosmopolitanism provides an alternate portrait of human beings as always-changing and as members of always-changing communities" (Commissiong, 2012, p. 2). Most importantly, for us, cosmopolitanism is an inherently intercultural and communicative philosophy. We share here a description that clearly illustrates why. According to Kurasawa (2011), cosmopolitanism:

> . . . signifies a capacity for multiperspectivism, that is to say, to move between and be able to decode a wide array of divergent socio-cultural practices and belief systems, as well as to be familiar with the self-understandings of various groups across the world. . . . such a cosmopolitan outlook seeks to translate seemingly incommensurable cultural frameworks to make them mutually intelligible. (p. 279)

Cosmopolitanism emphasizes Self–Other mutuality and the need to humanely forge meaningful communicative connections through empathy and with respect for difference. According to Mota (2012), "cosmopolitanism puts at the center of the human condition respect within and between peoples" (p. 491). Postcolonial and critical cosmopolitanism has a clear agenda—to fuel globalization from below (see Chapter 1). By problematizing the hegemony of the nation-state, which is a structure and system that actually aids neoliberal globalization and keeps unjust power hierarchies in place, critical cosmopolitanism encourages subnational, transnational and translocal (local-to-local) voices to emerge and push back against inequities and marginalization (Mignolo, 2000; Ono, 2010). Critical cosmopolitanism is dead set against nativisms and fundamentalisms that hurt already disadvantaged communities and cultures.

A key value of cosmopolitanism is what Nava (2007) calls "a positive engagement with difference" (p. 5). This does not mean playing down or exoticizing differences; rather, it means valuing and engaging with difference in complex ways that embrace the hope for good outcomes and intercultural learning. Like Appiah (1996), we do not equate cosmopolitanism with flat humanism where differences are downplayed, because cosmopolitanism "celebrates the fact that there are different local human ways of being, while humanism is consistent with the desire for global homogeneity" (Appiah, 2006, p. 25). What cosmopolitanism is not (and what it is often accused of being), according to van Hooft (2009), is:

—a quest for a single global culture, language, or religion;
—following of international fashion trends in an urban café society;
—growth in tourism and international travel;
—consumer interest in exotic products, clothes, world music and so on;
—Western liberalism with a global agenda;
—the imposition of Western morality in the form of moral universalism.

(pp. 13–14)

Instead, critical cosmopolitanism entails a deep appreciation for difference, the willingness to engage with cultural Others and be transformed by such experiences, kindness towards strangers, and the labor of the imagination to envision a world that aspires towards peace, possibilities and intercultural respect for those near and far. Thus cosmopolitanism is a planetary and moral vision that can help us move towards a world where we can be better intercultural neighbors and collectively look out for the wellbeing of the earth and its inhabitants.

Here we would like to alert our reader that the resurgent interest in cosmopolitanism has spawned a variety of labels related to cosmopolitanism such as vernacular cosmopolitanism, rooted cosmopolitanism, critical cosmopolitanism, discrepant cosmopolitanism and so on. To these labels we have added some of our own (such as *cosmopolitan communication* and *cosmopolitan peoplehood*). To reduce confusion and clarify these various labels, we have included a glossary for cosmopolitanism at the end of the book.

COSMOPOLITANISM AND INTERCULTURAL COMMUNICATION

The field of intercultural communication has produced much knowledge over the last 60 years about culture, communication and the dynamics of interacting with those who are culturally different from us. However, a major gap remains, and it must be addressed so we may respond to today's conditions of postcolonial globality. This gap is two-fold: First, its U.S. roots and the proclivity to draw mainly from Eurocentric knowledge bases keeps the field intellectually parochial, so to speak (Asante, 1980; Miike, 2003). Second, while much has been studied within the context of the U.S. and other countries, there remains a curious divide between "intercultural" and "international" communication; the assumption seems to be that there is some type of difference between the two (Shome, 2010). In a way, this assumption suggests that we are too ingrained in the habit of equating country with culture (and scholarship), something that cosmopolitanism terms "methodological nationalism" (Beck, 2006). We cannot afford this gap in our field if we are to make our work relevant from postcolonial and global perspectives. Sorrells' (2013) recent textbook provides a breath of fresh air in articulating intercultural communication from a critical globalization perspective. Other scholars working through postcolonial and critical global perspectives have also been making this call, especially over the last decade (e.g., Kraidy, 2005; Shome & Hegde, 2002). Recent work on cosmopolitanism is chock-full of contributions by scholars with diverse and hybrid cultural/country affiliations and who, in this sense, speak from multiple spaces around the world. We feel that in building planetary (not the same as homogenizing or Eurocentric) theoretical visions, intercultural communication can gain much from cosmopolitanism scholarship and its diverse voices.

The more recent critical turn in intercultural communication has also opened the door to cosmopolitanism by bringing up the issue that the field, for too long, has simplistically equated the nation-state with culture (Halualani, Mendoza, & Drzewiecka, 2009; Ono, 1998). Methodological nationalism shapes how we study other identity markers within intercultural communication, e.g., gender, race, religion, sexuality and so on. It stops us from clearly seeing the historical overlaps and continuities. This is not the same as saying that we should do away with national perspectives—it means that the national perspective should be of the kind that does not foreclose the vision of cosmopolitanism (Taylor, 1996) and allows us to understand the complexities of the global in the local and the local in the global. This is where cosmopolitanism, in its postcolonial form, can make a significant contribution. Furthermore, while it is crucial to carefully study how culture and communication are constrained by power, context and ideology, we need to further explore and theorize how people are still able to work together, with hope, across cultural and national borders to accomplish social and global justice goals. This means we have to find ways to theorize multiple differences outside the constraints of methodological nationalism and question if what we currently have in our theoretical toolbox is sufficient. The more recent scholarship on intersectionality and intercultural alliance-building is a hopeful movement in this direction, and we feel that this is one area to which the cosmopolitan moral and planetary vision can make a contribution (see Chapter 3).

In order to join cosmopolitanism with intercultural communication, we need to make careful decisions about how we approach culture and communication (our approach to culture has been explained in the section on globalization and postcolonialism). Along with viewing culture through the dimensions of mobility and difference, a transcendent and dialogic approach to communication is needed. The transcendent view sees communication as "*the simultaneous experience of the self and other*" through which one may transcend one's current self in order to become more than that through interaction with another (Shepherd, 2006, p. 22, italics in original). This is a dynamic, empowering and ethical view of communication which works well in relation to cosmopolitanism. According to Shepherd, this view is for those "who understand that identities are never fixed, but are rather under constant re-creation . . . " (2006, p. 28). A dialogic approach to communication complements the transcendent view. It focuses on what is produced in the spaces 'in-between' people during communication. It sees difference as the pivotal dynamic within the communication process, and as the source for the creation of meaning and new possibilities (Baxter, 2006). Together the transcendent and the dialogical views of communication enable us to think about cultural identities as ongoing productions which are capable of change and transformation (see Chapters 3 and 4). Such a view of identity and the Self in relation to the cultural Other, we argue, is central to the cosmopolitan vision and way of "being and becoming" (Hall, 1990).

In sum, cosmopolitanism can help us add the layer of critical global citizenship to all our other intersecting layers of identities, and bring a planetary moral vision to intercultural communication scholarship and praxis. It can teach us the meaning of "world belongingness" (Delanty, 2009) which is needed if we are to believe that we can indeed make another world possible through how we communicate and relate. As de Turk (2006) notes, " . . . possibilities for social change, to the extent that they exist, do so at the level of language or communication" (pp. 35–36). According to Cooks (2001), morality and intercultural communication are deeply tied, and how we engage with and perform difference involves moral decisions. She emphasizes that intercultural communication, as a field, needs to "develop a theoretical approach towards respect, ethics, and responsibility across differences" (Cooks, 2001, p. 339)—and to this we add that such theorizing needs to take the whole world into consideration. Cosmopolitanism is an ideal candidate to guide us in this direction.

ORGANIZATION OF THE BOOK

The first four chapters of this book form a theoretical unit. Through these chapters we do the work of building two concepts—*cosmopolitan communication* and *cosmopolitan peoplehood*. Together, these two concepts provide a guiding framework or vision for understanding intercultural communication through the lens of cosmopolitanism. The second half of the book is more programmatically focused on empirical, methodological and pedagogical issues that emerge in the linking of cosmopolitanism with intercultural communication. It draws crucial connections between cosmopolitan communication and peoplehood and extant and ongoing research involving cosmopolitanism within the field of communication, specifically intercultural communication. We especially draw from a research project currently being conducted by the first author, Miriam, in which she is engaging with Hostelling International–Chicago as an ethnographic site to study cosmopolitan communication, pedagogy and peoplehood.

In Chapter 1 we trace an interdisciplinary trajectory for cosmopolitan thought through the centuries in order to lay the foundation for its use in intercultural communication. While it is impossible to talk about cosmopolitanism without acknowledging the contributions of the ancient Greeks, we make it a point to demonstrate that cosmopolitan thought has existed outside the sweep of Western hegemony. We also make a case that cosmopolitanism, in its revised critical and postcolonial form, is not a Eurocentric, elite or imperialistic philosophy, and that it is well suited for the current critical turn in intercultural communication. In Chapter 2 we do the work of building a bridge between cosmopolitanism as an inherently communicative and intercultural philosophy and the field of intercultural communication. We focus specifically on the key concept of difference. We explain how each body of work can enhance the other in a symbiotic manner. At the end of this chapter, we present the assumptions and working definition for our concept of cosmopolitan communication.

Chapter 3 focuses on how the concept of identity has been approached in intercultural communication, and how it can gain from the cosmopolitan vision. We specifically focus on identity since identity orientation (or disposition) is a key issue within cosmopolitanism scholarship. Cosmopolitanism entails a specific world-oriented way of being and relating with the cultural Other. We provide an explication of the concepts of differential belonging, dialogism, agency, hybridity, intercultural bridgework and critical self-transformation and start the work of building our ontological concept of cosmopolitan peoplehood. In Chapter 4 we put the finishing touches on this concept by discussing the role of the imagination in cultivating a sense of cosmopolitan peoplehood, the importance of empathy and implicature and the overarching value of kindness to strangers necessary for engagement in cosmopolitan communication through cosmopolitan peoplehood. We provide a working definition and assumptions for cosmopolitan peoplehood and explain its co-constitutive relationship with cosmopolitan communication.

In Chapter 5 we devote our attention to differentiating cosmopolitan communication and peoplehood from similar-seeming concepts and models in intercultural communication. This is necessary to demonstrate that cosmopolitanism is more than a sum of the various parts that exist in various forms in extant models and concepts. We start with the notion of multiculturalism and then specifically focus on Y. Y. Kim's (2008) Intercultural Personhood model, Ting-Toomey's (1999) Intercultural Communication Competence model, M. J. Bennett's (1993) Developmental Model of Intercultural Sensitivity and Casmir's (1997) Third Culture Building model. Chapter 6 delves into issues of methodology and operationalization of cosmopolitanism for intercultural communication research. We describe cosmopolitanism as a method in and of itself (i.e., cosmopolitanism-as-method) and the various methods that can be fruitfully used to study cosmopolitanism (i.e., cosmopolitanism as phenomenon of study). We lean towards vernacular methodological cosmopolitanism and work with the example of Hostelling International–Chicago to show how a research project which uses both cosmopolitanism-as-method and cosmopolitanism as phenomenon of study may be designed. We also draw connections between some of the outcomes of the study and cosmopolitan communication and peoplehood.

In order to provide the reader with a sense of the extent to which cosmopolitanism is being incorporated into communication studies and specifically intercultural communication, Chapter 7 presents an analysis of seven recent studies. We describe how the authors apply cosmopolitanism, and discuss the implications of their findings and arguments for the field of intercultural communication. We also make connections between these studies and cosmopolitan communication and peoplehood. While pedagogy is not a primary focus of this book, in Chapter 8 we take a pedagogical focus and suggest a program for cosmopolitan pedagogy for intercultural communication. Here we draw specifically from Miriam's experience of researching the cosmopolitan pedagogy programs of Hostelling International–Chicago, as well as her experience of teaching a hybrid undergraduate-graduate level course on cosmopolitanism.

Pointing out what he sees as the naïve and uncritical fervor of its supporters, Parker (2003) writes: "Cosmopolitanism, in its desire to be all-embracing, can hug too hard" (p. 171). As we hope this book will demonstrate, cosmopolitanism can enable a critical as well as hopeful vision for intercultural communication. In order to be critical, one need not abandon hope. We do not wish to hug too hard, just a little bit harder than we normally would.

1 Tracing the Trajectories of Cosmopolitanism for Intercultural Communication

> The fact that the dream of cosmopolitan culture has been around so long attests to its power to excite the social consciousness. . . . As a cultural ideal, it also confronts scholarly imaginations and is currently an important topic in academic circles in the humanities and social sciences. (Kendall, Woodward, & Skrbis, 2009, p. 150)

> To be human is to face others, which makes human existence essentially ethical. (Stade, 2007, p. 229)

We would like to begin this first chapter with the word *hope* because hope opens the door to possibilities and can lead to empowerment. We need hope to envision and work towards creating a world where despite enduring differences and postcolonial complexities, people from different nationalities and cultural backgrounds are able to face one another in various contexts with the sense that ultimately, we all belong to the same planet and that our fates are interconnected. We need hope to rise above constraints that impede the moral vision that all human beings matter equally—no matter what their nationality or cultural background. When we blindly allow cultural constructs, such as nationality (or race, or religion, and so on), to naturalize differences, we also allow for the naturalizing of hierarchies that can be used to justify the oppression of fellow human beings. We begin to see Otherness as a threat and forget that we can learn much from cultural Others.

Cosmopolitanism advocates an Other-oriented approach and *openness towards the world*, and this notion of openness is the "driving force" behind it (Skrbis & Woodward, 2011). It promotes an *outward cultural and moral focus as well as the idea of being open to change through intercultural interaction.* This outward focus and openness is not an unthinking and naïve acceptance of all points of views, but a discerning approach which is willing to genuinely consider all points of view. It is a way of being (and becoming) in the world that is embedded in the local but opens out willingly to the Other and to the world instead of remaining constrained by the local. It is a way of being (and becoming) that considers the whole world to be historically interconnected, despite politically and culturally constructed divisions (such as nationality) which, in turn, hierarchize modes of belonging. In fact, a key notion within cosmopolitanism is the critical transcendence of the negative constraints of nation-state-centric thinking (e.g., divisive nativism) when it comes to cultural identity, social and global justice and communication. Following this notion, our moral and planetary vision for this book is that all human beings, in all their cultural complexities and not despite them, matter and that this mattering needs to be an inherent part of how we communicate across cultural differences—as critical global citizens. Communicating with an Other is a moral matter, and as Cooks (2001) reminds us, "To use language itself requires a certain degree of recognition of a moral other" (p. 344). This cosmopolitan moral vision does not downplay culture and difference, or the notion of nationalism; instead it challenges us to conceptualize culture, communication, power, identities and difference in world-oriented ways, i.e., in outward rather than inward ways, that allow us to see connections across differences, communicate ethically and grow as cultural and moral beings through these experiences.

By 'outward world-oriented ways' we mean an orientation that leans towards the cultural Other and the world in general with a willingness to learn, grow and change along with the shifting complexities of the world instead of insularly desiring to remain and communicate from within the bounded contours and logics of received culture. An outward orientation helps us see how the global is culturally changing the local and how local actions can have global implications. In fact, as American Indian author and poet Joy Harjo writes, cultures that we may think of as 'pure' contain "many threads leading all over the world" (2011, p. 88). Such a perspective encourages us to transcend static views of culture (and hence static views of the Self and Other), and think of communication and culture from an ecological perspective.

According to Rodriguez and Chawla (2010), an ecological view assumes cultures to be permeable, emergent and embedded in each other. Such a view sits well with cosmopolitanism's vision of the planet ultimately being one continuous space inhabited by diverse cultural beings who are ecologically interconnected despite their socially and historically constructed differences. The possibility for empathy, intercultural and moral growth, goodwill and solidarity with the cultural Other, both near and far, lies in the recognition of such basic connectedness. According to Chicana scholar Gloria Anzaldúa, "the knowledge that we are in a symbiotic relationship to all that exists and co-creators of ideologies—attitudes, beliefs and cultural values—motivates us to act collectively" (2002, p. 2). Without such knowledge and recognition, global problems that transcend national and cultural divides will continue to proliferate.

This type of openness and transcendence is something that many dream of and hope for in their lives, and yet it is one of the most difficult ideas to theorize within the field of intercultural communication without trivializing important differences. Nonetheless, it is not impossible. We find hope and possibility in the ethical vision of cosmopolitanism. In writing this book we wish to build a bridge between intercultural communication and the hope-inspiring values and ideals contained within cosmopolitanism, a philosophy that is inherently intercultural and communicative in nature (see Chapter 2). We demonstrate that cultivating the values of cosmopolitanism for intercultural communication can provide a hopeful communicative approach, and an ethical vision, for communicating as critical global citizens and for building community, intercultural dialogue and solidarity across national and other cultural differences.

One might argue that the goal of intercultural communication has always been to effectively and appropriately communicate with the cultural Other. What does cosmopolitanism add? Part of the answer lies in the scope of cosmopolitanism's ethical vision—the entire planet. Our collective consciousness of the world as a whole has been on the rise for a while now (Giddens, 1990), and it seems unlikely that the direction of this consciousness is suddenly going to move into reverse gear. Intercultural communication needs more theoretical visions that are able to critically grasp the phenomenon of globality. While postcolonial theory has opened some doors in this direction, cosmopolitanism adds a moral vision for humane Self–Other communication and growth at the planetary level. It adds the layer of critical global citizenship to our other cultural identities, and focuses on the commitments necessary for communicating outwardly as global citizens. By aligning with postcolonial theory, it attempts to reconfigure narrow understandings of nation, culture and difference, thereby widening the field for intercultural communication.

Second, cosmopolitanism applies to all levels and forms of communication—from the intrapersonal to the macro/societal. Within intercultural communication as well as the communication discipline in general, there is a need to more carefully theorize the relationship between micro- and macro-level communication practices that help bring about transformation and social change (Ganesh, Zoller, & Cheney, 2005). Cosmopolitanism, as we elaborate later in the book, works through all levels of intercultural communication and holds promise for such theorizing. Third, cosmopolitanism focuses on mutuality, intercultural growth and the expansion of one's cultural horizons through the cultural Other—these are qualities that are yet to be theorized adequately in intercultural communication. The primary focus of the field has been to predict, describe and critique how various cultural groups communicate amongst and across themselves. While this focus is very important indeed, precious little exists on how mutuality and intercultural growth, for the sake of social and global justice, is accomplished by people communicating jointly across cultural differences. Power asymmetries, oppressions and inequities no doubt need to be critiqued and resisted. However, without jettisoning critiques, what other visions can we include in our repertoire to understand how people and groups *jointly* build intercultural bridges between *asymmetrical* cultural locations and accomplish solidarity, critical self-transformation and change for social and global justice?

In this chapter, we accomplish two things. First, we trace the trajectories of cosmopolitan thought through the various epochs of histories. While we do begin with ancient Greece, we explore examples of cosmopolitan thought and praxis that have emerged before and outside the historic sweep of the

West and Western modernity. As Inglis (2012) reminds us, every intellectual field has a dominant telling of its history and cosmopolitanism studies is no different. However, "after a while certain orthodoxies in narration can arise, with subsequent authors reproducing, rather than interrogating, the histories offered by earlier contributors" (p. 11). Following voices such as Inglis', we trace the trajectory of cosmopolitanism in the spirit of questioning its dominant narrative. Second, and relatedly, we make the case that cosmopolitanism is not a Eurocentric, elitist and imperialistic philosophy which should be summarily dismissed as such. Its meaning and scope have changed with changing times and with more recent debates. We argue that the more recent critical and postcolonial turn in cosmopolitanism thought makes it a crucial body of work to incorporate within intercultural communication.

CLASSICAL COSMOPOLITANISM

Cosmopolitan thought is far from a recent phenomenon. In this section we trace, in an interdisciplinary manner, what we consider to be the key moments in the growth of cosmopolitan thought through the course of histories. While it is beyond the scope of this chapter to include all thinkers and theorists who have contributed to the intellectual and scholarly debates on cosmopolitanism, we identify those who we believe have had a significant impact.

The English term "cosmopolitanism" has its roots in the ancient Greek term for "citizen of the world." The Cynics, followed by the Stoics, in response to the more closed and exclusivist order of the ancient Greek "polis," advocated for a moral form of cosmopolitanism. They believed that one's primary moral anchor should not be just the city-state but should extend outward. Thinkers such as Antisthenes and Diogenes advocated that one should be outward-looking and concerned with the matters not just of the immediate circle of self, family or even the polis, but also of the larger community of human beings of this world. The conquests of Alexander the Great at that time, which brought disparate cultures all the way up to the Indian subcontinent under the fold of his empire, increased intercultural contact and made it possible to imagine humanity beyond the narrower confines and concerns of the Greek polis. But the Cynics were not mainstream or popular, and their ideas (such as arguing for citizenship for women) were not enthusiastically embraced. In practice, in ancient Greece, Athens was probably the most open of all the city-states, inclusivity was limited, and the status of citizen was not extended to women, slaves and foreigners. Eventually, the Roman Empire, which was more open to Greek Stoic thinking, evolved in a more cosmopolitan direction. This was aided by the fact that the empire was vast, ethnically diverse and more Mediterranean (Asian and African) than just simply European in its make up (Delanty, 2009; Fine & Cohen, 2002).

While the contributions of the ancient Greeks to cosmopolitan thought are well-documented in cosmopolitanism studies, Delanty (2009) reminds us that to keep the narrative of cosmopolitanism within Europe helps fuel claims that cosmopolitanism is a Eurocentric intellectual enterprise (see also Inglis & Robertson, 2011). He documents ancient Chinese thinkers such as Mo Tzu and Mencius who promoted universal love and global peace as well as Hindu, and later Islamic and Christian, civilizations that advocated for "an inclusive vision of human community" (p. 20). He and Brown (2012) document ancient Chinese concepts such as *tianxia* and explain its cosmopolitan dimensions. Pollock (2002) provides us with a comprehensive account of non-Western cosmopolitanism in the first millennium made possible through the vernacularization and wide circulation of the ancient Sanskrit language and culture within large parts of South and Southeast Asia (see also Giri, 2006).

Other evidence of the existence of cosmopolitanism before the rise and hegemony of Western modernity is well-documented in Hawley's (2008) edited collection titled *India in Africa, Africa in India: Indian Ocean Cosmopolitanisms*. The essays in this volume provide various viewpoints on the vibrant and open economic and cultural exchanges and mixtures that were ongoing for centuries before the rise of Western modernity between the cultures surrounding the Indian Ocean. Similarly, Ghosh (1994) offers an impressive historical account of the cosmopolitan connections during medieval times between South Asia, the Middle East and the Mediterranean. Abu-Lughod (1989) provides a book-length treatment of flourishing trade and cosmopolitan cultural exchange in the Old World during the 13th and 14th centuries. The domain of this world extended from northwestern Europe to China and the core was formed by the Middle East, the Indian subcontinent and China. However, no one power had hegemonic hold over the others, and Europe, according to Abu-Lughod, was at this time an " . . . upstart peripheral to an ongoing operation" (p. 12).

Intercultural communication scholar Molefi Kete Asante writes about the ancient African philosophy of Maat, which espouses living and communicating through constantly striving for "harmony, balance, order, justice, truth, righteousness, and reciprocity. Maat opens up possibilities that go beyond tolerance for the Other towards profound respect" (Asante, 2011, p. 49). A philosophy oriented towards peace and non-combative and non-dominative relations between Self and Others, Maat is known by many different names throughout Africa and has permeated culture and society in that part of the world for a very long time. The parallels between Maat and cosmopolitanism are not hard to detect.

What these histories and ancient philosophies tell us is that cultural cosmopolitanism was a thriving outlook well before the rise of Western modernity and hegemony, and that the narrative of cosmopolitanism can be retold from a non-Eurocentric perspective. They also tell us that the idea of the nation and nation-state, which has so naturalized our identities and views of difference over the recent centuries, has not always been the norm. Commenting on the value of pre-European expansionist histories, Clifford (1994) writes that such histories can help us imagine new ways of being within contemporary globalization, ways that are "non-Western, not-only-Western, models for cosmopolitan life . . . " (p. 328).

During the early modern and European Enlightenment age, there was a renewed interest in cosmopolitanism in Europe, and it was during this time that the ideas became somewhat more mainstream, politically-oriented and recognizable as we know them today. For example, Erasmus of Rotterdam drew from the ancient Greco-Roman ideas of cosmopolitanism to plead for national and religious tolerance and world peace. This was also a time of reaction by intellectuals against European dogmatism, and the openness inherent in cosmopolitan thought appealed to many writers and thinkers of that time. Furthermore, the outward colonial expansions of European states and the growth of trade and capitalism were further contexts that increased intercultural contact and paved the way for thinking in an outwardly (albeit colonial) manner (Kleingeld, 2003).

One of the prominent proponents of cosmopolitanism at that time was Immanuel Kant, who wrote on the topic for over a decade. His notable works are *Idea for a Universal History from a Cosmopolitan Point of View*, written in 1785, and *Perpetual Peace*, written in 1795. Kant was the first to advocate a rationalistic international order and cosmopolitan law. He saw the need for global civic order and relations between nations in order to avoid war and destruction. Cosmopolitan law, according to Kant, would guarantee the fundamental rights of every human even if their own state didn't. While Kant was writing at a time when nationalism hadn't taken hold in the way it did later, he foresaw the scope for violence. And while he was aware that his ideas were ahead of his time, he wrote with hope for lasting peace. But ironically, just as the ancient Greeks had their prejudices and did not believe everyone could be a citizen, Kant was limited in his vision of cosmopolitanism. Trapped in the Eurocentric thinking of his time, and specifically influenced by scientific racism, he did not believe in the equality of the races and was convinced that Europe should be on top in the cosmopolitan order. More specifically, he was heavily influenced by the racial taxonomies of the human species developed by northern European philosophers and scientists of his time (such as Hume, Buffon, Linnaeus and Bernier). In his own writings on race and moral development of 'man,' Kant firmly asserted that all but the white race were naturally incapable of developing moral faculties and, therefore, were naturally inferior and not capable of being educated (Eze, 2001).

Kant's cosmopolitanism was thus based in a tension between his beliefs in scientific racism and his outlook for cosmopolitan law. His version of cosmopolitanism did not embrace humankind but assumed a natural division between superior white and inferior non-white races. According to Eze (2001), Kant's assumption:

. . . that the lives of the so-called savages were governed by caprice, instinct, and violence rather than law left no room for Kant to imagine between the Europeans and the natives a system of international relations, established on the basis of equality and respect, and governed by non-unilaterally imposed systems of law. (p. 78)

So while Kant was deeply disturbed by the level of cruelty perpetrated upon non-white races through European colonization, he was perhaps more disturbed by the levels to which his white fellow men had stooped during the process of conquest. Arising from such a position, Kant's cosmopolitanism was an absolute Western, white, modernist and rationalist universalism, and imagined a world modeled after Europe in which the non-white races could never be equal to the white race (see also Fine & Cohen, 2002; Malcomson, 1998; Mignolo, 2002; Wood, 1998).

THE 20TH CENTURY

The rise of nationalism, and the fervent hold it took over public and political imagination, created a thick binary between the ideas of nation-state patriotism and cosmopolitanism in the war-torn and Cold War climate of the 20th century. Those advocating cosmopolitanism in political, moral or cultural senses came to be generally seen as elitist or as rootless outsiders. According to Delanty (2009):

The cosmopolitan was epitomized by the Jew and came to signify the outsider within. This anti-Semitic use of the term still informs popular French uses of the term in the present day. The xenophobic and racist climate that developed in Europe from the first World War onwards represented not merely a turning away from the cosmopolitanism of the nineteenth century . . . but a reversal of it. (p. 47)

In the former Soviet Union, the cosmopolitan project was perceived to be related to Anglo-American imperialism (Fine & Cohen, 2002).

The post-World War II Nuremberg trials and the establishment of the idea of "crimes against humanity" marked an important interruption in favor of cosmopolitan thought. The writings of Karl Jaspers and Hannah Arendt in debating the relevance of this idea were significant contributions. This category of crimes held Nazi perpetrators individually responsible for their actions, and challenged the oppressive authority of the nation-state. In other words, "crimes against humanity" helped establish the idea of justice beyond the boundaries of national sovereignty, and no one could anymore get away with the claim that they had perpetrated crimes in the name of the nation-state (Fine & Cohen, 2002). The Cold War, however, plunged the world back into the fervor of nationalism and cosmopolitanism, specifically political cosmopolitanism, continued to be regarded as the polar opposite of patriotism (Malcomson, 1998).

In the U.S., Martha Nussbaum's work on cosmopolitanism marked a key moment. An essay she wrote for the *Boston Review* in 1994 drew much criticism and stirred up an intense debate about the relevance of cosmopolitanism in a post-Cold War globalizing world. In her essay, in which she draws from ancient Stoic and Cynic ideas on cosmopolitanism, Nussbaum makes the point that U.S. Americans are too wedded to their national identity, to the extent of being blind to the larger humanity outside the U.S. Emphasizing the interdependent nature of humanity, and that cosmopolitan education helps us learn more about ourselves (also a core imperative of intercultural communication education, see Martin & Nakayama, 2012), she wrote: "Our nation is appallingly ignorant of most of the rest of the world. I think this means that it is also, in many crucial ways, ignorant of itself" (Nussbaum, 1996, p. 11). Nussbaum proposed that cosmopolitan reform in education curricula is a way of addressing this matter, and would help U.S. Americans become better citizens of the larger world. Critics were of the view that Nussbaum's take on patriotism was too naïve and narrow (Fine & Cohen, 2002). McConnell (1996), for example, wrote: "Humanity at large . . . is too abstract to be a strong focus for the affections" and that "abstract cosmopolitanism . . . is unlikely to create a substitute moral community" (p. 81). Others argued that cosmopolitanism need not be pitted against patriotism and that both are necessary. According to Taylor (1996), " . . . we have no choice but to be cosmopolitans and patriots, which means to fight for the kind of patriotism that is open to universal solidarities against other, more closed kinds" (p. 121, see also Sen, 1996).

Close to the end of the 20th century, the world's economic, cultural and political climate started undergoing radical change. The fall of the Berlin Wall, the sharp rise of market globalization and unprecedented innovations in communication, information and travel technologies started resulting in increasing cultural deterritorialization/reterritorialization and time–space compression (Harvey, 1989), thereby reconfiguring older structures, ideologies and imaginations (Appadurai, 1996). While nationalism has not disappeared, how the nation-state is conceived of is changing. Complex connectivity, defined by Tomlinson (1999) as the "the rapidly developing and ever-densening network of interconnections and interdependencies" that characterize globalization, is the pressing reality of the day (p. 2). According to Robertson and Khondker (1998), globalization, in its current form, "involves the compression of the entire world, on the one hand, and a rapid increase in consciousness of the whole world, on the other" (p. 29). Giddens (1990) describes globalization as "the intensification of worldwide social relations which link distinct localities in such a way that local happenings are shaped by events occurring far away and vice versa" (p. 64). While the events of 9/11 once again fueled inward-looking nationalism, we continue to live in a world where the centripetal forces of nationalism and the centrifugal forces of globalization exist simultaneously in tension with each other. As is evident from past debates on cosmopolitanism, the flavor of cosmopolitan thought at any point in time has been influenced by the political, economic and cultural currents of those times as well as by projections into the imaginable future. It is no different today, and it is urgent that we continue to debate the possibilities of cosmopolitanism for a more humane world for future generations.

Several scholars (e.g., Delanty; 2009; Hannerz, 1990; Inglis & Robertson, 2011; Malcomson, 1998; Tomlinson, 1999) are of the view that contemporary globalization is not the same as cosmopolitanism but that it is laying the groundwork for a non-absolute form of cosmopolitanism (evident in multiplicity of identities, interactions, ground-up structures and transnational coalitions) to emerge. In other words, the dynamics of contemporary globalization are producing conditions for a revised form of cosmopolitanism to emerge. Beck (2006), while he has been critiqued for leaning towards a Eurocentric view of cosmopolitanism (see Bhambra, 2011), puts forth a useful argument for a shift from "methodological nationalism" to "methodological cosmopolitanism" in the social sciences. Methodological nationalism, according to Beck, is the tendency to assume that the nation-state is the natural unit of analysis for society and culture (see also Chapter 6). He is of the view that we are already within a cosmopolitan age and that our methodological and epistemological assumptions need to shift to match this reality. Other scholars, such as Appadurai (1996), who have made arguments about the declining power of the nation-state ideology in public and political imagination, theorize the proliferation of global flows and disjunctures, and advocate for cosmopolitan conceptions of culture and society. Appadurai's work on the growing importance of the role of the social imagination in enabling outward senses of connections with cultural Others in the world is notable and, according to Theodossopoulos (2010), is making it possible for transnational and translocal (local-to-local) connections and learning to occur among people from different cultural backgrounds who feel united by common causes.

The cultural turn in cosmopolitan thought has been prominent in the 20th century. Culture, many (like Beck) argue, can no longer be seen as static, inward-looking and bounded by the nation-state. Culture must be understood as always in the process of transformation at the nexus of the global and the national/local. According to Hannerz (1990), another prominent writer on cosmopolitanism, we now live in a "one world culture" and the cosmopolitan is somewhat "footloose:"

> Cosmopolitans can be dilettantes as well as connoisseurs, and are often both, at different times. But the willingness to become involved with the Other, and the concern with achieving competence in cultures which are initially alien, relate to considerations of the self as well.

Cosmopolitanism often has a narcissistic streak; the self is constructed in the space where cultures mirror one another. (pp. 239–240)

Hannerz drew a clear distinction between "locals" and "cosmopolitans" in his earlier writings. This set up a binary that can, and is, being transcended for a more postcolonial, Other-oriented and critical conceptualization of cosmopolitanism. The characterization of the cosmopolitan as "footloose" and "narcissistic" is being revised (see Hannerz, 2006) to challenge the charge that the cosmopolitan is a surface-level sampler of 'exotic' cultures and is a globe-trotting elite (usually a white male), a weightless and free-floating figure without any loyalties or commitments (for this critique see Brennan, 2001; Calhoun, 2002). Furthermore, few would argue that we live in a "one world culture"—instead, the argument is that we now have a keener sense of the world as a single place which is chock-full of diverse and overlapping cultures (Featherstone, 1995). There is a perceived need to move from "thin" (top-down) to "thick" (ground-up) conceptualizations of cosmopolitanism (Delanty, 2009; Hannerz, 2006). Critics of post-national and one-world arguments have also made the point that nationalism is far from eroding, and that the new cosmopolitanism need not pit nationalism and patriotism against itself (Appiah, 1996; Cheah, 1998; Delanty, 2009). In fact, the more recent critical and postcolonial turn in cosmopolitanism scholarship recognizes that "Far from being a selfish, idiosyncratic or indulgent choice, to advocate, delimit and develop cosmopolitanism in a global age has become an urgent *moral necessity*—even if the pessimism of the intellect dictates an orange rather than a green light forward" (Fine & Cohen, 2002, p. 162, italics added). This recognition involves the conviction that theorizing about cosmopolitanism, reconfigured to inform the global justice goal of challenging neocolonial aspects of globalization, is a path worth following.

THE CRITICAL AND POSTCOLONIAL TURN

The critiques against cosmopolitanism in the past have mainly centered on charges of elitism, Eurocentrism and imperialism. If conceived as having its genesis purely in the West and developed through Western modernity, then cosmopolitanism can easily be castigated as elitist and accessible only to the privileged. Eurocentric brands of universalism, typical of cosmopolitanisms such as Kant's, *are* imperialistic and pay no heed to issues of power that produce and keep in place intercultural and global inequalities, exclusions and historically produced injustices (Mendieta, 2009). And most importantly, cosmopolitanism that does not engage with the material and symbolic realities of European colonialism and the postcolonial and neocolonial conditions in today's globality is simply inadequate (Bhambra, 2011). Stråth (2012) writes that, in general, the problem with most tellings of world history is Eurocentrism, and that for cosmopolitanism to be a viable ethical vision for the planet, it needs to be extracted from its "European distortion" and imbued with a social and global justice agenda (p. 73). The revised thinking and debates over the last two decades, including alternative narratives of cosmopolitanism, have to a large extent addressed these shortcomings and are reappropriating cosmopolitanism as an ethical intercultural orientation and vision that is critical, dialogical, transformative and reflexive. In current debates, it is positioned as a moral and postcolonial imperative, and the focus is on how people actually live cosmopolitan lives on an everyday basis rather than on simply theorizing cosmopolitanism as an abstract ideal (Rovisco & Nowicka, 2011). It is in this turn that we find hope for a joining between intercultural communication and cosmopolitan thought.

According to Argentinean postcolonial scholar Walter Mignolo (2000, 2002), reconceiving cosmopolitanism from the perspective of coloniality is a critical move much needed to rescue it from its Eurocentric influences. Furthermore, there resides in such a reconception major opportunities for cosmopolitanism to grow in directions that can help address the injustices and inequities of top-down neoliberal globalization. Globalization today is connected to and yet different from the globalizing movements in the past that have involved missionizing, civilizing, modernizing and economic imperialism (Mignolo, 2002). Despite obvious strains of these top-down "global designs" (Mignolo, 2000) in today's world, contemporary globalization also includes within itself tools and technologies that are enabling the postcolonial and the marginalized to push back. This has been especially true since the mass territorial decolonization of the mid-20th century, social movements such as the Civil Rights Movement in the U.S. and other emancipatory watershed events such as the formal end of apartheid in South Africa. In the words of Mignolo (2002):

> Today, silenced and marginalized voices are bringing themselves into the conversation of cosmopolitan projects, rather than waiting to be included. . . . Bringing themselves into the conversation is a transformative project that takes the form of border thinking or border epistemology—that is, the alternative to separatism is border thinking, the recognition and transformation of the hegemonic imaginary from the perspective of people in subaltern positions. Border thinking then becomes a 'tool' of the project of critical cosmopolitanism. (p. 174)

On the topic of borders, Cooper and Rumford (2011) note that globalization is leading not to a borderless world but to a proliferation of borders, and that there is a need to reorient traditional thinking about borders (especially the nation-state border) as divisions. Instead, they argue that borders are conduits that connect differences and are sites for cosmopolitan connections and creativity. As communication and performance studies scholar Dwight

Conquergood (1991) notes: "Borders bleed as much as they contain" (p. 184). Rumford (2012) further argues that borders and their meanings are not static, and that they are discursively produced and are always in process. Beck (2007) argues that being confined to the perspective that the nation-state is the natural container (i.e., a border that separates) for culture, politics, economics and diplomatic relations obscures our analytic vision of the macro global-level inequalities that have been (and continue to be) generated through centuries of uneven trade, colonialism, human migration patterns and war. Put another way, it is imperative to recognize, through postcolonial cosmopolitan vision, the globally interconnected nature of worldwide inequalities and that borders (wherever they may be produced) are critical zones of intercultural performance, communication, inquiry and hope.

In line with Mignolo's emphasis on border thinking, Delanty (2009) has advocated for a new critical theory of cosmopolitanism and the cultivation of a "cosmopolitan imagination" for bringing about social and global justice, intercultural understanding and change (see also Kurasawa, 2011). Such an imagination would have to interrogate questions of power and the agendas behind cosmopolitan-seeming visions and projects. For example, an outward-looking vision purporting to embrace humanity could very well be either emancipatory (e.g., transnational feminism) or coercive (e.g., European colonialism). Similarly, Nederveen Pieterse (2006) has called for "emancipatory cosmopolitanism" which, according to him, should involve critiques of Western domination and goals of emancipation for the postcolonial and marginalized peoples of the world. Delanty (2009) has proposed "post-universal" cosmopolitanism, and writes that " . . . cosmopolitan orientations simply take different forms and can be found in many different cultural contexts and historical periods" (p. 9). Pollock, Bhabha, Breckenridge, and Chakrabarty (2002) have used the phrase "diversity of universals" to emphasize the point that all claims of universality always arise out of particular locations. Therefore, cosmopolitanism should be about "diversality" or "pluriversality," i.e., a commitment to heeding diverse claims of universality (Mignolo, 2002, 2011). Such thinking directs us away from Cosmopolitanism with a capital 'C' (or Eurocentric cosmopolitanism) and towards cosmopolitanism*s* (in the plural and with a lower case 'c') and dialogue between multiple universalisms arising from various cultural viewpoints and locations from around the world. In other words, we need to provincialize universalisms and vigilantly deconstruct the hegemonic varieties in order to promote dialogue.

Thus it is obvious that cosmopolitan thought has benefited from the impetus of critical and postcolonial theory. While retaining its outward cultural focus, it is committed to applying that focus in service of social justice at the nexus of the local and the global. There is an obvious effort to disengage from the absolutist and universalizing assumptions of Western modernity. The proponents of the new cosmopolitanism(s), given the imperial and Eurocentric assumptions of the past, are bringing humility into their theoretical deliberations. Much of this humility involves the desire to include voices and cultures that have been historically erased or marginalized, and to decenter Western modernity. In order to accomplish this inclusion, it has been amply noted that cosmopolitanism can no longer be seen as an abstract, ahistorical and free-floating moral philosophy. Cosmopolitanism has to be "rooted" (Appiah, 1996) and "situated" (Delanty, 2009; Werbner, 2008). The contexts of specific cosmopolitan practices and projects matter since outward orientation does not occur in a vacuum: All cosmopolitanisms come from somewhere and from some perspective (Holton, 2009). In other words, some kind of perceived and meaningful connection is needed other than just an abstract appreciation for difference and for cultural Others.

For example, a collection of essays in the recent book *United in Discontent: Local Responses to Cosmopolitanism and Globalization* (Theodossopoulos & Kirtsoglou, 2010) provides cogent empirical evidence of cases where people from disparate national and cultural backgrounds have connected across differences to act for a joint cause, i.e., mostly discontent with some unjust aspect of top-down neoliberal globalization. Such initial connections can eventually lead to further appreciation of cultural differences and even critical transformation across borders. As Mignolo (2002) argues, the new cosmopolitanism, instead of starting with the abstract and anchorless notion of cultural relativism, should begin from specific locations of colonial and postcolonial *difference* in order to enable translocal and transnational connections between non-elites and allies. This emphasis on difference, conceived as a power dynamic that is not absolute but open to reconfiguration, is a key point (see Chapter 2).

The trend towards situated and non-elite cosmopolitanism has led to the growth of several labels, e.g., rooted, mundane, subaltern, minoritarian, marginal, working class, ordinary, vernacular, banal, decolonial, emancipatory, feminist and discrepant cosmopolitanism (Bhabha, 1996b; Clifford, 1992; Holton, 2009; Lamont & Aksartova, 2002; Nederveen Pieterse, 2006; Werbner, 2008). In fact, the labels of "ordinary," "mundane" and especially "vernacular" (Bhabha, 1996b) have gained momentum. Instead of positioning cosmopolitanism as a grand accomplishment or project, the need to look for everyday mundane forms of cosmopolitanisms routinely performed and accomplished by everyday people is being emphasized. According to Hannerz (2006), "It may be worth looking more closely for the signs of small, banal, or quotidian, or vernacular, or low-intensity cosmopolitanism" (Hannerz, 2006, p. 27). Others have advocated the need to include more non-Western figures and their philosophies into the ongoing retelling of the narrative of cosmopolitanism such as Vietnamese Buddhist monk Thich Nhat Hanh, Latin American intellectuals such as Simón Rodriguez, Indian literary figure Rabindranath Tagore and spiritualists and freedom fighters like Mohandas Gandhi and Sri Aurobindo, Japanese cultural commentator Okakura Tenshin and thinker Tsunesaburo Makiguchi, and many others (Giri, 2006; Hogan & Pandit, 2003; Holton, 2009).

In reference to vernacular cosmopolitanism, anthropologist Pnina Werbner (2008), like some other scholars (e.g., Cheah, 1998), does not see an opposition between cosmopolitanism and nationalism. According to her, people (whether travelers or non-travelers) find ways to engage with and make connections between ideas and values within and beyond their immediate locales. In her words:

> Vernacular cosmopolitanism—an apparent oxymoron that seems to join contradictory notions of local specificity and universal enlightenment—is at the crux of the current debates on cosmopolitanism. . . . [E]thnic rootedness does not negate openness to cultural differences or the fostering of a universal civic consciousness and a sense of moral responsibility beyond the local. . . . [Vernacular cosmopolitans] first make parochial interpretations of culture, religion and ethnicity in order to transcend them and assert wider cosmopolitan values. (Werbner, 2008, pp. 14, 15, 16)

Through an examination of various uneven forms of world travel (voluntary and involuntary) that have been produced through the historical forces of colonization, the capitalist circuits of neoliberal globalization and through postcolonial migration, Kaplan (1996) urges us to recognize that cultural displacement can occur in many complex ways, within one's national space and outside of it. Such a recognition, which involves the disturbance of a pure and romantic sense of the local (the local that the traveler has left behind as well as the local that the traveler enters), opens up space for a critical understanding of cosmopolitanism as a cultural orientation that is simultaneously local and outwardly directed towards the world. A disruption of the local is not equal to the destruction of the local, but creates space for that which is considered to be beyond the local. But what always remains crucial, Kaplan reminds us, is a critical understanding of the positionality of the traveler in relation to place, space and history so that privileged and non-privileged forms of travel are not conflated.

According to Aboulafia (2010), who makes a convincing case that attachment to one's own culture and those of others need not be seen as an either/or choice:

> . . . cosmopolitans are not necessarily rootless souls who have escaped their childhood cultures to dwell in the empyrean of a world community. A cosmopolitan may be someone who has developed a deep respect for the integrity and worth of different cultures while remaining attached to his or her own culture. (p. 2)

As we described earlier, reflexivity and self-critique lie at the heart of vernacular cosmopolitanisms that are dialogically-oriented. Such cosmopolitanisms are "cosmopolitanism[s] of the other," aspire towards mutual understanding and "entail a self-critique of one's prejudices, as a well as a confession and disclosure of one's own epistemic standpoint" (Mendieta, 2009, pp. 243, 250). In order for cosmopolitanism to be truly critical and dialogical, Delanty (2009) argues that critical self-transformation is necessary. According to him, cosmopolitanism occurs when interactions between Self and Other lead to "third cultures." In this process, self-critique, respect for and openness to the cultural Other could lead to transformation and learning on all sides. All cultures involved in the project or interaction could be "translated," which involves "more than interpretation and the transmission of meaning; it is also about the transformation of meaning and the creation of something new, for culture is never translated neutrally" (Delanty, 2009, p. 195). *Thus cosmopolitanism doesn't just reside in any one individual but is something that emerges in the 'in-between' spaces of difference and intercultural interactions and performances.* It is not a thing but a process involving an orientation that can mobilize bridge-building projects that draw upon the energies of "global/local mixture whose hope-generating resources can be marshaled to serve better ends than the xenophobic hegemony of mononations, monoraces and monocreeds" (Wilson, 1998, p. 360).

In sum, cosmopolitanism has been steadily reappropriated from the grips of Eurocentrism, and is evolving into an ethical vision and critical project for the present and the future, a vision that is careful to not forget the past. Our goal in this book is not to dismiss the valid critiques that have been mounted against Eurocentric conceptualizations of cosmopolitanism. Instead, it is to respect these critiques for what they have taught us and provide a descriptive framework for a new and non-imperialistic cosmopolitanism. The focus of this new cosmopolitanism is to imagine (in order to make possible) a world where the broadening of one's cultural horizons and engaging in solidarity across national and cultural differences for the sake of social and global justice is considered a moral imperative. Dialogism and critical transformation are key ideas guiding this non-imperialistic cosmopolitanism. We now turn to a crucial question: Despite the critical, activist and postcolonial turn in cosmopolitan thought, what are the realities on the ground and what are some realistic possibilities for non-imperialistic cosmopolitanism in today's world?

CAN COSMOPOLITANISM RISE ABOVE BEING A EUROCENTRIC, ELITE AND IMPERIAL PHILOSOPHY?

Consider the following cases based in empirical evidence. These are examples of what Robbins (1998) calls "actually existing cosmopolitanism" in today's world:

Muslim feminists in Indonesia, the country with the largest Muslim population, are demonstrating Islamic cosmopolitanism by dialoguing and creating alliances with secular and Muslim feminists and scholars within and outside Indonesia to address gender issues such as domestic violence, polygamy and marriage and divorce laws. While the connections spread outward, this work originates out of a specifically Indonesian Islamic understanding of gender relations. This is an example of translocal cosmopolitanism. (Robinson, 2008)

In Barcelona, Spain, non-elite Senegalese and Bangladeshi migrant workers (street peddlers) display simultaneous local and diasporic attachments to their own cultures and cosmopolitan connections with others in similar situations in order to strategically deal with discrimination and difficulties and survive in a new environment. By so doing, they challenge the parochial vs. cosmopolitan divide. Their cosmopolitanism is mundane—a matter of everyday existence that is socially produced and outwardly directed. This is an example of transnational cosmopolitanism. (Kothari, 2008)

In the Indian town of Bhilai, home to a large public sector steel plant, workers from all castes, religions and cultures from across the nation co-exist bound by the common goal of being part of the nation-building and industrialization narrative. Their children cross even more cultural boundaries in their social interactions. This community manages to maintain relative harmony, even in times of religious and communal violence in other parts of the country. Here the nationalism vs. cosmopolitanism binary is challenged. Cosmopolitanism does not always have to be transnational in nature and can exist within the formal borders of the nation-state. (Parry, 2008)

Coffee drinking is a common or growing practice in many parts of the world. The transnational Fair Trade coffee project was started to challenge the inflated profits of big corporations and to pay small farmers (geographically located mostly in the non-West) more for their labor and product. The conscious coffee drinker, in a Western (or non-Western) setting, who decides to buy Fair Trade coffee performs solidarity with unknown farmers (Others) around the world. This is an example of cosmopolitan solidarity with distant Others at the nexus of the global and the local. (Holton, 2009)

In Greece, against the backdrop of growing anti-neoliberal globalization rhetoric, Greeks are increasingly seeing themselves as transnationally connected to cultural groups normally considered to be rival Others, such as Turks, Palestinians and other Middle Eastern cultures. In this context, they feel "united in discontent." This is an example of regional and transnational cosmopolitanism. (Kirtsoglou & Theodossopoulos, 2010)

We present just a few examples here to make our point. These examples demonstrate that transnational, transregional, subnational and translocal cosmopolitan alliances, dialogue and transformative spaces of practice do actually exist in many contexts around the world (see also Nowicka & Rovisco, 2009). They all demonstrate that everyday people are able to transcend bounded notions of culture and identity (especially the nation-state) in order to come together, however tentatively, for a larger purpose. Intercultural interactions work in various ways across various registers of power, and unexpected alliances across differences, bound by the common goal of emancipation, are formed. All the cases are context-specific and occur in a variety of places/spaces—Western, non-Western and sites where both entangle. While these are cases of cosmopolitanism, they are certainly not cases of elite or Eurocentric cosmopolitanism.

Clifford (1992) was probably the first scholar to challenge the idea that cosmopolitanism is a phenomenon of the elite, specifically elite travelers. People travel in privileged (usually voluntary) and non-privileged ways (e.g., under the force of expulsion, exploitation or dire economic need), and these movements intersect to produce what he calls "discrepant cosmopolitanisms," or multiple articulations of cosmopolitanism that are not necessarily just Western or elite in nature. In today's globality, "cosmopolitical contact zones are traversed by new social movements and global corporations, tribal activists and cultural tourists, migrant worker remittances and e-mail" (Clifford, 1998, p. 369). Discrepant cosmopolitanisms are often strategies for survival, and while "nothing is guaranteed, except contamination, messy politics, and more translations," such cosmopolitanisms "make more visible a complex range of intercultural experiences, sites of appropriation and exchange" (Clifford, 1998, p. 369).

Others have more recently argued that it is time to stop taking for granted that cosmopolitanism is a Western elite privilege and realize that more cosmopolitan spaces exist in the global South (or the East) than the global North (or the West). The former are the postcolonial spaces where people have had their identities assaulted, their cultures displaced and have had to learn how to strategically (or 'tactically' if one were to follow de Certeau) work with externally imposed difference and think outwardly about culture for a much longer time (Bhabha, 1994; Canagarajah, 1999; Forte, 2010; Hannerz, 2006; Malcomson, 1998; Pollock et al., 2002; Thomas, 1992). In comparison, the global North/Europe has only recently begun to learn how to work with difference in its midst, especially since the 20th century when its postcolonial Others from former colonies increasingly started migrating into its own spaces.

Quoting Nandy, Hannerz (2006) makes an astute point: "Europe and North America have increasingly lost their cosmopolitanism, paradoxically because of a concept of cosmopolitanism that considers Western culture to be definitionally universal and therefore automatically cosmopolitanism" (p. 16). Delanty (2009) convincingly argues that today, some of cosmopolitanism's "most innovative expressions can be found in the non-Western world" (p. 12). Finally, in a quantitative study that used survey methodology to operationalize and measure cosmopolitanism, Furia (2005) found that the cosmopolitan outlook is more prevalent among people of non-Western nations and among underprivileged rather than privileged cultural groups in wealthy Western nations. The logic here is not hard to understand. Members of those cultures (usually marginalized or formerly colonized cultures) who have had their identities symbolically attacked or externally shaped by others cannot help but be aware of the arbitrary nature of identities and differences. Their "double consciousness," to use du Bois' term, puts them "in a unique position to achieve the impartiality of the spectator because of a heightened awareness of otherness and multiplicity" (Aboulafia, 2010, p. 99). Hence it is likely that they are more familiar with change and also more used to negotiating borders and differences.

TWO CAVEATS

At this point we would like to put forth two caveats. First, it is quite easy to fall too deep into the Western/non-Western binary in our postcolonial and critical commitment to bring social justice to the less privileged and marginalized cultures of the world. But as Shome and Hegde (2002), among others, remind us, in today's world of increasing migration and cultural deterritorialization/reterritorialization, the seemingly neat categories of West and non-West are often intricately tangled and harder to separate. They exist within, through and outside each other. Therefore, while we acknowledge the overall need for making this distinction at times for epistemological clarity, we do not subscribe to a rigid binary in how we apply these categories to cosmopolitan conceptualizations of intercultural communication. We feel that decisions about how to label certain spaces and practices of cultural cosmopolitanism should be done with great care and with specific attention to nuances and context.

Second, we feel that it is unrealistic and naïve to assume that individuals who engage in cosmopolitan endeavors in certain contexts will do so in all contexts (Beck, 2009; Nowicka & Rovisco, 2009). According to Skrbis and Woodward (2011), openness, which is the driving force behind cosmopolitanism, "as a cultural outlook and practice is context and object dependent" (p. 65). Universalizing assumptions about openness are reductive and undermine the importance of context and situatedness in critical cosmopolitan performance and action. Cosmopolitanism can arise out of certain situations and it can be mindfully cultivated, but it must also be discerning and *cannot and should not be forced*. This way of thinking about cosmopolitanism makes it less of a universal (in a top-down sense) and more of a ground-up and context-specific philosophy. But this does not change the fact that "there is a new need for a hermeneutics of the alien other in order to live and work in a world in which violent division and unprecedented intermingling coexists, and danger and opportunity vie" (Beck, 2009, pp. xi–xii). For the sake of opportunity, we need to invest more in hope and lean towards the cultural Other and the world.

We are well aware that we are up against a tall order in what we are attempting in this book. Cosmopolitanism thought has generated a high volume of critique, and we are mindful of these as we venture forward to cultivate cosmopolitanism's strengths for intercultural communication. Critics, such as Brennan (1997), have noted that while myriad global interconnections and outward cultural projections are becoming more possible and imaginable, we cannot forget that real inequalities, structural and material oppressions and imperialisms have not simply disappeared. Beck (2006) is also very clear in noting that cosmopolitanism can be either emancipatory or despotic in its orientation. Werbner (2008), for instance, offers the Iraq war example to show how cosmopolitanism can become hegemonic in the name of freedom and democracy. Cosmopolitanism is one of those concepts which, like the concept of hybridity, has the potential to do great good or great harm. Kraidy (2002) has worked hard to help us see the value of hybridity (a concept closely related to cosmopolitanism, see Chapter 3) for international and intercultural communication, and has suggested moving forward with caution, vigilance to context and a critical mind in further theorizing hybridity for our field. We too aspire to do something similar with cosmopolitanism.

The examples and arguments in this previous section tell us that practices of mundane and vernacular cosmopolitanism are not uncommon in today's world, and they are definitely not all elitist or Eurocentric in nature. As intercultural communication scholars, our challenge is to better understand and theorize the communicative dynamics of cosmopolitanism. With caveats, reflections and critiques in mind, we now move forward to establish links between cosmopolitanism and intercultural communication in order to explore what such a linking has to offer towards the goal of humane, transformative and ecological communication in conditions of postcolonial globality.

2 Establishing Links Between Cosmopolitanism and Intercultural Communication

> Cosmopolitanism, in its wide and wavering net, catches something of our need to ground our sense of mutuality in conditions of mutability, and to learn to love tenaciously in terrains of historical and cultural transition. (Pollock, Bhabha, Breckenridge, & Chakrabarty, 2002, p. 4)

As we begin this chapter, we would like to make one point very clear. Our ultimate goal, through our linking of cosmopolitanism and intercultural communication, is not to present a prescriptive and universalistic (i.e., one-size-fits-all) model or theoretical framework for communicating ethically as global citizens. This does not mean that we do not believe in the importance of being able to communicate as global citizens. What we offer through our intellectual labor, instead, are tentative suggestions for humane, transformative and ecological communication and ways of being and becoming in a world where, as the quote above indicates, we need to find mutuality (however tentative) across cultural differences within conditions of rapid change. We sincerely believe that our suggestions must be responsive to the intercultural politics and context of any given communicative situation.

That said, cosmopolitanism, in our view, is a promising philosophy for developing such suggestions that may aid in the forging of outwardly-oriented human (and humane) communicative connections, practices and structures across national and cultural divisions. Cosmopolitanism does exist, and we need to shed some light on its communicative dimensions. We find there to be a symbiotic relationship between the values and philosophical inclinations that are currently guiding the field of intercultural communication, specifically critical intercultural communication, and those that are guiding the critical/postcolonial turn in cosmopolitan thought. Cosmopolitanism is intercultural in its orientation and intercultural communication can benefit from incorporating cosmopolitanism and its world-oriented cultural outlook and ethical vision into its theoretical toolbox.

In this chapter, we first identify what we see to be a good entry point for cosmopolitanism into the field of intercultural communication. Next, we outline some of the prominent values of cosmopolitanism and explain how they are in tune with intercultural communication. We explain how cosmopolitanism is inherently communicative, and particularly focus on the notion of difference while highlighting the cosmopolitan possibilities that reside within a more 'entangled' view of difference. We conclude this chapter by presenting a working definition and assumptions for what we call *cosmopolitan communication*.

A BRIDGE AWAITS BUILDING

Intercultural communication, as a field of study, began in the U.S. (read: West) after World War II with the establishment of the Foreign Services Institute (FSI) in 1946. The FSI was charged with training overseas personnel, specifically government and business personnel, to be culturally competent. Early knowledge produced by FSI researchers was mostly practical (functional) in nature, and the practice of equating country with culture took hold during this period. The goal of the FSI was to produce knowledge about the 'Other' so the 'Self' could better 'manage' communication with such Others (Cooks, 2001).

During later years, in order to gain academic status (particularly in relation to the physical and social sciences), the field developed its body of knowledge along more social scientific lines. The nation-state remained the unquestioned container of culture in several quantitative and postpositivist studies from the late 1970s onwards (Leeds-Hurwitz, 1990; Moon, 1996). Culture and communication, according to this paradigm, are objectively conceptualized as *a priori* variables for the purpose of quantitative measurement and prediction (i.e., they are conceived of as fixed rather than ever-changing). Individuals who belong to a culture, it is assumed, are 'programmed' to communicate according to its rules and values. Difference is viewed as a neutral fact and not examined as a socially constructed and historical/contextual power dynamic. It was only in the latter part of the 1980s and 1990s, along with a larger interpretive and then critical turn in other related fields within the communication discipline, that the social scientific paradigm began to be problematized, and methodological nationalism began to be questioned. In 1998, Ono's critique of the field's reductive tendency to naturalize the nation-state and assume that country is equal to culture was a significant contribution (Ono, 1998; see also Asante, 1980). In a more recent essay, Ono (2010) reiterates his argument and notes that the taken-for-grantedness of the nation-state in intercultural communication research simply helps reify stereotypes and unequal power relations between nation-states. Furthermore, this assumption is unable to account for changes that are resulting through the plays of various transnational forces and phenomena. Rethinking the nation-state and its role in communication, according to Ono, is necessary and we fully agree with his assertion.

The interpretive paradigm of intercultural communication scholarship conceptualizes culture and communication as socially constructed and co-constitutive. The focus is on qualitatively understanding and describing how people within particular speech communities and identity groups are continuously involved in the creation and maintenance of culture through everyday social interaction, communication and meaning-making. Here, the conceptualization of culture and communication is not as objective, etic and rigid as in the social scientific paradigm, however, the focus is more on studying cultural patterns linked to rules and meanings that emerge through communication. Relatedly, the interpretive approach, while it considers culture to be fluid and dynamic, focuses less on change (including how cultural identities change) and more on description of the here and now. The 'in-between' complexities of intercultural interaction (or hybridity issues) are not the focus and nor does it significantly challenge methodological nationalism or put the notion of difference into motion.

The critical paradigm also subscribes to the view that culture and communication are co-constitutive, however, it focuses heavily on issues of power and macro context, thereby situating culture as always contested. This paradigm connects culture and communication to power, difference and structure, something the social scientific/functional and interpretive approaches are unable to well account for (Cargyle, 2005; Martin & Nakayama, 1999). However, what the critical approach is less able to account for, given its focus on macro perspectives of power and context, is the micro relational aspects of intercultural communication (Cooks, 2010). Critical intercultural communication is also mostly entrenched in static views of difference and methodological nationalism, e.g., the U.S.-centric focus of issues such as race, gender and power remain largely unproblematized (Shome, 2010; Shome & Hegde, 2002).

At this point in time, what we perceive is still needed within the critical paradigm, indeed within all the paradigms of intercultural communication study, is more *hopeful* and *world-oriented* ways to study intercultural communication that can help us theorize the communicative connections and dialogic possibilities across national and cultural differences *without* losing the critical imperative. The challenge is to find more ways to study how meaning is *jointly* produced by culturally different individuals through the willingness to engage in mutual and critical transformation. The challenge includes understanding how such mutuality is accomplished within the shifting plays of similarities and differences, i.e., without assuming that differences are always static and oppositional (or negative).

Postcolonial and postmodern approaches to culture, difference and communication have the potential to expand the critical paradigm in world-oriented ways because of the manners in which they can help us (re)conceptualize culture, nation, power, identity, communication, and especially difference in transnational contexts. As Shome and Hegde (2002) remind us, "postcoloniality has complicated the very meaning of interconnections between cultures" (p. 263). Differences constructed as pure and absolute binaries are usually entangled in complex ways which can be opened up to reconfiguration and change for decolonization and social justice (Grossberg, 2002). Postcolonial scholarship interrupts the logic of methodological nationalism since "it entails geopoliticizing the nation and locating it in larger (and unequal) histories and geographies of global power and culture" (Shome & Hegde, 2002, p. 253). This is necessary in the field of intercultural communication not only to avoid cultural reductionism, essentialism and nation-state-centrism in our scholarship, but also to make transparent *interconnected* transnational and historical power dynamics and allow for the emergence of subnational subaltern voices (Ono, 1998). However, and this is especially important for our purposes, mutuality, critical transformation, dialogue and how communicative solidarities are forged despite historical and geopolitical power differences remain understudied across all three paradigms of intercultural communication.

Several glimmers of hope are evident though. More than a decade ago, Cooks (2001) called for a reorientation of research and pedagogy in intercultural communication in ways that engage "cultural borderlands" and differences in more critical, heuristic and dynamic rather than in static and reifying ways. Furthermore, some scholars of critical intercultural communication are increasingly engaging intersectionality (Crenshaw, 1991), a notion which focuses on multiple interlocking oppressions and identities and the possibility of alliance-building across identity groups (e.g., see Carrillo Rowe, 2008, 2010; Chávez, 2012). Similarly, the works of scholars such as Anzaldúa (1990) and postcolonial studies scholar Homi Bhabha (1990, 1994) who have specifically labored to theorize the transformative space of the 'in-between' (i.e., the space where something new is created when cultural differences intersect) have also gained some ground within intercultural communication. Recent work on dialogue, including Mitra's (2011) dialogic framework for understanding performances of difference as a "strategic struggle," are paving the way for more complex views of difference (see also, Dempsey, Parker, & Krone, 2011; and special issue 4(2) of the *Journal of International and Intercultural Communication*) [Ganesh, 2011]).

Furthermore, Fred Casmir's (1993) work on third culture building suggests an 'in-between' transformative approach to intercultural communication at the interpersonal level, and Y. Y. Kim's (2008) Intercultural Personhood model is undoubtedly cosmopolitan in spirit (see Chapters 4 and 5 for more details). Also, more recently, organizational communication scholars have called for more complex theorizing of the communicative production of difference. By emphasizing that differences operate along multiple and not singular axes, they have called for more attention to intersectionality, especially when studying difference in transnational contexts (Dempsey, 2011). They are also emphasizing the need to study difference less as something that is a property of individuals and groups and more as a communicative and discursive production so that we may be able to explore the many nuanced ways in which difference is produced in various contexts (Putnam, Jahn, & Baker, 2011). These more recent trends are indications that the communicative and performative space of difference production, the space where mutuality and critical transformation may be possible, needs more theoretical and empirical attention within the field of intercultural communication. This is where cosmopolitanism comes into the picture.

Cosmopolitanism exhorts us to perform difference in ways that hold potential for intercultural and moral growth, creativity and mutual learning in an ever-changing world. With its intention to interrupt the logic of methodological nationalism and understand ways in which solidarity can be accomplished across national and cultural differences, the critical and postcolonial turn in cosmopolitanism can lend intercultural communication heuristic insights. It can help the field focus specifically on how to accomplish mutuality, dialogue and transformative connections within conditions of transnational and postcolonial complexities and power asymmetries without abandoning the critical perspective. Postcolonial scholarship has encouraged intercultural communication and critical media studies scholars to bring the politics of the transnational and transcultural into focus through the study of hybridity, diaspora, the global-local dialectic, subalternity, cultural deterritorialization/reterritorialization and other related phenomena (Shome & Hegde, 2002). Drawing upon anthropologist Clifford Geertz's work, Kraidy and Murphy (2008) have forwarded the notion of translocalism, or the dynamics of local-to-local communication, which helps us "refocus on the local, which is after all the site where meaning emerges, without disengaging from issues involving global forces" (p. 339). While these critical perspectives focus intensely on power and resistance, the role of mutuality, critical transformation and agency in forming difficult alliances across difference through communication needs more attention. These are issues cosmopolitanism can address to a certain extent. It catches these postcolonial and critical notions in its "wide and wavering net" (Pollock et al., 2002, p. 4) and stirs an ethical vision for communicating as global citizens into the mix. Cosmopolitanism offers critical hope.

But what can cosmopolitanism gain from intercultural communication? The answer is straightforward. Cosmopolitanism's inherently communicative and intercultural dimensions remain insufficiently theorized, and this is where it can benefit from a symbiosis with intercultural communication. A bridge waits to be built here. To start this interdisciplinary bridgework, we begin by highlighting some of the prominent values guiding cosmopolitanism thought in sociology, anthropology and political philosophy and foreground their inherently intercultural and communicative nature.

PROMINENT VALUES OF COSMOPOLITANISM

Cosmopolitan thought can be divided into two entwined clusters—cosmopolitanism and political philosophy and cultural cosmopolitanism. Our focus in this book, however, is on the cultural aspects of cosmopolitanism. The prominent values that underlie cultural cosmopolitanism can be distilled from the larger literature, and they could apply to interactions and discourses that range from the intra/interpersonal level to the macro discursive level of transnational public communication. At the heart of the various trajectories of cosmopolitanism are ideas about a certain kind of disposition and identity orientation towards the cultural Other and the world, including intercultural competencies and an ethical vision which may be mindfully cultivated. Some of the prominent values and competencies (and this is, by no means, an exhaustive list) that, according to the literature, mark such a disposition and orientation are as follows:

- An ability to cultivate an ethical vision or horizon (Werbner, 2008), and an outward orientation that is partly shaped but not bounded and controlled by the nation-state perspective (Nussbaum, 1996). This involves a commitment to social justice at and beyond local and national levels and developing skills of thinking, living and acting at the nexus of the global and local by striving for a balance between patriotism and world-belongingness (Cheah, 1998; Delanty, 2009; Werbner, 2008). This is a willingness and ability to "inhabit the world from afar" (Szerszynski & Urry, 2006, p. 113).
- A desire and commitment to expand one's sense of belonging from near to far, and to develop imagination skills necessary to understand the near and far implications of one's actions (Appadurai, 1996).
- The willingness and readiness to be (discerningly) open to and engage with the cultural Other (whether near or far), and be transformed through interaction (critical self-transformation) (Appiah, 2006; Delanty, 2009; Hannerz, 1990; Szerszynski & Urry, 2002).
- An optimism about learning, a willingness to take intellectual and emotional risks to do so and finding pleasure in learning new things (Hannerz, 2006).
- A desire and commitment to live by values such as equality, human rights, inclusion, humility, compassion, reflexivity, respect and empathy (Delanty, 2009; Mendieta, 2009; Werbner, 2008).
- A desire and ability to develop an Other-oriented sense of Self (Appiah, 2006; Delanty, 2009), and develop a sense of "allegiance . . . to the worldwide community of human beings" (Nussbaum, 1996, p. 4).
- A desire and ability to develop a sense of cultural belonging that can navigate the tension between multiple cultural attachments (Appiah, 2006; Hannerz, 2006). This entails cultivating a sense of cultural citizenship which dwells in the dialectic tension of imagining any place in the world as a possible homeplace (should that become a reality) and the commitments that arise from home/family being rooted in culture-specific contexts. This could be seen as the ability to participate with commitment in more than one culture without exclusively becoming a part of any of them (Vertovec & Cohen, 2002).
- An ability to recognize multiple cultural identities and affiliations in Self and Others (Vertovec & Cohen, 2002).

- A desire for dialogue and creating connections, however tenuous, across difference, i.e., the desire to take up an aesthetic and intellectual stance that searches for "contrasts rather than uniformity" (Hannerz, 1990, p. 239; or an equal appreciation for both). Or, as Werner (2008) puts it, cosmopolitanism involves the ability to devise ways for "living together with difference" (p. 2).
- An ability to build transnational and translocal intercultural alliances for developing agency and momentum for countering the negative effects of neoliberal globalization and attending to social and global justice issues.
- A commitment to "diversality" or regard for all "universals" (Mignolo, 2002).
- A commitment to decentering Western hegemony and engaging in decolonizing and emancipatory projects (Mignolo, 2002; Nederveen Pieterse, 2006; Theodossopoulos & Kirtsoglou, 2010; Werbner, 2008).

All these values (and the gestalt they produce) are inherently intercultural in that they all orient towards creating connections, however tenuous, with the cultural/national Other, and with Otherness, across what may seem to be enduring cultural differences. In fact, they collectively advocate *connection through difference rather than through sameness*, and embrace various dialectics with the ethical vision of transcending static and divisive conceptions of nation, culture, communication and the Other. One point to note here is that some may practice cosmopolitanism more intrinsically because history and circumstances have already taught them how, and some may strive to cultivate cosmopolitan skills. Either way, it is the actual performance of cosmopolitanism that ultimately matters. Cosmopolitanism, then, is about living life interculturally and in a world-oriented manner, through a certain disposition and ethical vision about the relation between the Self and the cultural Other. It is about taking an active interest in the cultural Other, being open to change and dialogue for social and global justice, and critically navigating multiple cultural attachments.

Since cosmopolitanism is a philosophy and cultural and ethical vision that is amenable to all levels and forms of communication—the intra/interpersonal to the global/societal, the values highlighted above are also applicable to various levels and forms of communication. Delanty (2009), for instance, notes that cosmopolitanism plays out both on the level of the Self–Other (the micro level of intercultural communication) and at the nexus of the global–local (the macro level of intercultural communication). Thus cosmopolitanism is suitable for development as a critically-oriented intercultural communication theory that moves across multiple levels and forms of communication. For instance, U.S. network NBC's decision to air an interview with U.S. swimming star Michael Phelps during that portion of the 2012 London Olympics opening ceremony which was a tribute to the victims of London's 7/7 terrorist attack was explained away as a choice "tailored for the U.S. audience" ("NBC's edit of Olympic opening ceremony," 2012). The assumption here is that the London terrorist attack and the suffering that it caused is not something the U.S. public can identify with and that they would rather see an interview with Phelps. This is an example of a decidedly uncosmopolitan communication decision made at the macro level (and at the nexus of the global and national/local) that used the nation-state as a natural divider to determine whose suffering is more relevant for whom. For a micro-level example, a colleague at work caring to enquire about the family of another colleague in a distant country suffering a major power outage demonstrates cosmopolitan empathy. Perhaps if this caring colleague had been in charge of making NBC's editing decisions, the outcome may have been different.

The micro–macro applicability of cosmopolitanism is an important strength from the point of view of intercultural communication since the field needs more critically-oriented theoretical visions that can span and be theorized across various levels and forms of communication. Relationships that are communicatively built and/or transformed at the micro level can set the tone for change at more macro and institutional levels—and philosophies and visions that can connect all levels are valuable. We are by no means suggesting causal reasoning but making the point that various levels and forms of communication are interrelated. For example, according to Casmir (1993), "all institutions initially, and always, are the results of the efforts of individual human beings" (p. 408). Using Giddens' structuration theory, Falkheimer (2007) explains that "social structures are reproduced or transformed through repetition (on a macro-level) of individual acts" (p. 288). In other words, cosmopolitan micropractices (Mumby, 1993) could, in a ground-up fashion, lead to creative macro-level cosmopolitan changes capable of addressing power inequities and social and global justice issues in the world.

COSMOPOLITANISM AS A COMMUNICATION PHILOSOPHY

If we are to build a bridge between cosmopolitanism and intercultural communication, we have to first draw out the communicative dimensions of cosmopolitanism. Sociologists, anthropologists and political philosophers, in their writings about cosmopolitanism, generally seem to acknowledge that cosmopolitanism is an intercultural and inherently communicative and performative philosophy. But given their disciplinary backgrounds, they do not theorize these aspects further. For example, Hannerz (1990), a social anthropologist and one of the earlier theorists of cosmopolitanism in current times, characterizes cosmopolitanism as "a mode of managing meaning" (p. 238). This succinct definition is often cited in the literature and attests to the inherently communicative nature of cosmopolitanism. As Martin and Nakayama (2012) note, "The defining characteristic of communication is meaning, and we could say that communication occurs whenever someone attributes meaning to another person's [or entity's] words or actions" (p. 96). Intercultural communication occurs when meaning production occurs in intercultural contexts, i.e., contexts in which there is a perception of cultural difference (see also Gudykunst & Y.Y. Kim, 2003). Therefore, it is obvious that cosmopolitanism falls squarely in the camp of communication, specifically intercultural communication. Cosmopolitan spaces, places, practices, discourse and institutions emerge through cosmopolitan performances of intercultural meaning-making.

Along with being concerned with meaning production, cosmopolitanism is communicative in other ways as well. As we have already explained in detail in Chapter 1, the revised critical cosmopolitanism is dialogic, reflexive, and involves openness to critical self-transformation and the ability to hear and see the cultural Other with empathy and respect. These are all qualities of ethical communication, specifically in intercultural contexts. Delanty (2009) writes:

> Inter-cultural communication conceived of in cosmopolitan terms has five main characteristics. First, it is a mode of communication that is deliberative. Second, it is reflective. Third, it is critical in its orientation. Fourth, it entails societal learning. Fifth, it concerns political practice that has a global relevance. (p. 261)

He further emphasizes that cosmopolitan dialogue, in intercultural terms, cannot occur unless it produces learning and new horizons.

Cosmopolitanism entails the production of a communicative reality that transcends the Cartesian 'I' to produce a mutual sense of intercultural 'We' within the conditions of postcolonial globality. According to anthropologist Werbner (2008), "Cosmopolitanism is itself a product of creativity and communication in the context of diversity; it must be ultimately understood not merely as individual, but as collective, relational, and thus historically located" (p. 2). Werbner's words underscore the point, as we did earlier, that cosmopolitanism is not just about individual disposition, i.e., something that people possess. It is something that is *relational* and *performed* by people and groups who desire to produce cosmopolitan meanings, spaces, places, practices and structures. Thus cosmopolitan discourses and practices are consequences of world-oriented intercultural communication performances. According to Kendall, Woodward and Skrbis (2009):

> . . . we need to think of cosmopolitanism as a more flexible application of a cultural outlook focused on strategically discerning and appreciating difference in relevant social settings. It is, then, a *disposition performed* in particular contexts and settings as required. (p. 107, italics in original)

The relational, performative and discursive aspects of cosmopolitanism are significant connections to communication. People and groups can accomplish cosmopolitanism by consciously 'doing' through communicative praxis. According to Holton (2009), "the emphasis on cosmopolitanism as performance . . . extends to the ways that cosmopolitan life is performed through conversation, song and consumption of goods, sexual preference and interpersonal relationships" (p. 15). Cosmopolitan performances and 'doings' can permeate various aspects of our personal and public lives and relationships.

For cosmopolitanism to emerge, we cannot engage in instrumental communication that intends to control or coerce the cultural Other. Communication has to be vulnerable and dialogic and engage the space of the 'in-between,' the space that is produced through the intersection of cultural differences, the space of mutuality and possible intercultural growth. Rodriguez (2006), in describing himself as a product of multiple cultural dislocations, attests to the value of practicing the art of dwelling and communicating in the space of the in-between. He calls for a less instrumental and more humane definition of communication that is vulnerable to the humanity of others and is not driven simply by the intentions of 'tolerating' differences and maintaining the status quo. This form of communication is driven by the intention to expand our humanity and our worlds "by constantly demanding of us new meanings, new understandings, new experiences, and, ultimately, new modes of being in world with others" (p. 16).

In the book titled *Communication Ethics: Between Cosmopolitanism and Provinciality* (Roberts & Arnett, 2008), various established communication scholars offer their views on cosmopolitanism. Much of what they have to say resonates with Rodriguez's approach to communication. Stewart (2008), in connecting cosmopolitanism to communication, draws on Martin Buber's work on dialogue to note that the space of the in-between is an important aspect of human reality. He writes that "humans can learn and can choose to attend to the between . . . " (p. 114). Since cosmopolitanism involves the nexus of the global and the local, Stewart emphasizes the importance of this space and the skills needed for dialogic communication within such spaces. However, he does note that such spaces and skills do not automatically exist and they need to be carefully and intentionally cultivated. Like Stewart, Fisher (2008) too relies on Buber to emphasize the importance of the space of the in-between for ethical communication. This may be a narrow space or a wide space, and he notes that those who are far should matter as much as those who are near. Drawing upon Dewey's writings on community, he describes dialogic communication as involving connections with others and working collectively to build genuine relations and community for a more humane world. Fisher emphasizes that no community is possible without interest in others, which can be extended to mean that interest in others is necessary for cosmopolitan spaces, places, practices, discourses and institutions to emerge.

In this same book, Langsdorf (2008) also draws upon Buber and the work of Ronald Arnett to focus on the phenomenological and rhetorical space of the in-between. She argues that difference does not reside so much in the people engaged in communication but in the meanings that are inter-subjectively created in the communicative constitution of the in-between. Ethical communication requires openness to interruptions of prior held assumptions. Langsdorf helps us focus on the ontological reality of being joined in communication rather than thinking of communication as a process involving separate entities engaging in transmission of messages. It is in this joining and mutuality that the potential for cosmopolitanism resides.

Delanty, a sociologist who writes about cosmopolitanism and recognizes the importance of cosmopolitanism's communicative dimensions, also stresses the importance of the space of the in-between where cultural differences intersect. According to Delanty (2009), this is where cultural translation occurs. This is a space where tensions between various cultural orientations play out through a communicative and dialogic "process of mutations, transferences, innovations, appropriations, borrowings, re-combinations, and substitution" (p. 196). Through such translations, critical transformations may occur, and new ways to work together through difference may emerge. This notion of cultural translation is closely linked to another notion—cultural hybridity—which is closely related to cosmopolitanism (see Bhabha, 1990, 1994; we explore hybridity in more detail in the next chapter).

By explaining the inherently communicative and intercultural nature of cosmopolitanism, we have taken the initial steps to link cosmopolitanism with intercultural communication. We now turn to the important concept of difference. This look at difference is crucial for the next steps of the linking process since how we produce cultural difference through our communicative performances determines to what extent mutuality, critical self-transformation, intercultural learning and cosmopolitanism may be possible through intercultural encounters.

A DIFFERENT LOOK AT DIFFERENCE

At the heart of cosmopolitanism lies the notion of difference. Cosmopolitanism perceives societies and cultures as plural, overlapping and related, and the cosmopolitan goal is to naturalize (not to be confused with glossing over) and work with and through difference rather than mostly position differences as obstacles that need to be surmounted. Difference, according to cosmopolitanism, is something that can help us learn and grow as critical and ethical global citizens. While this is a recurring theme throughout the literature, what is less prominent are explanations of how societies and cultures may learn to view and perform difference in less divisive ways. Views from communication, cultural and postcolonial studies help shed some light on this topic. By exploring and connecting these views with cosmopolitanism, we move towards our concept of cosmopolitan communication.

From a communication perspective, Rodriguez and Chawla (2010) explain that how we think about communication impacts how we think about and perform difference in our daily lives. They argue that if we are going to define communication as the act of separate rational and autonomous Cartesian selves transmitting messages from one to another then difference becomes a rigid matter—something that is clearly outside the Self (and therefore the Other is always responsible for it!). On the other hand, if we focus on compassion, mutuality, empathy, vulnerability (openness to change) and dialogue, and stress the connectedness between humans despite various symbolically-constructed differences, then the borders between inside and outside, between 'Us' and 'Them,' become more permeable. The locus of difference, then, moves to a more mutual terrain and difference becomes something that is naturally a part of all of us. However, as Rodriguez and Chawla (2010) note, the assumption in most intercultural communication literature is that:

> ... our differences are what ultimately make for strife and conflict. Our differences are cast as a set of dangerous and perilous rapids that demand vigilant and sensitive navigation. Any wrong act, movement, behavior, or word can presumably send us crashing into the rocks and currents of discord. (p. 29)

Theorizing and positioning difference as a negative phenomenon is a barrier in the way of developing more entangled and less defensive assumptions about cultural difference.

Why the Negative Focus?

Audre Lorde (1984/2007) writes that Western European history, over time, has taught us to think about difference in oppositional terms and that we have become programmed to respond to difference in three main ways: to ignore it, emulate it if we view it as dominant and destroy it if we see it as subordinate. None of these responses position difference as empowering or as the source of creative knowledge production. It is worth quoting Lorde at length here:

> Difference must not be merely tolerated, but seen as a fund of necessary polarities between which our creativity can spark like a dialectic. Only then does the necessity for interdependence become unthreatening. Only within that interdependency of different strengths, acknowledged and equal, can the power to seek new ways of being in the world generate. ... Within the interdependence of mutual (nondominant)

differences lies that security which enables us to descend into the chaos of knowledge and return with true visions of our future, along with the concomitant power to effect those changes which can bring that future into being. Difference is that raw and powerful connection from which our personal power is forged. (1984/2007, pp. 111–112)

Anzaldúa (1990) has shown us through her writings how differences should not be glossed over but nor should they lead to harmful tribalism and divisive barriers. Absolute or pure conceptualizations of difference tend to work in terms of binaries which always position the first part of the binary as positive and the second as negative (e.g., Self–Other). In this vein, difference becomes something that is outside the Self (or the Self's identity group), it threatens the identity of the Self, and needs to be guarded against (Derrida, 1981; Sarup, 1996). Also, situating the cultural Other outside the Self is an act of exclusion as well as an exercise of power that keeps in place visions of purity and contamination (see Laclau, 1990). Such a conception of difference rejects ambiguity, since ambiguity threatens the status quo, and works against recognizing overlaps, connections and new ways of being and becoming. It makes it difficult to imagine changing the status quo and leans towards keeping hierarchies of power intact.

Warren (2008), in focusing our attention on the deeply ontological nature of difference, also points out the generally negative and binary assumptions regarding the concept in communication studies. Noting the lack of careful and nuanced theorizing of difference in the discipline, he makes the case that a performative theory of difference can help us "understand 'what happens' within intercultural settings" (p. 302). Drawing upon Deleuze, he stresses the importance of better understanding how we actually perform and 'do' difference in our everyday lives so that we can "increase our ability to be agents of interruption, critique, and change" (p. 300). Warren's view is a hopeful one since it helps us imagine a more productive and dynamic approach to difference. Only if we move away from absolute, static and negative conceptualizations of difference, and see difference as something which we all do and can do differently, can we enter into the space of the in-between with others to work through and negotiate our differences in a manner that promises more hope, empathy and creativity. It is only then that meaningful connections across enduring differences will be possible, and the space of the in-between (or the 'inter' in intercultural communication) will become a more productive space. According to Carrillo Rowe (2010):

The inter of intercultural communication is a capacious site of unfolding interactions across lines of difference. It gestures towards the unknown and unknowable space between unevenly located subjects. . . . This is to say that the inter marks a process of becoming that is constituted *between* subjects, who, in engaging the inter are, in turn, reconstituted through their exchange. . . . The space of the inter into which we must insert ourselves in order to engage an/other is fraught, frightening, even as it brims with transformative possibilities. (p. 216, 224, italics in original)

This space of the 'inter' is well-theorized in postcolonial/cultural studies.

The Postcolonial View of Difference

The postcolonial studies approach to difference does not work in terms of polarizing binaries, but adopts a more entangled view of difference in order to recognize the complexities and possibilities involved (Grossberg, 2002). Pratt (1992), in her book *Imperial Eyes: Travel Writing and, Transcultura-tion*, does a remarkable job of demonstrating how both oppressors and those oppressed are changed across the lines of difference and power when contact occurs. This leads to the idea that identity and power lines may be guarded rigidly, but they can and do change in the face of ambiguity which is inevitably produced in the in-between spaces of all intercultural interactions (Bhabha, 1994). This is the space of cultural translation and transformation which can alter power hierarchies by interrupting claims of cultural purity and superiority by more powerful cultural groups. Thus the postcolonial position on difference clearly recognizes disparities and oppressions, is committed to addressing them, but instead of banging its head against rigid binaries, searches for overlaps, entanglements, ambiguities and border realities that hold hope for disruptions and change. It advocates a creative engagement with cultural difference minus the fear and anxiety that comes with the need to rigidly guard cultural boundaries of Us–Them and Self–Other. It is marked by an acceptance of ambivalence and a discerning openness to the cultural Other, values that cosmopolitanism embraces (Delanty, 2009). Such a view works to destabilize binaries in order to reconfigure and disrupt power hierarchies, and is committed to dismantling old systems and formations of power (e.g., the oppressor/oppressed form). It helps us see that there is no escape from these forms, even if power relations are inverted, unless the forms themselves are changed (see Grossberg, 1996; Laclau, 1992).

Stuart Hall's contributions are also helpful for arriving at less polarized views of difference. Hall (1990) draws upon Derrida's clever play on the word—"differ*a*nce" instead of "difference"—to show how a slight textual shift of the word shifts its meaning and suspends it between the pure/oppositional view of difference (i.e., how we are mostly used to thinking of difference) and the constant sliding or deferment of meaning which occurs through ongoing interactions between cultural differences. Acts of power attempt to fix the meanings of difference in oppositional, hierarchical and negative terms, but postcolonialism's political project involves disrupting such fixing through attention to the possibility of changing colonizing and oppressive meanings of difference.

Gupta and Ferguson (1992) challenge methodological nationalism and help trouble our settled ways of thinking about cultural difference at the global level. Noting there is nothing natural about mapping distinct cultures (often conflated with nation-states) onto distinct bodies, spaces and places, they write: "The distinctiveness of societies, nations, and cultures is based upon a seemingly unproblematic division of space, on the fact that they occupy 'naturally' discontinuous spaces" (p. 6). They question this unquestioned separation, or play of power, which they believe makes opposition possible and helps keep in place "natural" divisions between cultures which are actually interconnected through the power plays of history. Such assumptions result in the fallacy of a united 'Us' and entrench the "otherness of the 'other'" (p. 14). Gupta and Ferguson's argument helps us imagine a more continuous (albeit unequal) world marked by ongoing and overlapping cultural productions that cannot be neatly mapped. In a globalizing world, as "the 'here' and 'there' become blurred," all attempts to separate cultures are "bewildered by a dazzling array of postcolonial simulacra, doublings and redoublings" and the heightened pace of cultural deterritorialization and reterritorialization (p. 10). This view is supported by Shome and Hegde (2002):

> Whether it is high-speed communication systems, global migration, or the circulation of images, we are faced with the coming together of contradictory forces and incommensurable differences. The critical vein of postcolonial theory enables a complicating of these overlapping and interstitial spaces. (p. 260)

Postcolonial views on difference bring us to the notion of multiculturalism and its problematic assumptions about difference.

The Assumptions of Multiculturalism

The idea of multiculturalism and its assumptions about difference underlie the bulk of the current research in the field of intercultural communication. Since a great deal of the field is academically entrenched within the U.S., and multiculturalism is a cultural and political philosophy and discourse that is deeply ingrained in this society, the field has naturally leaned towards multiculturalism. However, as we will presently elaborate, multiculturalism's assumptions about difference actually pose an obstacle in the way of cosmopolitan visions of intercultural communication. Therefore, it is necessary that we interrupt the taken-for-grantedness of multiculturalism and its approach to difference (see Chapter 5 for more discussion on multiculturalism).

Multiculturalism, while it must be commended for valuing the notion of difference, also displays the fallacy of assuming a natural separateness between cultures. Multiculturalism tends to hold sacred cultural particularity (hence separateness), but unfortunately at the expense of ecological interconnectedness. According to Shome and Hegde (2002):

> The rhetoric of multiculturalism celebrates the diverse assemblage of cultures in their pristine flavors—colorful yet standing separate in their authenticity. . . . The discrete positioning of cultures without any sense of their interconnected histories reproduces the violence of colonial modernities and fixes difference in a spectacle of otherness. (pp. 261, 262)

Such a position on cultural difference produces a static view of the Self's identity group and that of the cultural Other and reduces the scope for imagining change, creativity and growth that may be possible through intercultural communication and mutual transformation (Delanty, 2009; Prato, 2009). Without attention to interconnectedness and mutuality, old oppressions and divisions are maintained and Otherness becomes reified. Furthermore, as Prato (2009) argues, the danger inherent in how multiculturalism views culture and difference is that in pursuit of political correctness and equality, the discourse of multiculturalism actually creates a conflict between individual and group (cultural) identity/ies. To uphold the identity of the cultural group, the individual is constrained from exploring how the Self changes through interaction with cultural differences at the individual level. Relatedly, the static view of culture that multiculturalism promotes also holds the potential for contributing to cultural stereotypes since according to this bounded view of culture, "culture is treated as a 'thing,' an object to be possessed and shared by a strictly defined group of people and which sets the group apart from other groups" (Prato, 2009, p. 3). The scope for intercultural understanding and growth can also be considerably reduced when communication and discourses take on 'My culture vs. Your Culture' (i.e., 'we are separate/competing') overtones and any form of change is perceived as contamination or even 'giving in' to another culture.

Bhabha's critique of multiculturalism is right on target. He argues that difference is not so much a discomfort when it is positioned as separate (as in 'yes, they are obviously very different from us'). It becomes an uncomfortable and "uncanny" problem when "cultural difference is ourselves-as-others, others-as-ourselves, that borderline" (Bhabha, 1989, p. 72), i.e., when we begin to (or are made to) see the connectedness despite the difference that postcolonialism and cosmopolitanism insist on. This discomfort is something which multiculturalism is unable to get at. Bhabha helps us see that it is a self-defeating logic to argue for equal respect and equal cultural worth without attention to unequal "cultural time," i.e., the historical processes that have produced intercultural inequities and injustices over centuries. When we argue that every culture is equal (and separate), we lose the vision that they are, in fact, actually not (Bhabha, 1996a; see also Sarup, 1996). While equality is a noble ideal, assuming it exists when it doesn't hampers honest conversations about intercultural politics and how they affect intercultural communication.

In addition to the postcolonial views of difference and the critique of multiculturalism, we need to address the notion of dialectics, and specifically how it applies to intercultural communication and cosmopolitanism. The notion is valuable for explaining the relationship between difference and dialogism (a value central to cosmopolitanism).

Dialectics, Difference and Dialogism

The notion of dialectics mainly involves the idea of negotiating the tension between unitary opposites or contradictory ideas. Unitary opposites are concepts that depend on each other for their meaning (Baxter & Montgomery, 1996). Hegel's classic work on dialectics posits that every concept (thesis) has its opposite (antithesis) and that people struggle to reach transcendent resolutions (synthesis). Syntheses, however, are not easy to reach, and in everyday life people are constantly caught up in managing the tensions and interplay between opposite-seeming ideas which often mark our intercultural differences. As Baxter and Montgomery note, dialectics help us get at the messiness that marks communication processes, and they subscribe to a dialogic view of dialectics which is based mainly on the work of Mikhail Bakhtin (explored in more detail in Chapter 3 in relation to identity). This approach does not assume an end-state (synthesis) but sees dialectic interplay as indeterminate and involving ongoing dialogic interaction wherein individuals or entities engage in "simultaneous differentiation from yet fusion with one another" with the possibility of change (Baxter & Montgomery, 1996, p. 24). The dialogic dialectic perspective is a process-oriented 'both/and' perspective. It urges us to focus on possibilities inherent in the tension between opposite-seeming (i.e., different) cultural forces. Thus difference, according to the dialectic view, is not necessarily a negative to be overcome but a reality that is charged with ambiguity, pregnant with possibility, and open to dialogue.

The notion of dialectics has come late to intercultural communication but it has now gained some support. According to Martin and Nakayama (1999), the dialectic approach to intercultural communication can help us transcend modernist dichotomies, because "it recognizes and accepts as ordinary, the interdependent and complementary aspects of the seeming opposites" (p. 14). They note that intercultural communication practice conceived of in dialectic terms is relational and allows us to see the world in multiple ways. To this we add that dialectics also help us transcend binary views of difference and move in a dialogic direction instead. Martin and Nakayama offer the following six dialectics for intercultural communication practice: (1) the cultural–individual dialectic, (2) the personal/social–contextual dialectic, (3) the similarities–differences dialectic, (4) the static–dynamic dialectic, (5) the present/future–history/past dialectic, and (6) the privilege–disadvantage dialectic. Building upon Martin and Nakayama, Cargyle (2005) makes the point that the dialectic approach to intercultural communication is well-equipped to get at the tensions between cultures which can be the source for change, creativity and innovation. He notes that by embracing contradiction, as dialectics does, "it becomes easy to recognize that seemingly distinct groups are nonetheless interdependent" (p. 116).

The dialectic perspective within intercultural communication is an open door that invites in cosmopolitanism. Its vision of dialogic communication across cultural difference ties in well with the inherently dialectic nature of cosmopolitanism. According to Rumford:

> Cosmopolitanism requires us to recognize that we are all positioned simultaneously as outsiders and insiders, as individuals and groups members, as Self and Other, as local and global. Cosmopolitanism is about relativizing our place within the global frame, positioning ourselves in relation to multiple communities, crossing and re-crossing territorial and community borders. (cited in Delanty, 2009, p. 250)

Thus dialectics are necessary for better understanding how cosmopolitan dialogue across seemingly opposite differences may be accomplished.

This section on how we think about, communicatively produce and engage with difference is a pivotal step in our effort to build a concept of cosmopolitan communication. *The postcolonial 'in-between' or interstitial view of difference (along with the critique of multiculturalism), if used to illuminate cosmopolitanism's vision of critical self-transformation and communicating dialogically and ethically as global citizens, can serve us better in a world where unequal differences are intersecting at a dizzying pace. In turn, when merged with a dialectic and ecological view of intercultural communication, cosmopolitanism enhanced by postcolonial insights can help us move towards a concept of cosmopolitan communication.* We now turn to the important task of offering a working definition for and the assumptions that we associate with what we call cosmopolitan communication.

COSMOPOLITAN COMMUNICATION

So far in this chapter, we have done the work of linking cosmopolitanism with intercultural communication. We now present a working definition of what we call *cosmopolitan communication* along with seven assumptions that inform this definition. We begin with the assumptions which are drawn from the linking of the two bodies of work.

Assumptions may be thought of as guiding principles. The following assumptions that underlie cosmopolitan communication could apply to all levels and forms of communication. They are based in a dialectic and ecological view of culture, and provide a vision for communicating ethically, dialogically and critically as global citizens. At this point we would like to note again, as we did at the start of this chapter, that what we offer here is by no means set in stone and nor do we desire that our concept of cosmopolitan communication be taken as such. We do not presume that the concept and its assumptions will always apply to all the myriad intercultural situations that exist and are possible in this world. But we strongly believe that they are sound, and theoretically informed, starting points.

Assumption 1

Cosmopolitan communication is world- and Other-oriented. It is not nation-state-centric (which is not the same as dismissing the nation-state) nor local-centric, and is able to navigate the dialectic tension between world-belongingness and local/national affiliations. It takes a space-based rather than place-based approach to culture and identity and affirms multiple cultural attachments on all sides.

Assumption 2

Cosmopolitan communication accomplishes mutuality. It focuses on the in-between space between culturally different interlocutors where the possibilities for change reside and where new meaning creation may be jointly accomplished.

Assumption 3

Cosmopolitan communication is attentive to power. It assumes that cultural Others who are near as well as those who are physically distant are worthy of moral consideration, and that our communication should reflect this moral vision and work towards redressing historical and newly emerging power inequities and social injustices at local and global levels.

Assumption 4

Cosmopolitan communication actively engages borders. It sees borders (e.g., those of nation-states) as connectors rather than dividers between cultures that can lead to new ways of thinking about Us–Other intercultural relationships.

Assumption 5

Cosmopolitan communication invests in a dialogical, emancipatory and non-oppositional view of cultural difference. It starts with the view that differences themselves are communicatively and discursively produced.

It attempts to engage contrasts and views differences positively, i.e., in a manner that looks for productive outcomes. The 'doing' or communicative production of difference is regarded as a moral matter. Furthermore, difference is engaged along multiple axes, i.e., cosmopolitan communication embraces an intersectional approach to difference. It is not threatened by and does not attempt to control ambiguities (or new meanings) that emerge at the intersections of multiple cultural differences.

Assumption 6

Cosmopolitan communication sees critical self-transformation as a key goal. Those wishing to engage in cosmopolitan communication need to be self-reflexive and open to interruptions of prior held assumptions. They need to be open to problematizing the Self and troubling values and notions they take for granted for the sake of intercultural growth and finding new and more hopeful ways of being, becoming and relating in a constantly changing world.

Assumption 7

Cosmopolitan communication is hopeful and deliberate. Those engaged in cosmopolitan communication are able to find hope in difference. They demonstrate an active, deliberate and genuine desire to learn about cultural Others and their worldviews in order to experience mutual intercultural and moral growth. Cosmopolitan communication is never, under any circumstance, coercive towards the cultural Other.

Based on the above assumptions, we present a working definition of cosmopolitan communication. *Cosmopolitan communication is a world- and Other-oriented practice of engaging in deliberate, dialogic, critical, non-coercive and ethical communication. Through the play of context-specific dialectics, cosmopolitan communication works with and through cultural differences and historical and emerging power inequities to achieve ongoing understanding, intercultural growth, mutuality, collaboration and social and global justice goals through critical self-transformation.* This definition includes a global ethical vision and is sensitive to issues of power and context. The 'Other' implied in the definition may be concrete or abstract and near or far. The communicative and moral relationship between the Self and the cultural Other lies at the heart of our definition and permeates all our assumptions. According to cosmopolitan communication, we need to move away from highly Cartesian modes of being and relating and see the Self as different from yet ecologically entangled with the cultural Other. Cosmopolitan communication encourages us to perceive the Self as not essentially bound by one's cultural assumptions but capable of making choices to expand the horizons of the Self beyond bounded (i.e., received) conceptions of cultural identity. It stresses the ability to be proficient in cultures one strongly affiliates with and yet be able to surrender some deeply entrenched assumptions when they are appropriately problematized.

In the next two chapters, we elaborate on this core aspect of Self–Other (or Us–Them) interconnectedness from a communication perspective. In Chapter 3 we focus on identity, belonging, dialogism, agency, hybridity, intercultural bridgework and the dynamics of critical self-transformation. In Chapter 4 we discuss the role of the imagination in cultivating a cosmopolitan outlook, empathy and implicature, and the overarching value of kindness to strangers necessary for engagement in cosmopolitan communication. The result of this elaboration is our ontological concept of *cosmopolitan peoplehood*, a way of being and becoming that we propose for accomplishing cosmopolitan communication. Through this concept we propose ways for envisioning an Other-oriented, decentered Self that is capable of contributing to a larger sense of world-oriented 'We' or cosmopolitan peoplehood. Cosmopolitan peoplehood and cosmopolitan communication are co-constitutive.

3 Cultural Identity, Communication and Critical Self-Transformation
Towards Cosmopolitan Peoplehood

> I have to find my way, like many of us, amongst many attachments, many identifications, none of them sufficient or complete. I have to recognize how limited that is. But it's obliged me to maintain what I would call an openness towards the horizon of that which I am not, the experiences I have not had—a sense of one's incompleteness, requiring for my own 'completeness' what is other to it. (Hall, 2008, p. 350)

Scholars of cosmopolitanism frequently use the term 'disposition' or outlook in relation to cosmopolitanism. They write about the importance of critical self-transformation and of an Other- and world-oriented disposition for cosmopolitanism to emerge. While they are careful not to fix cosmopolitanism as a concrete identity type (i.e., people do not carry cosmopolitanism within themselves), they do emphasize that a particular identity orientation (or disposition) could aid in the emergence of cosmopolitanism spaces, practices, discourses and institutions. However, they do not delve too much into what they mean by disposition, and related issues of selfhood and identity/ies remain under-addressed as well. But cosmopolitanism can gain in this area from intercultural communication. The topic of identity has increasingly become a central focus in the field of intercultural communication since how we perform and communicatively co-construct identities (and differences) lies at the heart of intercultural communication (see Bardhan & Orbe, 2012; Y. Y. Kim, 2007; Ting-Toomey, 2005). While cosmopolitanism is not a specific identity type, how identities are performed in communication does have a bearing on the possibilities for the production of cosmopolitan outcomes during intercultural encounters. A close look at the theoretical trajectories of identity research in intercultural communication can help us better understand the notion of critical self-transformation and what it means to be Other- and world-oriented in how we communicate as critical global citizens with cultural Others.

Identity tends to become a preoccupation when cultural identities are challenged, fragmented or when they proliferate in an explosion of possibilities (Hall, 1996). In today's conditions of postmodern and postcolonial globality, heightened movement (actual or virtual) across cultural borders is increasingly interrupting the power of national culture to remain a hegemonic identity category (Appadurai, 1996; Rosenau, 2004). People can and are simultaneously identifying with sub and supranational cultural entities (including virtual communities), and this is leading us away from a stable place-based received view of 'identity' to one of 'identities' that extend and shift across place and space (Hall, 1997; Shome, 2003, 2010). One major form of cultural and identity movement occurs through travel and migration. While the majority of the world's population does not actually travel and migrate, the percentage of those who do is on the rise ("How and why people move," n.d.). People move within and beyond the boundaries of the nation-state in privileged ways and for pragmatic reasons, as well as under oppressive and violent conditions (see Kaplan, 1996). The motivations and forces behind travel and migration are numerous—economic opportunity, leisure travel, missionary work, social service related travel, escape from war and ethnic conflict, escape from ecological disasters, corporate work related travel and sojourns, human trafficking of various forms, study related sojourns, diplomatic postings, military service and so on.

Historically, people have always traveled and moved, and the notion of the sedentary native or Other is a legacy of European colonization. However, in today's world, there are those who 'stay at home' and those who move for various reasons. Those who do not travel much or migrate find that the world is coming at them faster than ever before. As a result, they are increasingly coming into contact with cultural Others and finding themselves in situations where they have to find new ways to interact and live together with difference. In these heightened spaces of Self–Other identity intersections reside possibilities for cosmopolitan communication or conflict. In addition to actual travel, exposure to images, ideologies and information about other cultures through those who travel, the media and online sources is also a form of cultural movement that is widening our imagination about the world as a whole and the cultural beings who inhabit it (Appadurai, 1996; see Chapter 4). Thus culture, like identity, can no longer be thought of in fixed and sedentary ways. Along with identities, cultures are increasingly intersecting and dynamic. Our multiple senses of Self and Others are turning cultures and identities into multidimensional ongoing projects that are caught up in the play of various dialectics and registers of power, vacillating in particular directions depending on context.

Given this reality, some broad questions, specifically in relation to cosmopolitanism and 'disposition,' come to mind: What implications do these explosions of identity and culture hold for how we think of the Self in relation to the cultural Other? Why do some, through their discourses and interactions, feel the need to guard a static sense of 'I' and 'Us' while others open up and are willing to be transformed by the cultural Other? How can we move away from defensive views of cultural identity and move towards more dynamic and hopeful conceptualizations that emphasize the 'doing' and critical transformation of identity through cosmopolitan communication? These are key questions that we explore in this chapter. We have already emphasized in the previous chapter that cosmopolitan communication entails the recognition and affirmation of multiple identities and interconnected differences. Furthermore, a core value of cosmopolitanism is an open orientation towards the cultural Other and the world. Since the dynamic between the multiple Self and Others lies at the heart of our working definition of cosmopolitan communication, it deserves further attention.

In this chapter, we explore identity and the Self–Other dynamic from an intercultural communication perspective in order to theoretically bolster this core relationship that informs cosmopolitanism and cosmopolitan communication. We first broadly describe how the intercultural communication field has theorized identity. Next, we explore the strengths and the gaps in this theorizing, and demonstrate the connections between cosmopolitan 'disposition,' or ways of being and becoming, and intercultural identity theorizing. Then, through the notions of belonging, dialogism, agency, hybridity and intercultural bridgework, we move towards a cosmopolitan or Other- and world-oriented Self–Other view of being, becoming and relating which we call *cosmopolitan peoplehood*. Critical self-transformation, an assumption of cosmopolitan communication, is also elaborated upon. We hold that cosmopolitan peoplehood and cosmopolitan communication are co-constitutive. We invest in a social constructionist view that does not separate identity (or disposition) from communication. We begin the work of constructing the ontological concept of cosmopolitan peoplehood in this chapter and complete it in the next.

VIEWS OF IDENTITY IN INTERCULTURAL COMMUNICATION

In this section, we trace how the field of intercultural communication has theorized identity, and establish links with cosmopolitanism's take on the topic. We would like to note before proceeding further that culture works through many forms, and people identify (and disidentify) with various categories of culture related to ethnicity, nationality, race, gender, religion, sexual orientation, organizations, social and political issues and so on. Furthermore, these categories that shape identities are assuming more space-based rather than place-based meanings, and are intersecting rapidly from micro to transnational levels (Shome, 2003). Much work has been done on identity within intercultural communication, and it is beyond the scope of this chapter to cover all details. We offer some broad brush strokes with the aim of covering the main theoretical positions.

Earlier Theories

The question of identity is closely tied to how we perceive the Self in relation to the Self's cultural group(s), and in relation to cultural Others. According to Cupach and Imahori (1993), identity is "self conception—one's theory of oneself" (p. 113). The earlier theories were mostly functional and interpretivist in nature. According to Ting-Toomey (2005), "*Cultural identity* is defined as the emotional significance we attach to our sense of belonging or affiliation with the larger culture" (p. 214, italics in original). Early work on identity focused on the relation between the individual and cultural groups in the process of identity negotiation. Ting-Toomey's (1993) Identity Negotiation Theory sees identity as relational and context-based, and focuses on the intercultural communication skills required for positive and competent communication across identity groups. Collier's (1988) Cultural Identity Theory also focuses on the relation between the individual and cultural groups, and accords importance to context, relationality and the multidimensional nature of identities. Collier's work emphasizes that cultural identities emerge through everyday communicative interaction and discourse, they endure as well as change over time, and are transmitted to new cultural group members (see Collier, 1998). Cupach and Imahori's (1993) Identity Management Theory highlights effective identity negotiation skills through appropriate facework during the three interrelated and cyclical intercultural relationship stages of trial, enmeshment and renegotiation. While these theories mostly focus on identity first and communication second, the Communication Theory of Identity (Hecht, 1993; Hecht, Warren, Jung, & Krieger, 2005) puts communication before identity and notes that communication constructs particular identities rather than the other way around. According to this theory, four interrelated layers of identity—personal, enactment, relational and communal—work together and across various levels of communication. Additionally, scholars have also traced identity development models for particular majority, non-majority and bicultural identity groups in the U.S. (e.g., Cross, 1991; Poston, 1990; Ruiz, 1990).

Based on her many years of work on the cultural adaptation processes of immigrants in host societies (i.e., the U.S.), Y. Y. Kim (2008) has forwarded the Intercultural Personhood model of identity. This model emerges from "the experiences of acculturation, deculturation, and the stress-adaptation-growth dynamic," and it defines intercultural identity as an "open-ended, adaptive, and transformative self-other orientation" (2008, p. 364). Kim extends her model beyond the immigration context and claims that this model of intercultural identity is transnational in scope. She argues that since people are increasingly crossing cultural borders propelled by the dynamics of globalization, the Intercultural Personhood model can be applied to many contexts around the world. As Kim herself notes, this model is close to the cosmopolitan ideal (see Chapters 4 and 5 for an explanation of how we build on Kim's model).

What we can take away from these theories of identity in intercultural communication is that identities are multidimensional, relational, open to change and negotiable through communication. As R. L. Jackson (1999) notes, identity negotiation is the process through which "two or more individuals consider the exchange of ideas, values, and beliefs. . . . *Negotiation of cultural identity* is a process in which one considers the gain, loss, or exchange of his or her ability to interpret their own reality or worldview"

(p. 10, italics in original). We also learn that identity negotiation works at various levels (intrapersonal to communal), and that it is possible to actively cultivate intercultural communication competency skills to engage positively with cultural Others. What we don't get so much from these theories, some of which are still works in progress, is sufficient focus on issues of power, hegemony, privilege, spatial context, cultural deterritorialization/reterritorialization and the notion of difference. While context is acknowledged, it is generally studied as stable and unchanging (Y.Y. Kim's recent model is one exception), and larger historical, structural and political forces that impact identity-related communication are not investigated in depth (Mendoza, Halualani, & Drzewiecka, 2002; Shome, 2003). Due to their functional and interpretive nature, these theories are paradigmatically constrained from interrogating these issues (Martin & Nakayama, 2012; see Chapter 2). Furthermore, cultural difference is taken for granted and mostly assumed to be static in nature and a barrier that must be overcome (Rodriguez & Chawla, 2010). How the communicative intersection of differences can lead to identity transformation is not elucidated well enough (though Kim's model is a good start in this direction).

The Critical Turn

With the growth of the interpretive and critical paradigms in the 1990s, issues of power, privilege and hegemony were brought to the forefront. For example, Orbe's (1998) Co-cultural Theory is an identity-related theory that emerges from the viewpoint of muted non-dominant groups, or co-cultures, within the U.S. The focus of this theory is on an array of communication strategies deployed by co-cultural group members in their interactions with dominant cultural group members in various contexts. Co-cultural Theory has provided useful insights into identity negotiations enacted by groups in the U.S., transnational cultural groups with U.S. attachments and groups in non-U.S. locations (e.g., Matsunaga & Torigoe, 2008). R. L. Jackson's (2002) Cultural Contracts Theory, set in the context of U.S. race and power relations, posits that non-dominant cultures within society engage in strategic identity negotiations in contexts of inequality. They enter into metaphorical cultural contracts with dominant groups through which they assimilate, adapt or mutually value the Other's cultural worldview. This theory is applicable to all levels of communication, is influenced by Ting-Toomey's Identity Negotiation Theory and was developed from data on communication between African Americans and European Americans in U.S. contexts. In addition to these two more critically-oriented identity theories, whiteness studies, in the U.S. context, has made a major contribution to our understanding of identity by highlighting the racial privilege that is associated with the norm of whiteness as an invisible, and therefore unquestioned, identity category (e.g., see Nakayama & Krizek, 1995; Shin & R. L. Jackson, 2003; Warren, 2003). Others have elaborated on the discursive constructions of black masculine identity, again in the U.S. context, against the backdrop of whiteness as the norm, which produces anxiety and phobias regarding the black male body (e.g., see R. L. Jackson, 2006; R. L. Jackson & Dangerfield, 2002).

Within the critical trajectory, the more recent growth of identity research that employs the notion of intersectionality (Crenshaw, 1991), borrowed from feminist scholarship, is a move, as we noted in the previous chapter, towards the cosmopolitan ideal of finding ways of communicating and building alliances across cultural and ideological divides. For example, Carrillo Rowe (2008; 2010) has examined the possibilities of transracial alliance-building between feminists of color and Chávez (2012) has explored the possibilities of alliance-building among different identity groups with the common interest of immigrant rights in the U.S.

According to Chávez (2012), the notion of intersectionality and interlocking oppressions helps us transcend the purity logics of identity, and "coalition and alliance politics only emerges from acknowledging differences and finding ways to work with and through them toward various ends" (p. 30). Dempsey, Parker and Krone (2011), in the context of transnational feminism, use intersectionality to explore the political and cultural complexities of forming feminist alliances in transnational spaces and find that such efforts are compelling examples of "the ethical value of openness to interruptions by otherness" (p. 217). By focusing on interlocking oppressions and identities that could possibly bring cultural groups together for a common cause, this line of research is close in spirit to what we propose in our concept of cosmopolitan communication (see also Johnson & Bhatt, 2003; Pérez & Goltz, 2010). However, work on intersectionality does not yet sufficiently engage the vocabulary and philosophy of postcolonial/critical cosmopolitanism and world-orientedness. We see the possibility for a fruitful conversation between cosmopolitanism and work engaging the notion of intersectionality. Both challenge the purity logics of identity and advocate alliance- and agency-building through creative and non-oppositional performances of multiple differences. Specifically, cosmopolitanism can lend a transnational and translocal ethical vision to intercultural communication scholarship engaging intersectionality, and intersectionality can help sharpen the critical vision of cosmopolitanism (see also Assumption 2 of our concept of cosmopolitan peoplehood in Chapter 4).

To demonstrate that identity is a site of contested meanings and interests, and in order to move beyond received notions of identity towards ones that emphasize identity as an ongoing communicative production, Mendoza et al. (2002) bring in the notions of performativity, resignification and dynamic translation. Drawing upon Judith Butler's notion of performativity, they write that ethnic identities are linguistically performed and symbolically entrenched through linguistic repetitions which invoke sedimented meanings related to particular identities. This idea is also related to the narrative approach to identities which sees identity as a narrative performance and production, i.e., identities are produced through the stories we choose to tell about ourselves in particular contexts (see Chawla, 2012; Sarup, 1996). Sedimented meanings and set narratives may, however, be interrupted through particular linguistic performances. This point is further taken up by Warren (2008) who argues that by focusing on the interruptive possibilities of performance, we can start thinking about how hegemonic and oppressive performances of difference may be changed for emancipatory and hopeful performances of difference and identity (see also Bardhan, 2012; Holling & Calafell, 2007). Furthering Warren's work, Toyosaki (2012) writes that self-reflexive unpacking of identity as a dialectic between how we perform differences and similarities provides hope because such an understanding helps us focus on the fluid nature of identities and how we may engage in critical and emancipatory self-transformation. He writes:

> I have come to believe that the self is the key and ethical threshold in understanding the complexity of intercultural communication. . . . [H]uman growth becomes possible when we, human beings, understand our identity as an unstable construct and, thus, a conflictual site—the site of both the same and the different. How do we, human beings, change? (pp. 239, 241)

Mendoza et al. (2002) write that identities are double-sided and that while their meanings can be fixed through particular structural forces and symbolic exercises of power, they can also be unfixed and reconfigured through communicative acts of agency and resignification. Identities can also be dynamically translated, in order to excavate beyond surface meanings of identity avowals, by recognizing the politics behind decolonizing identitarian movements. All of this suggests that identities are not static, but dynamic, political, dialogic and performative productions.

More recent postcolonial and postmodern approaches to identity, culture and communication are also rupturing static conceptualizations (Sarup, 1996; Shome & Hegde, 2002). According to Yep (2002), identity is "political, fluid, and nonsummative" (p. 61). Notions of diaspora and hybridity are being increasingly utilized by several scholars to explore the 'in-between' and transnational nature of many identity groups within today's global ethnoscape (e.g., Bardhan, 2011; Drzewiecka & Halualani, 2002; Halualani, 2008; Hegde, 1998, Kraidy, 2002; Moreman, 2011; Witteborn, 2007). Furthermore, Shome (2003) emphasizes that "The relation between space and identity becomes especially important to investigate in contemporary times, when people's politics and actions cannot be located solely in their bodies and identities . . . " (p. 54). She underscores the point that we cannot assume that meanings of identities will remain the same across all spatial contexts since different configurations of space and human bodies produce varying meanings of identities. For example, the meanings associated with the brown body at the U.S.–Mexico border will likely be very different from meanings associated with the same body in the U.S. Midwest or in New York City (and meanings will shift even within particular spaces within the Midwest and New York City). Thus spatial shifts play a role in how identities are communicatively ascribed and even avowed.

The critical, postmodern and postcolonial approaches to cultural identity highlight the roles of power and difference in identity communication, two issues that are central to the more recent postcolonial turn in cosmopolitan thought. They suggest that identities are not set in stone, and that they can be performatively and communicatively reconfigured to bring about changes in perceptions about difference in ways that could open up possibilities for forming alliances across cultural divides. In other words, how we perform identities can interrupt and gradually change oppressive power hierarchies and structures—from the ground up. This move from identity as something people passively 'possess' to something they 'do' that can always be changed is a hopeful note for conceiving cultural identity and communication in cosmopolitan terms.

How identity is theorized is intricately linked to how culture and communication are conceptualized. How culture and communication are conceptualized is, in turn, linked to the paradigm within which they fall. As Y. Y. Kim (2007) has shown in her analysis of identity theories within intercultural communication, the approach to identity within the functional and interpretive paradigms falls into four categories: (a) cultural identity as an evolving and adaptive entity of an individual; (b) cultural identity as a flexible and negotiable entity of an individual; (c) cultural identity as a discrete social category and an individual choice; and (d) cultural identity as a distinct system of communal practices (p. 242). The critical paradigm puts cultural identity further into motion, and by highlighting issues of power, difference, oppression and hegemony puts an activist agenda firmly on the table for identity. Thus, the upshot of this is that if culture is conceptualized as static and individualistic, then so is identity. If culture and communication are conceptualized as dynamic, relational and always in the process of production, then so is identity. If issues of power, privilege, spatial politics and hegemony are taken out of the picture, then identity becomes merely passive and descriptive. If theorized critically, identity is mobilized and capable of doing critical work.

According to Martin and Nakayama (1999), it is heuristic to take a dialectic approach which helps us realize that all paradigms offer some useful knowledge. No paradigm is perfect or complete in itself. Descriptive knowledge about cultural identities and communication can enhance understanding about Self and Other and help generate dialogue while the critical impetus can help bring about needed change and critical self-transformation. We now move to the task of bringing cosmopolitanism into this literature on identity, culture and communication.

CULTURAL IDENTITY, COMMUNICATION, COSMOPOLITANISM

Identity theorizing in intercultural communication can enhance the notion of cosmopolitan disposition or identity orientation, and cosmopolitanism's approach to the matter can help move intercultural communication theorizing about identity in more outward and world-oriented directions, i.e., further open the process up to the Other and to the world by problematizing methodological nationalism.

Consider the following disposition/identity related statements by scholars of cosmopolitanism:

> Cosmopolitanism is infinite ways of being. (Pollock et al., 2002, p. 12)

> What is cosmopolitanism? . . . the word captures an open and receptive attitude towards the other. (Kendall et al., 2009, p. 1)

> . . . cosmopolitanism is dialogical—a collective, creative endeavor, beyond the individual. (Werbner, 2008, p. 25)

> It is in the interplay of the Self, Other and World that cosmopolitan processes come into play. (Delanty, 2009, p. 14)

> Action across borders, a heightened sense of the relativity of one's own social position and culture in a global setting, and interconnections between actors in diverse locations, lead us to an awareness of 'cosmopolitanism' . . . (Forte, 2010, p. 7)

> [Cosmopolitanism entails] conversations across boundaries of identity. . . . I'm using the word 'conversation' not only for literal talk but also as a metaphor for engagement with the experiences and the ideas of others. (Appiah, 2006, p. 85)

All of these statements express views about the need for the Self to be Other- and world-oriented and open to infinite possibilities (i.e., open to dialogue and critical self-transformation) for cosmopolitan performances and projects to be possible. The dialogical nature of identity orientation is emphasized, and the idea about being open to the experiences and realities of cultural Others and seeing the Self and cultural Others (whether near or far) as multiple, enmeshed and complex is central. Given that this is the kind of identity orientation (or disposition) being advocated by current scholars of cosmopolitanism, what can identity scholarship in intercultural communication offer to bolster these conceptions of cosmopolitan identity orientation?

First, the earlier identity scholarship tells us that people can and do make efforts to engage in identity negotiations in order to forge meaningful and positive connections across difference. This helps support the argument that it is possible to mindfully cultivate intercultural communication skills that can help generate cosmopolitan communication, spaces and projects. According to Ting-Toomey (2005), while all communicators involved need to make an effort for competent identity negotiation to occur, one person can set the process in motion. The same can be said for cosmopolitan communication. Second, we learn that people communicatively display multiple as well as hybridized identities that fall in between more fixed identity categories. This bodes well for cosmopolitanism since it suggests that particular contexts, the movement of human bodies and ideas, and particular spatial configurations can generate complex performances of identities that could bring about critical transformation in Self and Others.

Third, research on intersectionality (e.g., Carrillo Rowe, 2008, 2010; Chávez , 2012; Crenshaw, 1991; Malhotra & Pérez, 2005) shows that people from different identity groups, with interlocking oppressions, can come together in certain spaces and times to produce (perhaps tentative) alliances to achieve common emancipatory goals. Fourth, and relatedly, critical/ interpretive approaches to identity emphasize that identities are communicatively produced, are dialogic and relational and are driven by ideology and power (e.g., Mendoza et al., 2002). This shifting of identity theorizing from a received and individualistic notion to one that is always in production through communication with Others indicates that meanings of identities are not set in stone. Oppressive power configurations and perceptions of negative difference between identity groups can be changed for the better. Thus what we can take away from the intercultural communication literature on identity is that cosmopolitan identity orientations, if the willingness exists, are very possible and worth striving for in order to accomplish cosmopolitan goals and projects. At the same time, we remain cautious that such accomplishments may not always be possible. Much depends on the type of communication, context and the power configurations involved—key elements that must always be taken into account when gauging possibilities for cosmopolitan communication and identity performances.

The question we now turn to is: What gaps exist in identity scholarship in intercultural communication that can be addressed by cosmopolitan thought? First, methodological nationalism is still predominant within the theories and models of identity. Most of them were developed in the U.S. (read: nation-state) context and some have been applied in other country contexts. This is an 'inter-national' rather than a transnational approach to identity communication scholarship (Shome, 2010). A cosmopolitan approach to theorizing about identity, communication and culture requires a more world-oriented and historically and geopolitically interconnected outlook (see also Chapter 6). It should take into consideration the flows and disjunctures of globalization steeped in historical and emerging power relations and how they impact identity communication, and transcend the assumption that identities are bounded by the parameters of a nation-state. This is a postcolonial argument. Furthermore, it should focus on how mutuality, dialogue, intercultural learning and critical self-transformation are accomplished through, and despite, differences and power asymmetries. This is a cosmopolitan ideal. Simply put, cosmopolitanism, when conceived of as intercultural communication, can introduce another layer of identity—that of critical global citizenship, to all our other cultural identities and affiliations. If we can simultaneously have subnational and national identities, then why not extend outward towards the global?

Within the identity literature, and with the exception of Y. Y. Kim's (2008) Intercultural Personhood model, there is no conception of identity and culture that is planetary in scope. While Kim's model is a much needed move in this direction, it does not take into account larger issues of power and colonial and postcolonial difference (see Chapters 4 and 5). As mentioned earlier, in this chapter and the next, our goal is to develop a critically-oriented ontological concept of cosmopolitan peoplehood which can enable us to visualize how we may communicate as critical and ethical global citizens. Cosmopolitan peoplehood is a term that we borrow from Delanty (2009), and develop further, in order to move cultural identity and communication theorizing in a more outward, non-Cartesian and Other-oriented direction. According to Delanty (2009), "cosmopolitan peoplehood suggests . . . a reframing of identities, loyalties and self-understandings in ways that have no clear direction" (p. 59). We interpret this to be a process of selfhood that is perpetually aimed towards the horizon and discovers its cultural directions as life unfolds (Hall, 2008). Our goal is to position cultural identity not just as something an individual possesses but as an outwardly-oriented, dialogical, ethical, critical and ongoing communicative process that transcends Cartesian views of the Self in an effort to reach out and merge with (not the same as becoming one with) cultural Other(s) and the world.

Second, as some recent intercultural communication scholarship has argued, there is a need for more complex and less negative theorizing of how difference is produced in intercultural identity performances (Rodriguez & Chawla, 2010; Shome & Hegde, 2002; Warren, 2008). Cosmopolitanism advocates a more entangled, mutual, dialogic and less polarized view of the Self–Other relationship, or the relationship of difference. According to Kögler (2011), cosmopolitanism's dialogic approach stresses the "hermeneutic potential to move in-between and among contexts" and engage in a form of perspective taking that can "open up concrete life worlds of other" (p. 239). Our theories of intercultural communication and identity need to move beyond binaries and mainly negative understandings of difference, and consider the various nuanced, hopeful and emancipatory ways in which difference can and does work in different intercultural spaces. Identity production is closely tied to how we think about and perform difference in everyday mundane interactions and through various levels and forms of communication. As Hall notes in the opening quote of this chapter, the Other, in the play of identities, is an inherent part of the Self. Our concept of cosmopolitan peoplehood aspires towards such a view of the Self–Other identity relation.

Third, related to the issue of difference is the notion of dialectics. While the dialectic approach to intercultural communication practice has more recently gained some theoretical traction (see Chapter 2), we believe that there is a need to incorporate dialectics into how we theorize cultural identity and communication. Just assuming that the Self and Other exist in dialectic tension is not enough. We need to place this dialectic under a microscope and ask specific questions. How can dialectics point us towards a conception of Self and Other that can open up dialogic possibilities for cosmopolitan communication and projects? What role does agency play in whether we think about differences as dialectic (Self *and* Other) or as fixed opposites (Self *vs.* Other). How do the notions of belonging and agency work in relation to the Self–Other identity dialectic? In fact, the notions of agency and belonging are two key notions related to culture, communication and identity that remain underexplored in intercultural communication scholarship. However, they are central to our understanding of cosmopolitan identity orientation.

In the next sections, we further explore the notions of belonging, agency, hybridity and intercultural bridgework in an effort to move towards a cosmopolitan, i.e., Other- and world-oriented, dialectic sense of Self that can help us transcend (at least conceptually) the Cartesian 'I' of identity theorizing. In so doing, our aim is to shift our thinking from 'I am' to 'We are,' and to 'We are of this World.'

SHIFTING IDENTITY TO THE REALM OF THE OTHER

The ways people think about and experience identity and selfhood differ across cultures. The Self, according to M.-S. Kim (2002), "is an organized locus of the various, sometimes competing, understandings of how to be a person . . . " (p. 8). These understandings, in turn, influence the identity positions the Self takes up through ideological interpellations (Althusser, 1971) or resistance to interpellation/disidentification (Muñoz, 1999), and how the Self communicates with Others. Identity, in relation to selfhood, "is a concept that figuratively combines the intimate or personal world with the collective space of cultural forms and social relations" (Holland, Lachicotte, Skinner, & Cain, 1998, p. 5). The views of selfhood prevalent in the larger cultural environment the Self is embedded in influence this process.

For example, in cultures influenced by Greek philosophy, identity is mostly conceptualized and experienced in individualistic and oppositional terms ('I am this because I am not that'; Hecht et al., 2005). While the ancient Greeks themselves were more communal in their social relationships when compared to current modern Western cultures, the Enlightenment philosophies forwarded by thinkers such as Kant and Descartes in the 15th and 16th centuries marked a definite turn towards individualism, rationalism and a more mechanistic conception of the Self in relation to

Others, nature and the world (M.-S. Kim, 2002). As Allen (1997) writes, the modern Western Cartesian notion of the atomistic, highly individualistic and rational self ('I think, therefore I am') assumes a clear distinction between Self and Other. Most of the extant research on identity within the field of intercultural communication has emanated from within U.S./Western contexts, since the field itself is mostly U.S.-centered (Shome, 2010). Therefore, binary views of difference and Cartesian ontological assumptions influence much of this research. Most of our current theories and models, as reviewed earlier in this chapter, revolve around the individual and her relation to various cultural groups. Most of our methodologies, especially postpositivist ones, also lean towards individualism. For a more cosmopolitan conception of intercultural identity, we need a paradigmatic shift that is able to decenter individualism without losing the sense of Self, and move us towards a notion of identity guided by a sense of peoplehood (We-ness) rather than personhood. According to the notion of peoplehood, the Self and the Other are different yet dialogically connected.

Putting interdependent views of identity and selfhood in dialogue with individualistic ones can get us started in this direction. For instance, the Self (or even 'non-self') in Eastern philosophies, such as those influenced by Buddhism and Hinduism, is assumed to be more holistic and, in a cosmic sense, inseparable from Others and from nature (Allen, 1997). Similarly, in various African cultures, the Self is perceived as harmonious and coalesced with Others (Giri, 2009). In some Asian cultures, especially those rooted in Confucianism, the individual self is downplayed for the sake of collective (group) harmony and tradition (Hecht et al., 2005). Elaborating on Confucianism and its impact on how people relate and communicate, Yum (1988) notes that the cardinal principle of Confucianism is *jen* or humanism, which roughly translates into "warm human feelings between people" (p. 377). Practicing *jen* involves reciprocity, empathy and the desire to not hurt others. Another principle of Confucianism, *i*, stresses the importance of the common good over individual betterment. Proper behavior based on appropriate cultural codes, concern for others and saving the face of all involved and not just the Self are Confucian values that influence communication and interpersonal/group relationships. Yum (1988) does note that a potential drawback of this interdependent sense of Self is that individuality may be stifled. Furthermore, Yum notes that this sense of interdependent Self is not universalistic but particularistic, i.e., a strong in-group orientation could lead to discrimination against out-group members or cultural Others. A collectivist (Hofstede, 1980) or interdependent sense of Self does not mean everybody is included in the domain of interdependence.

M.-S. Kim (2002), in her book-length analysis of how communication (and theorizing about communication) is deeply influenced by cultural assumptions about selfhood, argues that since most communication theories have emanated out of the West, the individualistic assumption of selfhood undergirds them. She also critiques the unquestioned polar (either/

or) positioning of individualism and collectivism as modes of identity and communication in intercultural communication research. Pointing out the Western philosophical bias in this, she forwards the bidimensional model of identity, which calls for a dialectic consideration of both forms of self-hood—individualistic and interdependent. Asserting that the two forms are different but not opposite, she writes that "models that acknowledge differences without placing them in hierarchy or opposition" (p. 180) are necessary for more complex understandings of identity. Kim's model is conducive to a cosmopolitan approach to identity and selfhood. In a globalizing world of entangling cultures, views about how to be a person, and what personhood means, are also getting entangled. Thus the same Self can orient through individualism and/or collectivism depending on context.

But we want to go a little beyond what M.-S. Kim proposes and suggest that the Self be thought of as interdependent (Other-oriented) in a more outwardly (but discerning) way, and not just within the cultural in-group or nation-state. Only then can we connect Self and identity to the ideas of peoplehood and world-belongingness (Delanty, 2009). So while the sense of Self or how to be a person is not lost, the 'I' of identity is decentered in favor of being a more interdependent, Other- and world-oriented person in general. Giri (2009), in writing about cosmopolitanism and identity, calls for a transcendent notion of Self. In a postcolonial vein, he argues that humanity is not bounded by the nation-state but is planetary. Liberation from a type of Self that is 'I'- (or 'Us'-) centered and wants to dominate the Other must be achieved for the well-being of humanity. Giri advocates transcending modernistic humanism and striving for a type of planetary humanism that realizes the Self through non-violent connectedness with Others and with the world.

Drawing upon M.-S. Kim and Giri, we suggest that *cosmopolitan peoplehood entails a world-oriented, decentered sense of Self and identity. This Self learns and continuously engages in critical self-transformation through non-violent entanglement between Self and Others through cosmopolitan communication.* This description leads us to questions related to belonging. How can we envision belonging in ways that support cosmopolitan peoplehood and a decentered sense of Self? What does Other- and world-orientedness mean when it comes to experiencing and performing cultural belonging?

Belonging

Within intercultural communication identity literature, belonging is usually described in terms of feeling a sense of attachment, membership, identification and perceived acceptance in relation to a particular cultural group (e.g., Hecht, Collier, & Ribeau, 1993; R. L. Jackson, 1999; Ting-Toomey, 2005). But does belonging always have to work in relation to those who are culturally similar to us? Are we destined to belong to only those specific master and *a priori* categories of identity such as nationality, race, gender, sexual orientation, religion and so on which ideologically interpellate us (i.e., 'This is who you should be')? How narrow or wide does the domain of belonging have to be? Does belonging to one or more cultural groups at the local (or immediate) level rule out the possibility of cultivating a larger sense of world-belongingness and connectedness with the unknown or the far-away cultural Other? We argue that these two forms of belonging do not have to be mutually exclusive, and that belonging can take the form of belonging across difference. This view opens up possibilities for the formation of actual and virtual communities of people who do not have a whole lot in common in terms of culture and are yet able to connect across differences (Lingis, 1994). Belonging may be experienced through one's immediate environment as well as through the imagination and through empathy (Appadurai, 1996; Calloway-Thomas, 2010; see Chapter 4). As Tomlinson suggests, perhaps we could start thinking about belonging more in terms of "belonging to a specific [cosmopolitan and outward looking] identity position" (2007, p. 364) or, as Grossberg (1996) puts it, belonging does not necessarily have to be tied to the presence of similar cultural properties in Self and Other.

According to Carrillo Rowe (2005), if rational individualism and the 'I'-centered identity is central to colonial modernity, then belonging can be made to work in service of the decolonial imaginary. In other words, the rational modern 'I' entails a form of individualism that sees the Self as being atomistically separate from cultural Others, a form of being that generates modern forms of colonizing power (Grossberg, 1996). Others may be perceived as inferior, to be consumed, controlled and colonized by the Self (and Self's culture). Relatedly, such a colonizing 'I' also presumes we belong in purist ways to specific superior (Self) and inferior (Other) cultural categories. If the 'I' and meanings of belonging are decentered, then the very meaning of culturally colonizing and oppressing a distinct Other changes since the Other is inherently entangled with the Self.

Carrillo Rowe argues that we need not assume that we have to belong, in some hegemonic way, to certain *a priori* cultural categories. Belonging, according to Carrillo Rowe, is a "*movement in the direction of the other*" (p. 27, italics added) and towards "the edge of one's self" (p. 17) which can lead to collective and shared agency in the form of alliances across cultural and power lines for political and emotional reasons. Drawing upon Chela Sandoval's work, she offers the concept of "differential belonging" which allows us to explore different modes of belonging without feeling trapped by any one (p. 33). In this way, belonging is put into motion, and "identity is an *effect* of our belongings" (Carrillo Rowe, 2010, p. 218, italics in original). Through differential belonging, "power over" which is oppressive can be remade into "power with" which is creative and signals possibilities for change (p. 37). For example, a heterosexual male (privileged identity) joining in solidarity with a gay activist group to raise consciousness about violence against gay men is a move from 'power over' to 'power with.' This individual leans towards the edge of his identity as a straight male and towards the Other with the desire to be an ally. *This reconfiguration of how we think about belonging, not just to the Self's group but as an outward movement towards the Other, carries potential for decentering the Cartesian 'I' of identity that pervades current intercultural identity scholarship, and for opening the Self up to the world in a cosmopolitan spirit.* It is also a decolonizing line of thought since it positions belonging as a mode of connecting with likely and unlikely cultural Others across various registers of power for the common purpose of interrupting oppressions.

Martin Buber's work on the relationship of I–You (Self and Other) can further add to the notion of Other-oriented belonging. While Buber (1970) does not take culture into specific account, his focus on the primacy of the I–You encounter and relationship resonates with the idea of decentering the I and moving towards the You. According to Buber (1970), "The basic word I–You establishes the world of relation," (p. 56) and it is impossible to realize the I without You. But he does not suggest that the I should be absorbed into the You. The duality, which is not necessarily an opposition and can be understood as a dialectic way of being, is necessary.

Buber further elaborates that the relationship of I–You is established not in any one body but "*between* an I and a You" (p. 129, italics added). He makes a distinction between the "It" world where the Self experiences the Other as an object available for study, for the Self's use, and even for domination, and the "You" world which involves engaging with the Other with one's whole being. He acknowledges that the intensity of the pure I–You relationship is too much to sustain at all times, and that we vacillate between the two worlds. But the key, according to Buber, is to not give up or turn away from the "You" world and get locked into the "It" world. He stresses the importance of engaging in the I–You encounter whenever possible even if it makes life "heavy," because such encounters make life "heavy with meaning" (p. 158). The in-between space of the Self–Other encounter, which Buber describes as the heart and soul of the encounter, may be seen as the space where belonging may occur, where we recognize the Self in the Other, and where cosmopolitan possibility in born.

Mikhail Bakhtin's work on dialogism is another view that helps us decenter the monologic 'I.' While Bakhtin's work is in the realm of linguistics, his views have great value for understanding cultural worlds and identity interactions. According to Bakhtin (1981), we live amidst social "heteroglossia" ridden with the unifying (centripetal) and diverging (centrifugal) forces of languages, cultures and meanings, and that " . . . we must deal with the life and behavior of discourse in a contradictory and multi-languaged world" (p. 275). Unified forms (such as languages, cultures and identities) are constantly challenged by diverging forces which bring in other possible meanings of any given object or phenomenon. Thus, as Bakhtin writes: "The word [or Self] lives, as it were, on the boundary between its own context and another, alien, context" (1981, p. 284). In this way, languages, cultures and identities are constantly dialogized. This is especially true in eras of high flux wherein unified forms are harder to discursively maintain due to the intensity of intercultural contact and communication. Additionally, Bakhtin notes that when different cultures and identities come into contact with each other, each monologic form is experienced differently from how it would be been experienced just on its own. In other words, culture/identity ceases to be "sealed off and self sufficient" and becomes "conscious of itself as only one among *other* cultures" through dialogism (Bakhtin, p. 370, italics in original). Such dialogism opens up possibility for change and cosmopolitan communication. Working with Bakhtin and the dialectic nature of the Self–Other relationship, Baxter and Montgomery (1996) write:

> The self is constructed in the ongoing interplay of the centripetal and the centrifugal. According to Bakhtin, the self is possible only in fusion with the other. . . . But fusion with another needs to be complemented by differentiation from him or her. . . . In other words, the self is constructed out of two contradictory necessities—the need to connect with another (the centripetal force) and the simultaneous need to separate from the other (the centrifugal force). The centripetal–centrifugal dialogue is the indeterminate process in which the self is in a perpetual state of becoming as a consequence of the ongoing interplay between fusion and separation with others. (pp. 25–26)

What we can take away from Bakhtin is that the Self and cultural Other are not autonomous and sovereign, as Cartesian individualism suggests. They may be different, but they are inevitably entangled through dialogism and could belong to each other. Such a view helps us further see the need to decenter the monologic 'I' of identity or personhood and move towards the notion of cosmopolitan peoplehood which is steeped in a dialogic ethic. This move from the notion of personhood to peoplehood is an inherently dialogic move which recognizes the relational nature of identity and meaning construction and sets the stage for a coalitional perspective of difference and agency.

Agency, Hybridity and Intercultural Bridgework

Agency is a central concept when it comes to cosmopolitan orientation. For instance, in the prominent values within cosmopolitanism that we presented in Chapter 2, each and every value suggests agency and will, i.e., the *ability to be willing* to be open to Others and the world, the *ability to engage* in cosmopolitan action that aims to decenter Western hegemony and so on. But can we take agency, will and ability for granted? Here we address the notion of agency in relation to the Self–Other dialectic, identity and belonging through the lens of hybridity. We do so because the concept of hybridity, which is related to third space subjectivity (Bhabha, 1990), highlights a type of agency that is relevant for micro- to macro-level communicative interactions involving *asymmetrical* power relations. Furthermore, the concept is capable of explaining collective rather than individual agency, as we will explain shortly. In the current postcolonial turn in cosmopolitan thought, the emphasis is on ground-up efforts for addressing disparities and top-down social injustices and oppressions at local, translocal and worldwide levels. Since such efforts always involve the powerful and the less powerful, we need to find ways to discuss agency that can work with and through power asymmetry with the intention of change. Additionally, hybridity also helps us further get at in-between and third space views of subjectivity and identity, something we have been emphasizing throughout. This form of subjectivity and the kind of agency for which it holds potential aligns with the postcolonial view of difference (see Chapter 2) and is conducive to our notion of cosmopolitan peoplehood.

Normally, when we speak of agency in relation to identity, we mean the power and ability of an individual to speak, be heard and define her own cultural identity and reality without fear of oppression. This is an 'either/or' individualistic view of agency—one either has it or doesn't. But what about the in-between or collective view? Can agency be exercised only by those in obvious positions of cultural power in society? Does it have to always be understood at the level of the individual (Ganesh, Zoller, & Cheney, 2005)? It seems like it would be more heuristic to think of agency in terms of degrees, that is, how much agency one has relative to others. Also, a collective or intersectional view of agency, as Crenshaw (1991) writes, can help us "better acknowledge and ground the differences among us and negotiate the means by which these differences will find expression in constructing group politics" (p. 1299).

Agency is a pivotal issue that needs to be addressed further in critical intercultural identity theorizing (Shome & Hedge, 2002). We need to focus more on how those in non-dominant identity positions creatively and resourcefully exercise agency. Holland et al. (1998) write that agency, in relation to identity, is the ability to improvise and create openings for change which can interrupt the oppressor–oppressed binary. A similar view has been forwarded by intercultural communication scholars Mendoza et al. (2002) who argue and empirically demonstrate that while dominant structures may attempt to ideologically fix identities through exercises of power, agency exercised by non-dominant groups can transform, resist, elaborate and resignify identities imposed upon them. Non-dominant groups can also interrupt the identities of dominant groups through creative exercises of agency. This can be done through alliance-building across power lines for the purpose of addressing social injustices (Carrillo Rowe, 2008; Sandoval, 2000). This form of coalitional effort could lead to collective 'in-between' or intersectional agency which involves the combined efforts of those coming together from across different cultural and social locations of power. In this process, cultural identities of Self and Other are enjoined in solidarity (or peoplehood) that transcends just the individualistic Self.

The concept of cultural hybridity helps us further theorize this form of collective agency and decentered subjectivity. It is a central postcolonial concept that troubles the Us–Other dichotomy with the aim of transgressing divisive and/or oppressive boundaries. The term has a racist semantic history which has been creatively appropriated by postcolonial studies scholars. In the 19th century, at the height of European colonialism and scientific racism, it was used to justify theories of racial purity. The racial hybrid was considered to be contaminated, someone who produced border anxiety (Young, 1995). Today, the meaning of hybridity has been reconfigured to celebrate the power of contamination in all cultural forms, and is considered to be a cultural strategy that can subvert dominant canons (Bhabha, 1994; Brah & Coombes, 2000; Kraidy, 2005).

Hybrid subjectivity is formed in the "contact zone" through the process of transculturation (Pratt, 1992). A contact zone is a space where previously separated cultures intersect, usually in the context of colonization or some form of domination. These are spaces of "copresence, interaction, interlocking understandings and practices, often within radically asymmetrical relations of power" (Pratt, 1992, p. 7). Pratt (1992) explains that while those with less power cannot control the encounter, this does not mean they have no form of agency at all. According to her, "they do determine to varying extents what they absorb into their own, and what they use it for" (Pratt, 1992, p. 6). When the colonizer beholds that the hybrid is almost like the Self, the purity and unquestioned superiority of the colonizer's identity is also challenged: the hybrid is "almost the same, *but not quite*" (Bhabha, 1994, p. 123, italics in original). In this way, the unitary-seeming identities of both the colonizer and the colonized are interrupted, decentered and put into motion. This occurs in the space of the 'inter' in intercultural communication, is marked by cultural translation and holds the possibility of transformation of subjectivities. According to Bhabha (1994), "Translation is the performative nature of cultural communication. . . . Cultural translation desacralizes the transparent assumptions of cultural supremacy . . . " (pp. 326–327). Translation's outcome is the shift in meanings, identities and power. Through such translation, colonizing identities and relations can be reconfigured in decolonizing ways.

Thus the agency of hybridity is "oblique" and not direct, and it works to reconfigure power rather than to dominate or counter-dominate (Canclini, 2005; see also Bhabha, 1994). Hybrid subjects possess cultural and communication skills to survive tactically, and subvert when possible. This form of agency involves the recognition and acceptance that identities are not sovereign and that they can be entangled and reconfigured to interrupt oppressive binaries. Hybridity produces third space subjectivity, and according to Bhabha (1990) " . . . the importance of hybridity is not to be able to trace two original moments from which the third emerges, rather hybridity is the 'third space' which enables other positions to emerge" (p. 211). Hybridity brings together the Self and the cultural Other into an ambivalent third space of interaction and intersubjectivity. It entails an entangled sense of difference, and in its very ambivalence resides the possibility of interstitial or in-between collective agency.

However, there is one key concern we need to address here. In the play of hybridity, how willing are the powerful, who see their identities as intact and dominant, to interrupt their own sense of Self and question their own power? First, we must not assume that the more powerful are always unwilling to question their own power and privilege and will not respond to calls to be allies with non-dominant Others. Furthermore, it is helpful to remind ourselves of the privilege–disadvantage dialectic, i.e., no one, whatever cultural groups(s) they might primarily identity with, is all-powerful all the time or vice versa (Lorde, 1984/2007; Martin & Nakayama, 1999). People have multiple identities, and all of them may not be dominant. Tying this in with intersectionality, it is not unreasonable to argue that generally dominant identities, depending on context, may be open to dialogue and the interruption of their own identities for the purpose of attaining common emancipatory or social and global justice goals.

Second, it is the responsibility of those interested in cosmopolitan action and communication, wherever they may fall within the power and culture matrix, to seek and welcome allies from diverse cultural backgrounds who are willing to sincerely and self-reflexively join in solidarity and peoplehood for common causes. In colonial situations, the more powerful actively initiate the contact zone. In the play of hybridity, the less powerful are in a good position to take the first step towards the in-between space with decolonizing intentions and invite the more powerful (and willing) Other to enter this space for the larger purpose of realizing common goals. Performance artist Guillermo Gómez-Peña (1996), who is a proponent of hybrid cultural politics, writes that for the more powerful, the commitment to equity must be genuine and that the less powerful "will have to acknowledge their efforts, slowly bring our guard down, change the strident tone of our discourse, and begin another heroic project—that of forgiving, and therefore healing our colonial and post-colonial wounds" (p. 11). In this venture, dialogism could be a potential outcome. Kraidy (2005), in support of the agentic potential of hybridity in an unequal world, writes that:

> . . . agency must be grasped in terms of people's ability to accomplish things in the world they inhabit. If culture represents the meanings, ways of action, and ways to evaluate the value of actions in a society, and if cultural hybridity entails a change in those meanings and actions, then attention ought to be paid to hybridity's ability or inability to empower social groups [or individuals] to have influence over the

course of their lives. Ultimately, then, the value of a theory of hybridity resides in the extent to which it emphasizes human agency. (p. 151)

Hybridity has been subject to much criticism. It has been labeled as a privilege of elite postcolonials, the charge has been made that hybridity is not parity, that it is valuable only for critiquing essentialism, and that it is trivial to note that all cultures are mixed (Anthias, 2001; Friedman, 1999). Nederveen Pieterse (2009) responds to such charges and writes that there is plenty of oppressive essentialism at work in our world today that needs to be interrupted, that even if hybridity is not parity it is a move towards it, and that there are many examples of non-elite cultural hybridity around the world today. We find hybridity valuable since it helps us further collapse the binary between the individualistic Self and cultural Other, and move towards a sense of cosmopolitan peoplehood in a world where power asymmetries are common. The hybrid subject inhabits more than one cultural world with the aim of building 'power with' (an act of agency and mutual empowerment) rather than gaining 'power over' (an act of domination). According to Gómez-Peña (1996), "From a disadvantaged position, the hybrid expropriates elements from all sides to create more open and fluid systems" (p. 12). This brings us to Anzaldúa's notion of intercultural bridgework.

According to Anzaldúa, who does not use the term hybridity but prefers liminality, "Twenty-one years ago we struggled with the recognition of difference within the context of commonality. Today we grapple with the recognition of commonality within the context of difference" (2002, p. 2). She uses the term *nepantla* "to theorize liminality and to talk about those who facilitate passages between worlds . . . " (2002, p. 1). She notes that bridgework involves agency and empowerment since "to bridge is an act of will, an act of love, an attempt towards compassion and reconciliation . . . " (2002, p. 4). She further elaborates:

> To bridge means to loosen our borders, not closing off to others. Bridging is the work of opening the gate to the stranger, within and without. . . . Effective bridging comes from knowing when to close ranks to those outside our home, group, community, nation, and when to keep the gates open. (Anzaldúa, 2002, p. 3)

Bridgework may be seen as a discerning invitation to third space subjectivity and to engage in cosmopolitan communication and peoplehood.

Bridgework enables entry into the space of the 'inter' in intercultural communication, and:

> . . . it is marked by a fertile tension that opens up opportunities for individuals from non-dominant and dislocated cultural groups . . . to imagine, enunciate and enact agency in creative ways that affirm their split identities, and simultaneously invite (maybe compel) the unevenly

located cultural other on to the bridge to jointly engage in possible transformation. The communicative construction of this fertile tension is the first step toward possiblizing connection across difference. (Bardhan, 2012, pp. 153, 154)

Similarly, Malhotra and Pérez (2005) write that "A bridge enables a third space that allows one to connect across locations, even as we recognize the liminality of our locations," and that "one of the main functions of a bridge is to provide access between different locations. It facilitates crossings between two dissimilar realities" (pp. 50, 59). They, like us, assert that "bridgework is powerful and transformative when it is done in the spirit Anzaldúa envisioned for bridging . . . when it is both an act of will and an act of love" (Malhotra & Pérez, 2005, p. 65).

CRITICAL SELF-TRANSFORMATION AND COSMOPOLITAN PEOPLEHOOD

In this chapter, we have reviewed relevant identity research in intercultural communication, views of identity orientation or disposition within cosmopolitan thought, and explained the concepts of differential belonging, dialogism, agency, cultural hybridity and intercultural bridgework. In so doing, we have gradually built towards our concept of cosmopolitan peoplehood. We conclude this chapter with the notion of critical self-transformation which is a necessary aspect of cosmopolitan peoplehood. While we have implied this notion throughout this and previous chapters, we would like to make it specific here.

According to Delanty (2009), critical self-transformation "does not simply involve accepting the views of the Other but requires in some way a problematization of one's own assumptions as well as those of the Other" (p. 16). Through such reflexive work, it is possible to achieve "shifts in self-understanding that arise when both Self and Other are transformed" (Delanty, 2009, p. 11). Nowicka and Rovisco (2009) provide an articulate description:

. . . cosmopolitanism can be seen as a *mode of self-transformation*, which occurs when individuals and groups engage in concrete struggles to protect a common humanity and become more reflexive about their experiences of otherness. This capability enables people to reflexively rework the boundaries between self and other, us and them . . . and, thus, come closer to the reality of others and the world taken as a whole in fields often loaded with tensions and emotions. Self-transformation implies a sense of continuous self-scrutiny both with regards to the ways one committed to the building of a more just world in conditions of uneven globalization. A key assumption here is that people can *actually* become more cosmopolitan in ways that are both reflexive and emotional. (p. 6, italics in original)

Nowicka and Rovisco assume that this kind of identity orientation, or disposition, can be mindfully cultivated and we concur with them.

In the next chapter, we further build upon and complete our notion of cosmopolitan peoplehood for intercultural communication, but at this point, this is where we stand: *Cosmopolitan peoplehood is an open-ended, Other- and world-oriented, dialogic ('in-between') identity orientation that is morally committed to addressing social and global injustices in their many forms. Through non-violent entanglement between Self and cultural Others (near and far), it entails differential belonging, continuous engagement in critical self-transformation and intercultural bridgework (coalition and agency building) through cosmopolitan communication.* We now move on to discuss the role of the imagination in cultivating a sense of cosmopolitan peoplehood, the importance of empathy and implicature and the overarching value of kindness to strangers necessary for engagement in cosmopolitan communication through cosmopolitan peoplehood.

4 The Role of the Imagination and Kindness to Strangers
Cosmopolitan Peoplehood

The world we live in today is characterized by a new role for the imagination in social life. (Appadurai, 1996, p. 31)

Strangely, the foreigner lives within us: [s]he is the hidden face of our identity, the space that wrecks our abode, the time in which understanding and affinity founder. By recognizing [her]him within ourselves, we are spared detesting [her]him in [her]himself. (Kristeva, 1991, p. 1)

What I am trying to say is that humanity needs a cosmopolitan story of peoplehood. . . . (Sánchez-Flores, 2010, p. 11)

All human beings, near and far and from disparate cultures and nations, should be within our domain of moral consideration, and this consideration needs to be an inherent part of how we communicatively make our way through this world. This is the cosmopolitan vision that guides our work. But what about the critiques against this position? Isn't 'all of humanity' too abstract or thin a vision for one to feel morally engaged? Is it even possible to feel a sense of moral connection with strangers, cultural Others, whom we don't know and have never met? And even when they are nearby and within our locality, why should they matter as much as those familiar members of our family or our own cultural groups to whom we are connected through blood, kinship and other forms of cultural belongingness? Many may argue this way. But we would like to take a different path and ask, in the spirit of cosmopolitanism, does this matter of caring and moral consideration have to be an either/or problem? Is our well of humanity so dry that we have to carefully ration our compassion and empathy and let borders of family, culture and nation-state dictate who is worthy of moral consideration? Is the stranger really that strange, especially in today's world?

Our world is no longer the world it was as recently as 50 years ago when it wasn't uncommon to travel mainly by ship to a distant land and overseas phone calls cost an arm and a leg. Satellite television was barely in the picture yet, the Internet was still a brand new experiment, and the cell phone (or iPhone) and connective technologies such as Skype belonged to the future. Overall, there was still a good deal of distance, mental and physical, between 'here' and 'there' and 'Us' and 'Other.' But a lot has changed in the last half century. People, media images, ideas, communication technologies and ideologies are crisscrossing the world making it a place that we can envision more as a single entity. The ways in which people, processes and institutions across the globe are interdependent are becoming more and more apparent as the economies and political fates of nation-states and regions become increasingly entangled every day and alter the more closed, place-based and self-sufficient perceptions of the local and the nation. What we do 'here' could have a deep impact on the lives of people 'there' (and vice versa), and we are more aware of this than ever before. In the transnational realm, there has been a surge in the numbers of non-nation-state actors and organizations in the last two decades that are laboring daily across cultural and national borders to address global crises, social and humanitarian issues and the inequities of neoliberal globalization. If visionary thinkers in different times could have imagined world-oriented ways of being and relating, should it not be a whole lot easier for us to do so today, especially since there is an urgent need for social and global justice action?

Postcolonial globality is ripe ground for critical cosmopolitanism, and it is our responsibility as scholars of intercultural communication to envision and debate ways in which we could orient ourselves towards cultural Others so that they fall more within our moral radar. To accomplish such inclusion, we need to realize that we do not have to give up our local and national ties and cultural affiliations/identities as though we are caught up in a zero sum game; rather, we need to expand our sense of humanity and move towards an ontology of *cosmopolitan peoplehood*. In the last chapter, we started building this concept and in this chapter we put the finishing touches on it by discussing the notion of the stranger, the work of the imagination as moral and cosmopolitan labor, and how intercultural empathy and implicature can help elevate the idea of kindness to strangers. Finally, we present our working definition and assumptions for cosmopolitan peoplehood. We explain its co-constitutive relationship with cosmopolitan communication, and the value of both these concepts for intercultural communication and for communicating as critical and ethical global citizens with distant and proximate Others.

THE STRANGER

Back to our question: Is the stranger, or the cultural Other, really that strange in today's world? To answer this question, we need to take a closer look at how the stranger has been culturally and academically positioned over time. Historically, in many cultures around the world, the stranger has been viewed in a mixed light, and this ambivalence towards the stranger persists in our everyday sense-making of the cultural Other. On the one hand, the stranger is one who generates suspicion since he or she does not belong and has come from the outside. On the other hand the stranger, in many traditions, is simultaneously associated with bringing good luck from the mysterious outside. In some cultures (e.g., in Japanese and Hindu folk religion and culture), the stranger is associated with god appearing in disguise to perform a moral check on human beings. Ostracizing the stranger, therefore, could result in divine retribution (Yoshida, 1981). The stranger can be far away or can enter our own locality, but wherever he or she may be, the stranger is not like us in his or her values, beliefs and behaviors. We are not sure quite what to do with the stranger.

German sociologist Georg Simmel's ideas about the stranger have been very influential within the Western social sciences over the last century. Simmel was at the height of his intellectual performance during the latter part of the 19th century and the first half of the 20th century. Many of his ideas and concepts were imported from Germany into the U.S. by leading Chicago School of Sociology scholars such as such as George Herbert Mead and Robert E. Parks, and they had a significant influence on the course of sociology as well as the social sciences (Rogers, 1999). The concept of the stranger was particularly influential.

According to Simmel, the stranger is not an "owner of soil," both literally and figuratively (Wolff, 1950, p. 403). He or she is mobile, has objective distance from the local culture, to which he or she is not organically tied by way of kinship or locality. The stranger may be near physically but is far in a social sense and according to Simmel, this is actually a positive relation with the local culture since the stranger is able to offer objective views about the local culture (Wolff, 1950). But what happens when the stranger does not go back to the place he or she came from and decides to reside among locals? This stranger is now a threat to order, culture and the familiar ways of life. But this is also the kind of stranger (the one who stays or tries to stay) that the world sees more of today. Some strangers arrive voluntarily (the privileged stranger) and others are pushed into this category (the unprivileged stranger) through violent political expulsion, natural catastrophes, ethnic conflict or some other form of human violence or need to escape locality. Strangers can come from within the nation-state and beyond.

Simmel's stranger is more of a sojourner, i.e., not a threat to how things are. However, Schuetz's (1944) description gets closer to the more negative construction of the stranger, or the cultural Other. Schuetz's stranger comes from elsewhere and tries to stay. Despite trying to learn the ways of the local culture, he or she can never be accepted as authentic. This is compounded by the fact, as Sarup (1996) elaborates, that for the local culture, the stranger is ambiguously located between the binary of friend and foe: "The stranger is an anomaly, standing between the inside and the outside, order and chaos, friend and enemy" (p. 10). Using Derrida's term, Sarup describes this stranger as an "undecidable," one who is a source of discomfort and must be kept at a mental distance and somehow controlled. This stranger, in the meantime, develops a sense of cultural in-betweenness and critical distance from both home and host cultures and, therefore, becomes a stranger in his or her own eyes as well (Kristeva, 1991; Ossewaarde, 2007). This too doesn't sit too well with members of the local culture.

Within intercultural communication scholarship, the notion of the stranger has been equated to the notion of the cultural Other (Rogers, 1999). Influenced by Simmel, veteran scholars Gudykunst and Y.Y. Kim (2003) titled their popular intercultural communication textbook *Communicating With Strangers: An Approach to Intercultural Communication*. Citing Simmel, they position anyone entering a new culture as a stranger. However, as in the bulk of intercultural communication literature, their description of the stranger and his or her interactions with members of local (or host) culture assumes difference to be a problem that needs to be surmounted (Rodriguez & Chawla, 2010). For members of the host culture (the 'Us') the stranger invokes uncertainty, anxiety and even fear. This is mainly because the 'Us' are unable to predict how the 'Other' will behave and, therefore, are unsure how to interact with him/her. The stranger "surprises" 'Us' with his or her unexpected behaviors and this exacerbates the uncertainty and anxiety. Gudykunst and Kim write that the stranger is "rarely seen as a source of reward" by host culture members (2003, p. 31), and note that being unable to predict a stranger's behaviors is a problem that needs to be corrected. Furthermore, they make the point that despite globalization:

> When faced with new circumstances, however, most of us prefer to continue in our familiar cultural ways without a clear and objective vision and without a readiness to embrace the different and the unfamiliar. (Gudykunst & Kim, 2003, p. 375)

What does such a positioning of the stranger (i.e., cultural Other) and the negative view of difference imply for how we conceptualize the Self in relation to the cultural Other? Why should the Self be inspired to connect with and care about such a stranger who upsets the 'normal' order of things?

In the concluding chapters, and sometimes earlier in the text, Gudykunst and Kim address this matter and emphasize the value of cultivating skills such as mindfulness, empathy, being giving of the Self and tolerance for ambiguity in order to build intercultural communities and deal better with the uncertainty, anxiety and fear that the stranger may produce in 'Us.' These are helpful Other-oriented suggestions, and we wholly agree with them. The authors make an important point: "Lack of concern for strangers' interests leads to moral exclusion" (p. 391). Borrowing from Buber, they stress the importance of being able to walk a "narrow bridge" which "involves taking both our own and strangers' viewpoints into consideration in our dealings with strangers" (pp. 393). They emphasize that differences should be confronted and celebrated for the sake of understanding, tolerance and reaching consensus and add that "if we are to tolerate strangers, we must begin by accepting our own mistakes" (p. 408). They move on to the notion of Intercultural Personhood which involves transcendence and the ability to not view cultural differences as polar opposites but to seek non-dichotomous definitions of Self and Other and find "creative way[s] to reconcile seemingly contradictory elements of peoples and cultures and transform them into complementary parts of an integrated whole" (p. 384; see also Y.Y. Kim, 2008). We find some of these views, especially the Other-oriented ones, very helpful in our construction of cosmopolitan people-hood, but we also note some gaps and a contradiction.

First, and most importantly, this functionalist notion of the stranger does not take into account issues of power and colonial and postcolonial difference. It does not acknowledge that globalization, through the circuits of which the stranger moves, is an uneven process, or the fact that different strangers may be perceived and received differently based on context and historical and geo-political relations. For instance, the position of the Other is constantly con-tingent and the very notion of the Other is an anthropological myth based on Enlightenment thinking (Fabian, 1983/2002). Furthermore, the distinction between neoliberal (top-down) globalization and globalization from below is not touched upon. In short, the critical/postcolonial perspective is missing. Next, why stop short at understanding and tolerance, i.e., is tolerance enough when the stranger is in our midst and living with us? Doesn't tolerance simply entrench present inequities and maintain the status quo (i.e., 'I will tolerate your differences, and nothing more')? And while consensus without coercion is a good thing, how often does that happen?

Third, the Cartesian individualistic sense of the Self is prevalent in how the stranger is positioned in relation to the Self. There is an ontological gulf between the Self and the stranger. This obstructs discussions of mutual-ity, reflexivity and critical self-transformation in an Other-oriented way. It also positions difference as something that is outside the Self, something the stranger brings and not something that is produced through communica-tion between the Self and the cultural Other in particular contexts. How the stranger is thought of is related to how we think of difference. Therefore, if we think of difference as a problem (something that produces uncertainty, anxi-ety and even fear because we are unable to predict strange behavior), then inherent in that is the assumption that the stranger brings a problem for 'Us.' While this is not Gudykunst and Kim's explicit stand, and the Self is advised to be giving, mindful, empathetic and open to ambiguity, these become acts of benevolence bestowed upon the stranger (the Other). Those bestowing this benevolence are in a position of power over the stranger. What contribution does the stranger make in all of this?

Regarding the contradiction, if the stranger cannot be seen as a "source of reward" to 'Us,' why should the stranger matter even if we say he or she should? It seems like towards the end of the book and in describing Inter-cultural Personhood, Gudykunst and Kim strive to move towards a more cosmopolitan view of the Self in relation to the stranger. However, the indi-vidualistic Cartesian construction of the Self stands in the way of clearly con-ceptualizing what Sánchez-Flores (2010) calls "one-in-anotherness," (p. 12), i.e., the view that the Self and cultural Other are entangled and not autonomous units, and that they are joined together in how cultural difference and identities are communicatively produced and navigated. Ultimately, according to Gudykunst and Kim, the Self is responsible for becoming more intercultural—and this Self is still in Cartesian mode. The stranger remains the outsider, the Other, the bearer of difference, to whom the Self should adjust. A cosmopolitan view of the stranger could help address this contradiction.

The Cosmopolitan View of the Stranger

According to the cosmopolitan view, the stranger is welcome, and is not perceived as someone who interrupts culture and order, or the Self/Us. A basic cosmopolitan value is to take a willing and active interest in the stranger in order to grow and transform along with the stranger. Cosmopolitanism is "undeterred by traits that are strange," and those engaged in cosmopolitan interactions desire "to understand and appreciate humanity in its strange guises" (Ossewaarde, 2007, p. 368). According to Hall (2008), the cultural Other, or stranger, is necessary for the ongoing production of the Self. Also, from a critical perspective, our world now has more distressed strangers in it than ever before—people cast out of their localities and countries through human and natural violence. For those of us who are privileged enough to not be in this position, it becomes a moral imperative to include those strangers in the spirit of social and global justice (Derrida, 1997). Ossewaarde (2007) argues that the global mediascape has made it impossible for us to pretend that we are not aware of distressed and dislocated strangers (near and far) in our world. Stories about their plight are evident everywhere and every day.

Putting an interesting twist on the notion of the stranger, Bauman (1997) points out that within conditions of postmodern and postcolonial globality, strangerhood is becoming a more common experience as cultures and people move and mix in predictable and unpredictable ways. In other words, the stranger is not just a label reserved for the cultural Other anymore but could very well be applicable to the Self as well—if not today then tomorrow perhaps (see also Kristeva, 1991). Samir Amin notes that we are all strangers in a way as we move through life and diverse cultural spaces experiencing the ongoing production of identity (cited in Ossewaarde, 2007). Drawing upon Kristeva, Cavallaro (2001) writes that:

> . . . instead of trying to make sense of the other [stranger] as a menace or, at best, a nuisance to be kept at bay, we should learn to respect what we cannot know or understand. Fear of the Other far too often generates into blind hatred: fascism, racism, genocide, and a fetishistic attachment to national identities, languages and territories. . . . *It is by accepting the unknown in us that we are most likely to learn how to accept and value the unknown in others.* (p. 129–130, italics added)

This view of the stranger as not being very different from the Self in a deeply human way brings us to the issues of trust and compassion necessary for ontological enmeshment with the stranger or cultural Other.

Cosmopolitanism takes a thoughtfully optimistic approach to placing trust in the stranger, and according to Sánchez-Flores (2010), this includes the ability to compassionately and morally extend ourselves into Others. She elaborates that being able to trust a stranger is a moral (rather than a strategic) approach to trust which in itself is an attitude towards life and is deeply connected to appreciating Others and Otherness. She writes: "In order to trust in strangers one must have a well-developed appreciation of others (even distant others) and hold them as important in our own scheme of things" (p. 79). No doubt this is risky (and caution need not be thrown to the wind), but as intercultural communication scholar Mary Jane Collier (2003) reminds us, alliances across differences that are transformative require risk and vulnerability but are worth the effort. The willingness to trust is the key first step, and requires a certain vulnerability to start a conversation with the Other. Drawing upon past research, Sánchez-Flores argues that in various situations, people do trust strangers and this leads them to interact with people they normally wouldn't consider getting to know. Adding to her view, as more and more people experience and share the condition of strangerhood, the stranger may start to appear less strange and extending moral trust may begin to seem less risky.

In sum, according to the cosmopolitan view, the stranger (near or far) is ontologically enmeshed with the Self. The stranger is not distant, objective, a source of anxiety and fear or a menace to be controlled. The stranger is someone from whom we can learn what we don't know. There is a give and take, i.e., a sense of mutuality, between the Self and the stranger and both have something to contribute. It is our moral obligation to recognize that the stranger is already in us and we are in the stranger, and join in solidarity against oppression of the stranger. The non-Cartesian Self and stranger, or cultural Other, are joined in a state of peoplehood rather than separated as autonomous individuals. Here lies the shift from the 'I' of personhood to the 'We' of cosmopolitan peoplehood. This open-ended state gives up the driving need for certainty and prediction, and ambiguity is seen as an opportunity for new meanings to emerge, for intercultural growth and critical self-transformation.

Does this outwardly-directed moral identification with strangers mean that the meaning of the local and our local and national identities are threatened? Not if we reject the polarity and fixed view of culture and identity involved in this argument, and instead subscribe to the argument that the local and the global, and the Self and the cultural Other, are always already entangled within conditions of postcolonial globality. As Buber reminds us, we can be joined with the Thou and yet maintain the duality (not opposition) of the I–Thou relationship. Through this lens, inclusion of the stranger does not wipe out the Self or the local but may, in fact, enhance both.

Further, appreciation of the stranger and the condition of strangerhood within Self and Other can open up the imagination from the local towards more outwardly directions. We now turn to the role of the imagination in contemporary globalization, and how it can further help us move towards a sense of cosmopolitan peoplehood.

THE IMAGINATION AS A SOCIAL AND MORAL FORCE

The role the imagination plays in how we orient to cultural Others and the world is something that could be explored more within intercultural communication. How we imagine various cultural Others, and how generously and creatively we do so, shapes how we think of and perform difference and Otherness. The imagination is a force that can help us enter into worlds beyond our own and sympathetically and empathetically understand global issues and problems that cut across borders of culture and nation-states (Robbins, 1998). Harjo (2011) writes that because of the way humans are able to mobilize their imagination, "overall there's an expanded sense of the global" in peoples' minds today (p. 37). In fact, the exercising of the imagination may be thought of as an intellectual and moral form of labor that we perform in order to move beyond our own immediate realities and reach outward in the spirit of peoplehood. Holton (2009) describes the work of the imagination as a form of mobility and travel, and Szerszynski and Urry (2006) see it as a practice related to "inhabiting the world from afar" (p. 113). In this section, we elaborate on the role of the imagination in helping us 'travel' across borders and envisioning creative solutions to social and global justice issues through solidarity with cultural Others, both near and far.

Appadurai's (1996, 2000) work on the imagination as a social practice in current world conditions is helpful for understanding the changing role of the imagination and how it supports the cosmopolitan vision. He describes the imagination as being intertwined with subjectivity, and as a form of labor and a practice that "has a projective sense about it" (1996, p. 7). The imagination carries us beyond our localities and helps us form connections between what we are familiar with and what we are not. The various flows (of people, media, technology and ideologies) and disjunctures of globalization, according to Appadurai, aid in the work of the imagination. In other words, the imagination helps us establish connections between the local and the global and grasp the interrelatedness of social, political, economic and cultural phenomena in our world. It helps us understand, contextually, how the global enters and alters the local and how the local can move outward and alter the global. In this way, the imagination is a creative practice and a form of social labor that helps us develop "scripts for possible lives" and connections across cultural borders (1996, p. 3). This labor makes it possible for individuals as well as institutions to reach across cultural and ideological divides with goodwill and the desire to accomplish projects that require intercultural alliances and solidarity.

Appadurai extends B. Anderson's (1991) notion of "imagined communities of anonymity" to apply to the larger world. According to Anderson, the rise of "print capitalism" was a key factor in entrenching the idea of nation and eventually the nation-state. By reading materials about those who fell within the boundaries of the nation, people were able to feel a sense of patriotic connection with those many others whom they had never met before located in places they were unlikely to visit. This force of the imagination, according to Anderson, went a long way in creating "imagined communities" of disparate groups and people unknown to each other who felt somehow bound together as one nation. Appadurai's argument is that much has changed over the last century, especially the last few decades, and that the transnational mediascape and technoscape, along with heightened migration, is now making it possible for people and institutions to imagine creatively beyond the nation-state. This is becoming evident in the increasing forms of transnational life and work, civil society organizing and translocal connections being formed to address social and global justice issues (Theodossopoulos, 2010). Further, Appadurai argues that today people no longer depend on visionary leaders (they, of course, still remain important) and extraordinary global events to mobilize the outward work of the imagination. People's imaginations are taking them virtually and actually into other worlds in mundane and everyday ways, and according to Appadurai, this social practice is enabling new kinds of agency and possibilities in various intercultural spaces and allowing "people to consider migration, resist state violence, seek social redress, and design new forms of civic association and collaboration, often across national boundaries" (2000, p. 6).

An emerging interdisciplinary trajectory of study called the mobilities program has been critical of Appadurai's concept of global flows and disjunctures and what scholars working from this perspective see as his effusive support of contemporary globalization. Mobility scholars contend that his views subscribe to a sedentarist approach which assumes that places are fixed and unchanging and everything else moves and flows. They could also be read as a colonial as well as romantic approach to travel and movement (i.e., those who are able to move with the flows are able to access other static places). According to the mobilities program, everything is in motion within globalization, and places transform as well. Further, they argue that a mobilities approach is better equipped to get at the inequities of global movements than the more sedentarist approaches (Heyman & Campbell, 2009; Sheller & Urry, 2006). We must consider the implications of these arguments for the work of the imagination. We believe that while the critique of sedentariness is a valid one, it does not lessen the value of Appadurai's theorization of the imagination.

Delanty's (2009) views on the imagination are similar to Appadurai's. Specifically using the term "cosmopolitan imagination," he too notes that such a form of imagination is needed in today's world for people to grasp new social realities and the rapidly emerging challenges of globalization. Delanty focuses on the critical aspect of cosmopolitan imagination by emphasizing that the goal of this labor should be ongoing self-constitution and critical self-transformation "which can be realized only by taking the cosmopolitan perspective of the Other as well as global principles of justice" (p. 3). Being a sociologist, he elaborates on the four dimensions of the social that are constitutive of the cosmopolitan imagination. First, the social needs to be understood as a web of overlapping cultural differences and pluralities which can have positive outcomes rather than viewed in homogenous ways. Second, the relation between the local and the global and the social complexities of that nexus need to be a key focus. The cosmopolitan view does not consider one without the other. Third, the world needs to be imagined more in terms of borders and their ongoing spatial reconfigurations, along with the ambivalences that such processes produce, rather than in just territorial or place-based ways. Finally, a focus on reorientation of politics for the sake of global ethics is necessary.

Delanty and Appadurai's views are in the realm of the conceptual, and at this point one may wonder if such theorizing about the imagination actually pans out in people's lives and minds. Is it possible to feel the same level of moral connection that we feel, say, with fellow national citizens (as B. Anderson would argue), with people from other countries and cultures? Is the imagination a strong enough force without actual contact and interaction? Some empirical evidence is available in a study conducted by sociologists Szerszynski and Urry (2002) who, through focus groups in the U.K., investigated to what extent participants were able to extend themselves into the world through the work of their imagination and feel a sense of cosmopolitan and moral connection with distant Others. The results provide some evidence for simultaneous local/national–global imaginations. While participants were more easily able to connect with the local, the results show that what they consumed through the media did encourage them to imagine the world as an interconnected whole, and respond positively to various global justice and humanitarian issues as well as global crises. This outward projection was apparent in all respondents and not just those who had traveled widely and had international connections through their work. Their sense of moral connectedness, however, became more abstract as they extended outward from the locality. Despite demonstrating a keen sense of global consciousness, they were unable to imagine how they could personally make a difference in projects of larger magnitude. Szerszynski and Urry conclude that the results are encouraging and show that since the imagination is helping people think more transnationally and globally, this work is laying positive ground for the future emergence of more cosmopolitan spaces, projects and practices.

While the above results do not fully support the optimism of Appadurai's arguments, they are definitely not discouraging. They show that people are increasingly capable of intelligently and thoughtfully imagining the world and its interconnected issues as well as the distant Other (see also Nowicka & Rovisco, 2009). They also demonstrate, as the vernacular turn in cosmopolitanism argues, that it is possible to have moral consideration for both the local/national and the global simultaneously—this need not be an either/or choice. The catch, however, seems to be that people are at a bit of a loss when it comes to imagining their own specific involvement in global justice issues and how exactly to work together in solidarity with distant cultural Others.

The cosmopolitan hope is that such involvement will eventually become more possible if we keep imagining in this direction, develop a clearer sense of how the local/national and the global entangle and better learn how to impact the global through concrete local action from below. The Battle in Seattle in 1999, and more recently the Egyptian revolution of 2011, showed us how numerous committed cosmopolitan actors on the ground level, armed with new media technologies, the power of the social media and their imaginations, were able to make a global-level difference. When ordinary people are able to come together across borders and make such a macro-level difference, the sense of accomplishment produced can inspire agency and further visions of possibility. Further, if global consciousness is already present, when faced with concrete situations that entangle the local(Us) and the global(Other), it is likely that people will find ways to (inter)act. As we argued through the examples of mundane cosmopolitanism in Chapter 1, they already do. Finally, Szerszynski and Urry's study is more than a decade old and it was conducted in one location. More such studies are needed in various contexts and locations for a better sense of how morally connected to the global whole people in different parts of the world imagine themselves to be, and explore some of the reasons behind different ways of imagining.

What we can take away from this discussion is that the imagination as a moral and social force can contribute towards a sense of cosmopolitan peoplehood wherein the Self can imagine coming together with the cultural Other in a form of "one-in-anotherness" to accomplish larger social and global justice goals through cosmopolitan communication. This would have been beyond the imagination of the ordinary person and marginalized groups say a hundred or so years ago; today, it seems to have entered imagination's field of vision. This, we hope, bodes well for the future of cosmopolitanism conceived of as intercultural communication. Strangers, perhaps, will not seem so strange anymore if we can work together in certain contexts to accomplish common goals. We now turn to a quintessential cosmopolitan value—that of kindness to strangers.

KINDNESS TO STRANGERS THROUGH
EMPATHY AND IMPLICATURE

The last chapter of Appiah's book *Cosmopolitanism: Ethics in a World of Strangers* (2006) is titled "Kindness to Strangers." Building upon his various arguments throughout the book, in this chapter he eloquently debates what it means to be kind and charitable to strangers, distant and proximate cultural Others. He reminds us that to be kind to strangers requires an intelligent form of empathy and an informed moral outlook. What is needed "is the exercise of reason, not just explosions of feeling" (p. 170).

The world's problems are intensely complex. In many cases, people simply donate money thinking they are participating in alleviating pain and suffering among cultural Others. Donating money is not a bad thing and sometimes that's the best we can do. But Appiah's point is that we need to make the additional effort to understand, through empathy and intelligence, the economic, cultural and political complexities of the lives of distant Others. By so doing, we may realize that rather than just donating money, voting locally against policies that hurt distant others, making careful consumption choices, writing letters to the editor to express our views or getting involved at the grassroots through transnational/translocal efforts to change unfair trade policies might be more effective donations. Empathy, according to Appiah, is not about the Golden Rule that is available in many cultures—do unto others what you would have them do unto you; rather, empathy is about doing for others what they would like us to do for them, even if it is from a distance. *That*, in the cosmopolitan view, is kindness to strangers.

Understanding what empathy means is essential so we don't confuse it with sympathy or even pity. Aboulafia (2010) draws upon George Herbert Mead's work on perspective-taking or role-taking to elaborate that it is through such role-taking that we are able to enter into the worlds of others and develop the ability to abstract from the local to the global (or even see the global in the local). Respecting what others have to offer and reaching out to those who experience suffering helps the moral growth of the Self as well. Empathy, Aboulafia elaborates, if practiced meaningfully, can become a habit that grows and results in inclusiveness and even solidarity with cultural Others. Calloway-Thomas (2010) defines what she calls "intercultural empathy" as " . . . the ability to 'imaginatively' enter into and participate in the world of the cultural Other cognitively, affectively, and behaviorally" (p. 8). Similar to Appadurai, she too elevates the role of the imagination in enabling empathetic engagement. The imagination, according to her, helps us meaningfully participate in the lives of cultural Others as well as respect their dignity. She writes:

> Empathy helps us to understand people whose values, views, and behavior are different from our own. Feeling sorrow for individuals who lose their homes in a hurricane, grieving for children affected by cholera in India, feeling joy over a high school drama team winning a national

contest, and cheering when the villain in a motion picture is wounded are among the ways that we express empathy. A feeling of pleasure or distress, then, is not limited to those closest to us. (p. 7)

According to Calloway-Thomas, generosity of the imagination allows us to emotionally connect with, and therefore empathize with, distant and proximate others.

There has been some amount of research in communication studies on the role of empathy in human communication. Dace and McPhail (2002) describe empathetic communication as the ability to "feel with" other human beings. Scholars such as Benjamin Broome, Brant Burleson (interpersonal communication), Charles Kelly (rhetoric), Larry Samovar, Richard Porter, Myron Lustig, Jolene Koester (intercultural communication) and Ronald Pelias (performance studies) have all written about the role of empathy in their respective areas of study. They highlight the importance of empathetic listening, communication that is non-judgmental of behaviors and values that are different from our own, motivation to feel and share with others, emotional empathy and trying to get close to the reasons and contexts that shape the worldviews and feelings of others, thus positioning empathy as a communicative, emotional and intellectual endeavor (for details see Dace & McPhail, 2002). In order to better get at the idea of "feeling with" rather than just "feeling for" cultural Others, Dace and McPhail (2002) offer the very useful notion of implicature. They explain that traditional notions of empathy view the Self and the cultural Other as separate and distinct. But noting that this Cartesian separateness is an illusion, they offer a view of empathy that involves implicature:

> From this perspective, empathy is a state of mind that reflects an underlying state of being, an experience of reality that is defined not by separateness but by wholeness, or what we have chosen to call 'implicature.' . . . Implicature extends the notion of empathy from the psychological to the physical [embodied] by acknowledging that self and other are never separate and distinct, but are always interdependent and interrelated. (Dace & McPhail, 2002, p. 349, 350)

According to the authors, through empathy and embodied implicature, Otherness may be experienced in meaningful, fulfilling and productive ways. As Lingis (1994) reminds us, entering into conversation with Others calls for "lay[ing] down one's arms and one's defenses; to throw open the gates of one's own positions; to expose oneself to the other, the outsider; and to lay oneself open to surprises, contestation, and inculpation" (p. 87).

These views on empathy and implicature put the finishing touches on our concept of cosmopolitan peoplehood. They illuminate that kindness to cultural Others is not something 'We' magnanimously bestow upon 'Them.' Instead, it is an imaginative and empathetic form of communicative and embodied engagement that is accomplished through implicature and an intelligent read of how and why Others' lives and realities are different from our own. Cosmopolitan peoplehood involves communicating and feeling *with* Others (near and far), in solidarity, and with the ontological and moral vision that we are all different and yet inevitably entangled in an ever-changing world in which there is much need for kindness.

We now turn to an important task, that of providing our working definition and underlying assumptions for cosmopolitan peoplehood, and illuminating its relationship with cosmopolitan communication.

COSMOPOLITAN PEOPLEHOOD

In this section we bring together the theoretical developments of the last two chapters and present the working definition for as well as the assumptions which underlie our ontological concept of *cosmopolitan peoplehood*. As in the case of our concept of cosmopolitan communication, we do not assume this definition to be set in stone. Rather, it is a theoretically informed guiding vision, in the spirit of cosmopolitanism, that we could refer to in how we engage with distant and proximate cultural Others as we move through this world. We start with our five assumptions of cosmopolitan peoplehood and then provide the working definition.

Assumption 1

Cosmopolitan peoplehood assumes people have multiple cultural identities. Cultural identity, within this ontological position, is an open-ended and ongoing lifetime project that occurs through enmeshment with cultural Others, both near and far. Through this process, the Self develops complex and varied identity positions.

Assumption 2

Cosmopolitan peoplehood assumes a dialogic and dialectic relationship between Self and cultural Other. It transcends the Cartesian 'I' and focuses on the relational and embodied 'We' that constitute this world. The Self and cultural Other are interdependent through non-violent and dialectic entanglement. Critical self-transformation through differential belonging, intercultural bridgework and coalitional agency building is a goal of cosmopolitan peoplehood.

Assumption 3

Cosmopolitan peoplehood does not aim for certainty and prediction. Ambiguity is seen as an opportunity for intercultural and moral growth and for new meanings to emerge about how we relate with various cultural Others and accomplish cosmopolitan goals. Learning about the Self in relation to the stranger and the world is an ongoing journey full of possibilities we need to sincerely and mutually search for.

Assumption 4

Cosmopolitan peoplehood views the imagination as a positive moral and social force. It assumes that the labor of the imagination can help us make intelligent and creative connections between the local/national and the global, understand the complexities of Others' cultural positions, become more empathetic, and produce agency and visions of possibility through kindness to strangers.

Assumption 5

Cosmopolitan peoplehood is committed to postcolonial difference and to social and global justice goals. It privileges the perspectives of the margins (or border perspectives) and aspires towards solidarity with distant and proximate cultural Others to address historical and newly emerging social and global justices. Furthermore, it assumes that anyone, from any cultural location, can participate in cosmopolitan peoplehood if they are self-reflexive and respectful allies in causes they feel committed to.

Based on the above assumptions, our working definition for cosmopolitan peoplehood is as follows: *Cosmopolitan peoplehood is an open-ended, Other- and world-oriented and dialogic ('in-between') identity orientation that is morally committed to addressing social and global injustices in their many forms. It is an embodied way of being in the world that engages views from the margins, celebrates the powers of empathy and the imagination to connect the local/national with the global, and sees ambiguity as opportunity for intercultural growth and learning. Through non-violent entanglement between Self and cultural Others (near and far), it entails differential belonging, intercultural bridgework, kindness to strangers, and continuous engagement in critical self-transformation through cosmopolitan communication.* This working definition, in our view, embraces what it means to be simultaneously critical and hopeful in how we communicatively move through this world, alongside cultural Others, with the desire to make it a better place in the future.

COSMOPOLITAN COMMUNICATION AND COSMOPOLITAN PEOPLEHOOD: AN INTERCULTURAL COMMUNICATION PERSPECTIVE

So far in this book, we have accomplished the task of building a bridge between cosmopolitanism and the field of intercultural communication. We have traced the trajectories of cosmopolitan thought from ancient to present times in disparate cultural contexts, and provided an in-depth explication of the critical and postcolonial turn that is currently energizing debates about the heuristic value of cosmopolitanism within conditions of postcolonial globality. We have elucidated how cosmopolitanism is an inherently communicative and intercultural philosophy as well as how the field of intercultural communication can develop a more Other- and world-oriented ethical perspective by incorporating cosmopolitanism into its theoretical toolbox. We have explored the notions of identity, difference, dialogism, dialectics, agency, belonging and cultural hybridity in the attempt to carve out an ontological position for cosmopolitanism (or, a cosmopolitan way of being and becoming). We have discussed the concept of the stranger and how it applies to today's world, the role of the imagination and of empathy and implicature in making possible Other- and world-oriented peoplehood, and the importance of kindness to strangers who are near and far. In this process, we have offered two concepts—cosmopolitan communication and cosmopolitan peoplehood—that are co-constitutive. The first concept provides us with a vision for how to communicate ethically and critically as global citizens, and the second concept focuses on a cosmopolitan Self–Other way of being and becoming that transcends the Cartesian 'I' and moves towards a world-oriented 'We' committed to addressing social and global injustices. Together, they make each other possible.

Overall, cosmopolitan communication and cosmopolitan peoplehood constitute a frame of reference for communicating and relating ethically and critically as global citizens. Such intercultural communication entails being able to intelligently and empathetically connect the local/national and the global, understand where the cultural Other comes from (not just literally), engage difference positively and creatively, value border views and remain open to newness, possibility and critical self-transformation through enmeshment with the cultural Other. Culture and difference, here, are not 'things' within people but power-infused phenomena that are produced through communication and discourse. Culture is ecological and socially constructed and it travels with people, i.e., culture can be deterritorialized and reterritorialized. This takes culture into the realm of space in addition to place. Communication, in relation to culture, is understood as performative, dialogic, meaning-producing and accomplished in the space of the 'inter' (or the in-between) in intercultural communication. Cosmopolitan communication and peoplehood can be seen as infusing all levels and forms of intercultural communication—from the intra/interpersonal to the macro/global. Such a view makes it possible to imagine how cosmopolitan spaces of praxis may be engendered in micro and macro ways—during face-to-face encounters between people from different cultures as well as in discursive forms involving various cultural actors located near and far.

For intercultural communication, the cosmopolitan communication and peoplehood frame of reference provides a world-oriented moral vision for communicating within conditions of postcolonial globality. This vision is not obstructed by borders, especially borders of the nation-state. It adds another layer to our various identities (national, racial, gender, religious, sexual, ethnic and so on) that links the local/national with the global—that of critical and ethical global citizenship. Ritzer (2007) writes: "Globalization is an accelerating set of processes involving flows that encompass ever-greater numbers of the world's spaces and that lead to increasing integration and interconnectivity between these spaces" (p. 1). Globalization, according to Ritzer, is here to stay, and we have to take proactive steps to steer globalization in more humane directions. How we communicate across differences in various interconnected world spaces is a crucial part of this effort. However, as we have already noted, global visions for intercultural communication are sorely lacking and we see our contribution as addressing this gap.

Furthermore, we join in with other scholars who have already started problematizing polarized and negative views of difference, and position difference as a duality rather than as an opposition. Difference, according to cosmopolitan communication and peoplehood, is fraught with possibilities, and performing difference as differential belonging can produce collective agency for addressing social and global justice issues. We build on Martin and Nakayama's (1999) notion of dialectics within intercultural communication practice and suggest adding the Self–Other dialectic, which we explored in the last two chapters. Finally, we enhance Y.Y. Kim's (2008) Intercultural Personhood model, which is cosmopolitan in spirit, and take it from the confines of Cartesian individualism to the level of peoplehood which entails the Self and cultural Other enmeshed in dialectic fusion and differentiation (Baxter & Montgomery, 1996). Thus cosmopolitan communication and peoplehood, as a world-oriented intercultural communication framework, offers critical hope for building a better world for future generations. It is by no means a framework set in stone; rather we offer it as a vision of hope.

We now move our attention to other important matters. The rest of the book is dedicated to differentiating cosmopolitanism from other similar-seeming intercultural communication concepts and models; discussing issues of methodology and operationalization of cosmopolitanism for intercultural communication; reviewing some of the emerging research within communication that is beginning to recognize the value of cosmopolitanism; and constructing a vision for cosmopolitan pedagogy within intercultural communication.

5 Differentiating Cosmopolitanism from Other Intercultural Communication Concepts

So far in this book, we have established connections between intercultural communication and cosmopolitanism and shown the benefits of merging the two bodies of work. We have offered a conceptual framework for understanding, studying and practicing intercultural communication in the spirit of cosmopolitanism. Most importantly, we have argued all along that the recent postcolonial and critical turn in cosmopolitanism has helped this body of work rise above its past elitist and Eurocentric assumptions and reputation, and that this makes it especially suitable for intercultural communication scholarship within the conditions of postcolonial globality.

Before we move on to the remaining issues of methodology, operationalization and pedagogy and describe some emerging studies which combine cosmopolitanism and communication, we need to do one very important thing. We need to demonstrate that what we have offered as cosmopolitan communication and cosmopolitan peoplehood is not simply a reordering of concepts and models that already exist within the field of intercultural communication, and that they do indeed add something that is lacking in these models and concepts. For this purpose, in this chapter, we identify five models and concepts that we believe are closest to our concepts of cosmopolitan communication and cosmopolitan peoplehood. First we focus on the notion of multiculturalism and its assumptions and how they influence extant intercultural communication scholarship. Next, we discuss Y. Y. Kim's (2008) model of Intercultural Personhood. Third, we turn to Ting-Toomey's (1999) Intercultural Communication Competence model. Next we discuss M. J. Bennett's (1993) Developmental Model of Intercultural Sensitivity, and then finally Casmir's (1997) Third Culture Building model. For each of these five concepts and models we show how they overlap with as well as differ from what we have offered. We conclude this chapter by asserting that while all of these concepts and models reflect various aspects of cosmopolitanism, none of them replace what we have offered. We are indebted to the scholars who have authored these models and concepts and made it possible for us to work with and build on them.

MULTICULTURALISM

We decided to focus first on multiculturalism because this notion and its assumptions underlie much of current intercultural communication scholarship (multiculturalism was discussed briefly in Chapter 2 with regards to the notion of difference). On the surface multiculturalism may resemble cosmopolitanism, but digging deeper shows that it is not the same. Just as trying to define cosmopolitanism often feels like trying to bottle air or using one's hands to hold water, multiculturalism similarly has multiple definitions and critiques that make one meaning difficult to pin down. Both multiculturalism and cosmopolitanism defy concrete classifications and this, in our view, is a strength rather than a weakness.

Generally speaking, multiculturalism is a fundamentally late-liberal, democratic principle, which privileges pluralistic experience as a recognition of difference within a nationalist framework (Pollock, Bhabha, Breckenridge, & Chakrabarty, 2002, p. 6). The United Nations Educational, Scientific, and Cultural Organization (UNESCO) defines multiculturalism as the demographic make-up of modern nation-states, as norms upholding individual rights to equal access and participation in social and cultural life, and as a government strategy or political policy to implement these individual norms as rights to difference and diversity (Berman & Paradies, 2008, p. 7). Adler (1977), whose work has been influential in intercultural communication, described the concept of multiculturalism through the notion of multicultural "man:" "A man with a self-consciousness especially suited to working across cultures" (p. 26), thereby locating multiculturalism at the individual or identity-state level. Such a multicultural "man," according to Adler, embodies the ability to facilitate intercultural contact between cultures, as well as the knowledge of what it feels like to be a stranger in any particular nation-state or locality. It has been similarly argued that adopting a cosmopolitan disposition can be a lonely business since one cannot completely commit oneself to any one culture forever (Nussbaum, 1996).

On the surface level, these descriptions and embodiments sound similar to what is advocated by cosmopolitanism and by our working definitions and assumptions of cosmopolitan communication and peoplehood: A focus on recognition and privileging of cultural difference and an acknowledgement of and advocacy for equal rights across cultural differences. However, scholarly critiques of both multiculturalism in general, and Adler's multicultural "man" in particular, elucidate the crucial differences. For example, Berman and Paradies (2008) note that multiculturalism reinforces "binary notions of identity within a community, potentially focusing on the exotic, and failing to recognize and allow for the presence of multiple identities" (p. 7) (see also Shome & Hegde, 2002; Chapter 2). That is, multiculturalism focuses on culture-general notions of difference that tend towards either/or categories that don't allow for postmodern and postcolonial complexities of cultural overlaps, interstices, cultural deterritorialization/reterritorialization and hybridity.

In other words, while upholding difference, multiculturalism ends up reifying difference and conceptualizing culture in a static manner. Specifically critiquing multicultural "man," Sparrow (2008) advocates for identity as a space of in-betweenness, and supports "views of identity which are interactive with and responsive to context, in which the construction of identity is less conscious than it is intuitive, and wherein self-awareness comes after the fact as reflection, rather than as a 'choice' in immediate response to a new context" (p. 191). Generally speaking, multiculturalism tends to define culture at the individual and nation-state levels in terms of bounded categories, similar to islands of specific cultural pluralities existing in a larger sea of a nation-state configuration.

In this manner, then, multiculturalism sharply differs from cosmopolitanism and its more postmodern and postcolonial approach to culture, difference and identity. That is, cosmopolitanism advocates an outward- and world-oriented focus of actively and positively engaging with cultural Others, and bridgework across differences in order to create connections and be open to critical transformations rather than maintaining cultural separateness. And it is across these bridges that various cultural identities travel, shift, merge, separate, transform and flow in a manner that is more fluid than bounded. Delanty (2006) notes that "cosmopolitanism is not a generalized version of multiculturalism where plurality is simply the goal;" rather, "the cultural dimension of cosmopolitanism consists more in the creation and articulation of communicative models of world openness in which societies undergo transformation" (p. 35).

Multiculturalism looks inward and does not discuss transformation while cosmopolitanism looks outward—towards the cultural Other and the world— with a hope for and willingness to change. Therefore, cosmopolitan communication and peoplehood, which are based in these ideas of connection and transformation rather than separation, move beyond the mere recognition of bounded cultural differences towards a deliberate, dialogical, critical and ethical engagement between the complex and unbounded cultural Self and Other. Furthermore, the notion of world-orientedness underlying cosmopolitan communication and peoplehood moves beyond the idea of facilitation of cultural contact between groups within the boundaries of the nation-state to a larger transnational and global realm. Having established these key differences, we now turn to Y.Y. Kim's (2008) model of Intercultural Personhood, the intercultural communication model we believe is closest in spirit to our concepts of cosmopolitan communication and peoplehood.

INTERCULTURAL PERSONHOOD

The Intercultural Personhood model (Y.Y. Kim, 2008) evolved from earlier functionalist understandings of intercultural identity and development. Like multiculturalism, Intercultural Personhood takes cultural pluralism as a basic assumption and contextual framework in order to understand identity development from the level of the cultural to intercultural. That is, cultural pluralism creates a foil against assimilationist notions of cultural identity, like the melting pot notion. Kim (2008) defines intercultural identity as an individualistic identity-state, or a way of moving through and being in the world. The model entails stages of stress, adaptation and growth that lead to identity transitions towards an evolving state of intercultural personhood. This state can be described as one that experiences both functional fitness and psychological well-being in the process of moving through the world and through varying cultural groups. Intercultural identity, thus, involves the internal transformation of the individual who has to make personal as well as communicative adjustments to her own identity to continuously adapt to larger pluralistic environments.

Kim's model is certainly similar to cosmopolitanism in several aspects, particularly since it advocates engaging with multiple cultural Others and the constant seeking of personal transformation through intercultural communication. Like cosmopolitan communication and peoplehood, it involves an outward world orientation and willingness on the part of the individual to change. Kim describes an ethical obligation to the world and its people that is similar to those found in many discussions of cosmopolitanism. However, Kim's focus is mainly on the identity development of the individual, i.e., the Cartesian 'I' (see Chapter 4). More recent scholarship on postcolonial cosmopolitanism repeatedly stresses that cosmopolitanism is greater than the Self (or Self's identity)—it is mainly relational, dialogical and always takes into account the cultural Other (with which the Self is interdependent), historical location and other postcolonial power dynamics (Werbner, 2008). In this vein, our concept of cosmopolitan communication, and specifically our concept of cosmopolitan peoplehood, moves the focus out from the Cartesian individual to the social, the national, the transnational, all the way to the global through a critical and collective sense of peoplehood rather than personhood.

While the Intercultural Personhood model may quite closely resemble some early and more individualistic conceptions of cosmopolitanism such as those described by the Sophists of ancient Greece, Kant, and even more recently by Hannerz, cosmopolitanism from a critical and postcolonial perspective focuses more on ethical considerations that are larger than the individualistic Self, such as empowering the subaltern and engaging border perspectives for building translocal and transnational alliances for decolonizing and social justice projects (Mignolo, 2002). The Intercultural Personhood model is unable to account for postcolonial and neocolonial power dynamics which come into play when one moves beyond the individual level and takes into consideration historical location, macro structures and geopolitics. Intercultural personhood, similar to multiculturalism, does not focus on connections across difference and the relational and communicative complexities of in-betweenness. Despite its outward focus on one level, the model still remains inward in its focus on the individual.

In sum, our concepts of cosmopolitan communication and peoplehood enhance what Kim has already offered through her model of Intercultural Personhood. They do so by moving beyond a Cartesian sense of 'I' to a relational sense of 'We' by taking into consideration context, engagement with the cultural Other, and postcolonial and neocolonial power dynamics. We next turn to a more outwardly-directed intercultural communication model of competence.

INTERCULTURAL COMMUNICATION COMPETENCE

Ting-Toomey's (1999) Intercultural Communication Competence model is a classic communication studies model focusing on appropriateness and effectiveness in intercultural interactions. Intercultural communication competence involves acquiring "in-depth knowledge, heightened mindfulness, and competent communication skills—and, most critically, applying them ethically in a diverse range of intercultural situations" (Ting-Toomey, 1999, pp. 265–266). Under the rubric of intercultural communication competence, Ting-Toomey describes five communication competencies that are imperative for building bridges across cultural differences. First, she focuses on global perspectives on politics and culture, which manifest as an interest in and understanding of local and global politics and culture and how they mutually influence one another. The second competence involves the ability to take multiple perspectives in intercultural relationships. This speaks to the ability to embody empathetic communicative responses and to avoid ethnocentrism in attributing explanations for behaviors and interaction styles. This leads logically to the third competency, that of attaining skills in communicating with multiple cultural groups. This pertains not only to linguistic skills, but also to competence in non-verbal communication as well as varying communication styles, including elaborate/succinct or high context/low context communication.

The fourth competency is described as an ability to adapt comfortably to living in other cultures. This involves the ability to adapt one's identity across cultural boundaries in a way that allows the individual to feel at home in any locale within the world. The fifth and final competency is articulated as an embodied understanding of the necessity of equal treatment and respect for multiple points of view. This relates strongly to the notion of an ethical and empathetic engagement with others' political, cultural, social and economic perspectives, regardless of the distance of such perspectives from one's own. These five competencies, when taken together, increase knowledge, mindfulness and skills in intercultural interactions (Ting-Toomey, 1999; see also Collier, 2005).

Right off the bat it is easy to see similarities between the competencies that make up Ting-Toomey's Intercultural Communication Competence model and the values and ethics that guide cosmopolitanism. The first competency's focus on the global and local in terms of engagement in national and international political and cultural worlds seems quite similar to cosmopolitan perspectives that emphasize a local–global focus in how we move through the world. It also speaks to the notion of cosmopolitics, or "the concept of a world politics based on shared democratic values . . . a domain of contested politics" located "both within and beyond the nation . . . that is inhabited by a variety of cosmopolitanisms" (Hodgson, 2008, p. 225). In other words, this first competency encourages a cosmopolitical orientation to national and international political culture. The second competency describes a cosmopolitan-like empathy at the interpersonal level. This intercultural communication competency can be understood through Appiah's (2006) description of kindness to strangers (see Chapter 4), according to which those with cosmopolitan inclinations understand what it is like to be a stranger themselves and, therefore, are able to understand the necessity of kindness to strangers through empathetic response.

The third competency of communicating with multiple cultural groups is quite straightforward in nature. It reduces intercultural interaction to variables such as linguistic and non-verbal competence and communication styles and advocates competencies in these areas. Pedagogical approaches to cosmopolitanism often highlight these kinds of pragmatic competencies as skills related to educating for global competency (see Reimers, 2010). The fourth competency's notion of feeling at home in the world through cultural adaptability and functional fitness speaks to Hannerz's (1996) description of the cosmopolitan individual as a global citizen. And the fifth competency's focus on ethical and empathetic engagement with multiple points of view is addressed in Nussbaum's (1994) discussion of ethical obligations towards not just those within one's local sphere or those similar to us, but also towards people throughout the world.

Given these overlaps, what then is the difference between cosmopolitanism and intercultural communication competence? We argue that the difference lies at the level of focus. Cosmopolitanism can be viewed as a philosophical framework through which to understand intercultural communication competence; conversely, intercultural communication competence can also be considered important for engaging in cosmopolitan communication and peoplehood. However, the Intercultural Communication Competence model makes several assumptions that are not shared by our concepts of cosmopolitan communication and peoplehood. First, the assumption that multiple perspectives are skills that can be clearly and precisely taught is inherently problematic from a non-positivist view. According to this assumption, only those with access to such formal pedagogy can effectively engage in competent intercultural communication. Further, this model also assumes that these five competencies can be measured in a postpositivistic manner. Through our concepts, we propose a shift from a more traditional individualistic model of intercultural communication competence (such as Ting-Toomey's) towards an embodied and relational understanding more akin to relational empathy (Broome, 1991), which is described in more detail below. While we are not against the idea that aspects of cosmopolitanism can be taught in the classroom or in other pedagogical settings (see Chapter 8), we focus less on specific measurable outcomes seen as properties within an individual and more on reflexive syntheses of experiences that can lead to a lifelong process of cosmopolitanism. As we have explained earlier, cosmopolitanism does not reside within individuals but is produced through communicative performance.

DEVELOPMENTAL MODEL OF INTERCULTURAL SENSITIVITY

Milton Bennett's (1993) Developmental Model of Intercultural Sensitivity (DMIS) is the first of the intercultural communication models to address directly the transition from ethnocentrism to ethnorelativism. M. J. Bennett created the DMIS to serve as "a framework to explain the observed and reported experiences of people in intercultural situations" (J. M. Bennett & M. J. Bennett, 2004, p. 152). This model takes an interpretivist and constructivist approach to intercultural communication (although it does contain predictive elements), and therefore it differs from the more postpositivist models developed by scholars such as Y.Y. Kim and Ting-Toomey. Similar to Y.Y. Kim's Intercultural Personhood model, the DMIS "straddles the dividing line between cultural adaptation as a process of recovery and learning" (L. E. Anderson, 1994, p. 295).

The DMIS describes culture as existing in a space of dialectic tension between the objective and the subjective. It states that both subjective and objective conceptualizations of culture are required for intercultural competence. Objective culture entails the institutional aspects of culture, including politics and economics; and various folk and popular products of culture such as art, music and food. These objective cultural dimensions are internalized through socialization and education. On the other hand, subjective culture involves the varying and socially constructed experiences of social reality influenced by the systems and institutions of society as well as by interactions with members within and outside of a particular society. In other words, subjective culture can be described as the worldview developed by members of particular cultures, and objective culture has more to do with institutional norms and cultural products.

The DMIS is illustrated through attitudes and behaviors associated with the configuration of a worldview as individuals become aware of cultures other than their own. The model predicts that an individual will first go through three ethnocentric states—that is, three stages in which one's own culture is central to one's perspective of reality and serves as a framework for evaluation. The first stage involves denial, in which cultural differences go unnoticed or are ignored. The second stage is one of defense, in which other cultures are viewed through an 'Us–Them' distinction and one is protective of one's own cultural privilege. The third stage is called minimization, in which superficial cultural differences (such as style of dress) are acknowledged, but the individual still claims overwhelming similarity across cultures beneath the surface (i.e., 'We seemed different until I got to know her, and then found out we are really the same underneath the surface'). At this point, then, if the individual continues to develop, s/he will experience three ethnorelative stages during which one's own culture is experienced through the context of other cultures.

The first of these is acceptance, or the initial reconfiguration to ethnorelativism, in which equal but different complexity of others is recognized. This is followed by adaptation, but this stage does not occur until the individual learns to loosen her/himself from her/his own cultural context, and thus begins to embody cultural empathy. This empathy must be present not only in actions, but also in the intent behind actions. The final stage of the DMIS is called integration. This stage involves a developmental emphasis on cultural identity. J.M. Bennett and M. J. Bennett (2004) note that "at some point, [the individual's] sense of cultural identity may have been loosed from any particular cultural mooring, and they need to reestablish identity in a way that encompasses their broadened experience" (p. 157). This final stage (and indeed several of the ethnorelative stages) takes an almost hybridized position towards integrated identities and cross-cultural adaptation, as the authors note that "People dealing with integration issues are generally already bicultural or multicultural in their worldviews" (p. 157). Thus, it may seem that people experiencing integration maybe be quite similar in disposition to those engaging in cosmopolitan communication and peoplehood.

However, there are certain important distinctions to be made. The DMIS does not pay as much attention to local culture as do postcolonial and critical discussions of cosmopolitanism. That is, while cosmopolitanism certainly advocates for an outward orientation towards the world that embraces difference with the willingness to change, the critical turn emphasizes the importance of keeping a foot immersed in local culture in a dialectic tension between local and global. Furthermore, the kind of loosening from cultural moorings described by the DMIS does not speak to any possibility of translocalism (local-to-local cultural connections) often advocated for by scholars of cosmopolitanism for alliance-building purposes (see Kirtsoglou, 2010; Kraidy & Murphy, 2008).

Another point of difference is that the DMIS (which is identified as an intercultural training model) presupposes that the various stages can be taught/learned and measured. This, as we argued in the case of Ting-Toomey's Intercultural Communication Competence model, is not an assumption shared by our more critical and interpretive concepts of cosmopolitan communication and peoplehood. Finally, cosmopolitanism has a strong emphasis on social justice at a global systemic level, while the DMIS focuses largely on the identity/interpersonal communication level. Indeed, the DMIS tends to be presented in an ahistorical and apolitical context, making it inherently different from—and in many ways open to critique by—the critical and postcolonial focus of cosmopolitanism conceived in terms of intercultural communication. This is not to say that the DMIS's orientations towards empathy and humility cannot be harnessed to engage social justice issues and transform systemic oppression—just that in the context in which it was developed and is often applied, its scope is not so broad.

Overall, in its transformative orientation towards difference, embracing of the values of empathy and humility, and advocacy for cultural relativity, the DMIS is quite similar to cosmopolitanism, particularly as it advocates moving from ethnocentrism to ethnorelativism. In this manner, then, the DMIS can be useful to scholars interested in cosmopolitanism since it allows us to conceptualize the movement of individuals from ethnocentrism to empathy and humility, and towards an orientation that will make them more likely to engage in cosmopolitan communication and social and global justice efforts at the systemic level.

THIRD CULTURE BUILDING

Third culture building as a construct began with research in anthropology on the global nomad—i.e., an individual who is constantly migrating from culture to culture, with little affiliation with any one particular country or culture. The nomadic conception (similar to earlier descriptions of the cosmopolitan person as rootless) was first described in the 1960s as a "third culture" by Useem, Donaghue, and Useem (1963). Useem and Downie (1976) in particular furthered this work when they identified the Third-Culture Kid, or TCK, as a child of one culture who is raised in another. They described TCKs as possessing unique intercultural perspectives and skills, and as being more interculturally competent in some aspects of communication than others; however, they noted this was also somewhat of a lonely position, without national identity or affiliation. It was Fred Casmir (1997) who took Useem's focus on TCKs and worked on it from a communication perspective, creating an interactive process model of Third Culture Building. In this model, Casmir describes how two individuals from different cultures (cultures A & B) can combine their perspectives to create a unique third culture (culture C) in a constructionist process of mutually negotiated meaning-making (see also Starosta, 1991).

This model is somewhat similar to Bhabha's (1994) description of the third space, which has been defined as "a mode of articulation, a way of describing a *productive*, and not merely reflective, space that engenders new *possibility*" through hybridization between two or more cultures (Meredith, 1998, p. 3, italics in original). However, Third Culture Building is presented as an interpretive/social constructionist communication model while Bhabha's writing about third space sits squarely within postcolonial scholarship and takes the form of cultural critique. Shome and Hegde (2002) have critiqued the notion of third space by arguing that it assumes a temporal linear logic and a clear Us/Other binary. They state: "We live in a time of constant re/placement and reterritorialization as global capital connects, disconnects, and reconnects spaces in new ways and through constantly shifting lines of power" (p. 258) and, therefore, fourth, fifth and sixth spaces may make more sense. This critique can apply to Third Culture Building as well. Why not fourth, fifth or sixth culture building?

Third Culture Building also focuses on intercultural ethics and the creation of what Broome (1991) terms relational empathy, in which the 'third' culture produced can be used as a 'third' space that allows members from two cultures in conflict to experience empathy for one another outside of their particular cultural contexts, in order to fruitfully move towards conflict resolution in ways their positionality as belonging to distinct cultures would not allow. Evanoff (2006) describes how normative approaches "typically suggest that individuals should either adapt themselves to the norms of their host-cultures . . . or maintain their own norms while respecting those of the host-culture" (p. 421). He sees Third Culture Building as a useful alternative model. As in our concepts of cosmopolitan communication and peoplehood, mutual transformation and the willingness to change are key notions that guide Third Culture Building.

Third Culture Building is a classical intercultural communication model, in which several themes of cosmopolitanism are evident, such as empathizing with cultural Others, communicating across difference through this empathy, understanding and embodying an ethical approach to intercultural interaction, and the ability to move across rooted contexts into spaces of mutual transformation. However, Third Culture Building entails the communicative movement towards and engagement with cultural Others mainly at the interpersonal level of communication, and it conceptualizes culture as a bounded and discrete entity (see our earlier critiques of multiculturalism). In contrast, cosmopolitan communication, more like Bhabha's (1994) notion of third space, can be focused anywhere from the intra/interpersonal level to the macro-global level (i.e., cosmopolitan communication creates a discursive context through which to frame engagements with cultural Others), and generally exhibits a dialectic tension between the individual/local and the macro/global.

Cosmopolitan communication and peoplehood do not assume culture to be homogenous or bounded and nor do they assume that it is possible to completely shift back into one's original discrete culture once the goal of dialogue has been met. Rather, cosmopolitan communication must be mapped on intercultural and postcolonial transitions, in which cultures are (often involuntarily) merged, overlapped and marked in hybridized ways and cannot be simply returned to previous states. Cosmopolitan communication exists in the tension of the local and global simultaneously, and culture is assumed to be dynamic. Therefore, it can be stated that cosmopolitan communication involves third-cultural dialogic and communicative practices; however, Third Culture Building and the ontological position it assumes, in and of itself, is not the same as cosmopolitan communication and peoplehood.

COSMOPOLITAN COMMUNICATION AND
PEOPLEHOOD AS MORE THAN A SUM OF THE PARTS

The reader may have noticed that the concepts and models discussed in this chapter tend to take one of two directions: Functionalist and social scientific; interpretive and relativistic. Specifically, Y. Y. Kim's Intercultural Personhood and Ting-Toomey's Intercultural Communication Competence models take traditional intercultural communication perspectives of postpositivism. That is, according to these models, culture and communication are discrete measurable variables. Further, they assume that competence can be taught, measured and predicted through analysis of behavior. Indeed, these perspectives take the notions of culture, communication and intercultural contact as notions of directional movement forward through the measurement of various variables (i.e., knowledge, motivation, skill, stress, adaptation, growth and so on) which can be manipulated in ways designed to make intercultural contact beneficial and less stressful.

The DMIS and Third Culture Building model can be described as taking an interpretive turn towards social constructions of culture, identity and communication. These concepts and models examine culture and communication as mutually constituted, with the outcome of empathy, shared understanding, ethnorelativism and humble engagement across difference. Finally, all of these models and concepts (except the notion of multiculturalism) position difference as a problem that needs to be surmounted, and difference is treated as a given rather than something that is communicatively produced. Nor do they take into sufficient consideration issues of power and privilege, or challenge methodological nationalism. While each of these concepts and models incorporates aspects of cosmopolitanism, none of them is the same as what we have proposed as cosmopolitan communication and peoplehood.

From our perspective, our concepts of cosmopolitan communication and peoplehood fall more into the critical, postmodern and postcolonial realm in how they conceive of culture, identity, difference and communication. In the spirit of cosmopolitanism, we challenge methodological nationalism, we do not view cultural difference as a negative that needs to be surmounted but as a dynamic of Otherness that is communicatively produced and we take into account power, privilege and issues of social justice within conditions of postcolonial globality. In the spirit of vernacular cosmopolitanism, we advocate a bottom-up rather than top-down perspective—that is, cosmopolitanism cannot be taught from the top but rather must be experienced and learned on the ground. From this perspective, cultural identities are less individualistic and lean towards the cultural Other in the spirit of peoplehood rather than personhood. Belonging is also interdependent with the cultural Other and not a matter of just the Self (i.e., differential belonging; see Chapter 3).

In conclusion, the concepts and models analyzed in this chapter demonstrate that several of the values, already a part of cosmopolitanism's repertoire, are spread across a variety of intercultural communication models and concepts. Briefly, these values are:

- The importance of cultural self/awareness in pluralistic societies;
- The importance of an identity orientation which embraces interaction with cultural Others as a site of personal growth;
- The need to focus on both the local and the global in building the knowledge, motivation and skills needed to communicate across difference;
- The need to loosen oneself from ethnocentrism in order to move towards empathetic cultural engagement; and
- The importance of creating spaces of dialogue across difference that allow for orientations of intercultural empathy.

However, as we hope we have adequately demonstrated, cosmopolitan communication and peoplehood, together, are more than a sum of the individual parts of the concepts and models discussed in this chapter.

6 Cosmopolitanism, Methods and Operationalization

> The dualities of the global and the local, national and international, us and them, have dissolved and merged together in new forms that require conceptual and empirical analysis. (Beck & Sznaider, 2006, p. 3)

Kwame Anthony Appiah (2006) addresses the idea that cosmopolitanism as a philosophical framework exists as a response to positivism, to linear visions of the world, to Truths with a capital 'T' and to the assumption that facts are equal to values. Indeed, Holliday (2009) states that "a non-critical, post-positivist sociology has for too long carried out research which is led by researcher-generated questions in interviews and questionnaires, and has not made room for people who are being researched to express their own agendas" (p. 147). As an alternative, Holliday calls for a critical methodological cosmopolitanism "that requires restraint from defining and categorizing culture so that the margins can find space to claim the world in their own terms" (p. 146). Similarly, Beck and Sznaider (2006) also propose methodological cosmopolitanism in response to methodological nationalism.

Methodological cosmopolitanism stresses the necessity of moving beyond the bounded category of the nation-state in culture-related research, and conceptualizing and operationalizing culture and society in ways that take into consideration the complex connectivities that mark our world at local, national, transnational and global levels. Specifically, Beck and Sznaider (2006) posit that methodological nationalism is the practice of argument or research that presupposes the natural sociological unit of analysis to be the national society, the nation-state or a combination of both. In other words, methodological nationalism is the unquestioned assumption in social research that nation-states mark natural boundaries for cultures and societies.

Alternatively, methodological cosmopolitanism entails the notion of openness towards national and other borders, the ability to conceptualize cultural borders as connections rather than separations, the ability to work through and with many versions of universalism, or in Mignolo's words, with "diversalisms" (Mignolo, 2002), and the vision to work in the in-between spaces of taken-for-granted cultural categories. Methodological cosmopolitanism, when applied to intercultural communication, needs to be able to conceptualize and operationalize culture and communication at the local, national, transnational/translocal and global levels, and in some cases multiple levels as well as the interstices. Therefore, methodological cosmopolitanism involves conducting research in the liminal spaces of dialectic tensions and with blurred and shifting boundaries with an eye on postcolonial and neocolonial operations of power and social justice issues.

In this chapter, we address how cosmopolitanism as a cultural philosophy can be methodologically employed in framing and conducting intercultural communication research. We see two main ways in which we may discuss cosmopolitanism from a methodological standpoint. The first involves cosmopolitanism as a method in and of itself (i.e., cosmopolitanism as *method* of study). Cosmopolitanism-as-method should be conceived, elaborated and practiced in an inclusive rather than an exclusive manner. It must take a postcolonial, socially constructed, critical and transformative approach towards culture, communication, difference, power and identity. This approach does not intend to throw the notion of the nation-state out altogether, but to understand how nation-states are transformed in the cosmopolitan constellation and how new structures and reconfigurations of culture arise from the blurring and transcending of nation-state boundaries. Or, as Shome and Hegde (2002) explain, the nation-state as actor in global events has not disappeared, but rather it has shifted in meaning into something different from its earlier meanings. The challenge, therefore, for research based in cosmopolitanism-as-method, is to get a grasp on how to design research projects that are able to do justice to such complexity.

The second view of cosmopolitanism in the realm of method involves the various methods themselves through which cosmopolitanism as a phenomenon can be studied in intercultural communication (i.e., cosmopolitanism as *phenomenon* of study). Since cosmopolitanism is an outwardly-oriented and inclusive philosophy that is open to fluidity, dialectic tensions and transformation, it lends itself easily to study through the multiple methods embraced by intercultural communication scholarship. In this chapter, we first describe how cosmopolitanism-as-method can be used as an epistemological approach to intercultural communication research. We illustrate how different related disciplines approach cosmopolitanism-as-method and why intercultural communication scholars are in an ideal position to embrace this framework, which is capable of navigating multiple paradigmatic perspectives. Next, we describe how cosmopolitanism can exist as a *phenomenon* of study from social scientific, interpretivist, critical and postmodern/postcolonial perspectives and some of the methods attached to these perspectives. We provide a discussion of how cosmopolitanism can be operationalized for various levels of communication (individual/interpersonal to public, local to global) within intercultural communication scholarship. Finally, we describe how an intercultural communication study which explores cosmopolitanism as a phenomenon might be designed.

METHODOLOGICAL COSMOPOLITANISM: ADVOCATES AND CRITICS

Within the field of sociology, methodological cosmopolitanism has been proposed as a critique of and alternative to methodological nationalism (see Beck, 2006; Beck & Sznaider, 2006). In methodological nationalism, society's unit of analysis is the nation-state; in other words, the nation-state acts as a containment mechanism for studies of culture, according to which, for instance, U.S. Americans act one way and display certain cultural values while the Japanese act another way (Morris, 2009). Beck began his work on methodological cosmopolitanism in 2000 by describing what he sees as an epoch in the global world system which he calls the second age of modernity. In a world in which nation-state boundaries are blurring and weakening through the mobility of capital and people, Beck posits that modernist concepts of political, social and economic worlds no longer hold. Specifically, in this critique, Beck (2000) calls into question the contemporary state of political and social science. He then guides readers through what he describes as a "world-in-transition." This transition is the move from the modernist notion of the nation-state as the main unit of analysis in studying social systems (i.e., culture is described as bound by nation-state boundaries) to a cosmopolitan framework representative of multiple modernities (i.e., culture is dynamic and shifts across nation-states and there are multiple interpretations of modernity in addition to the Eurocentric one). This conceptualization of multiple modernities draws into question the very principles that constitute modern society, politics, territorial boundaries and collective communities (Beck, 2000, pp. 87–88).

In later and related work, Beck and Sznaider (2006) explain the need for a reconceptualization of the social sciences by asking for a cosmopolitan turn, in which social scientific findings are not bound by the nation-state but are influenced by and made available to the 'global' world. Methodological cosmopolitanism is defined as the opening up of new horizons by demonstrating how we can make the empirical investigation of transnational phenomena a transnational phenomenon in and of itself. Beck and Sznaider (2006) call for methodological cosmopolitanism as a necessary alternative to nationalism (in research) in the current era of accelerated globalization. This alternative is open to hybrid methods, conducting research across and through national boundaries, and working with a both/and rather than either/or approach to difference. This kind of move would involve, for instance, studying the tension between international law and human rights, and how human rights may exist along boundary lines other than the nation-state, such as race, ethnicity, gender, religion, status and class (Beck, 2000, pp. 83–84). Examples of this in contemporary politics and culture can be seen in the work of

Rainbow Planet, the international gay rights movement that has investigated the state of LGBTQ issues in 20 countries around the world in order to create informed analyses of global injustices and strive towards coalition-building across nation-state boundaries ("International Gay Rights Movement," 2012). It can also be seen in writings such as that of Anzaldúa, which focus on "borderlands" (the Texas–Mexican border) as hybridized cultural spaces that serve as sites of resistance. Anzaldúa describes her own hybrid *mestiza* identity as a site of exhilaration and critical transformation (cited in Sorrells, 2013, p. 94).

While Beck and colleagues' work is arguably the most prominent in calling for methodological cosmopolitanism, theirs is not the only movement in this direction (e.g., see Chernilo, 2006; Kendall, Skrbis, & Woodward, 2008), and nor is it without critique. Specifically, Beck's work overstates the 'death' of the nation-state. The nation-state may be changing in nature, but its impact on the world is still highly present and must be acknowledged and accounted for. Postcolonial communication scholars Shome and Hegde (2002) repeatedly emphasize that the nation-state still exists but must be reconceptualized "in new ways in the global that make us 'think' the nation is imploding, while in reality the nation is being redone through global processes that cannot be understood *only* through the nation" (p. 179, italics added). Bhambra (2011) directly confronts Beck's version of cosmopolitanism as being Eurocentric, and argues that postcolonialism, "with its critique of Eurocentrism in particular, provides more adequate resources for making sense of our contemporary world" (p. 314). Bhambra (as well as Chernilo, 2006) notes that Beck's focus of methodological cosmopolitanism primarily emerges from the viewpoints of Western Europe and the U.S., and as such reifies the very norming of the nation-state in its attempt to transcend it; she asserts that "methodological Eurocentrism" might be a better description than methodological nationalism, since Eurocentrism has been more problematic (and for a much longer time) than nationalism in how knowledge is produced about cultures around the world.

Furthermore, social anthropologists such as Werbner (2008) call for "the need to theorise the engagement of the people we study with the colonial and postcolonial state" (p. 6). Werbner offers a "new anthropological cosmopolitanism," which contrasts with what she calls the "new normative cosmopolitanism" proposed by Beck. Focusing on postcolonial approaches that attempt to create space for transformative dialogue through method, Werbner argues that "in a world of unequal power relations cosmopolitan intervention in the affairs of other states, however lofty its stated ideals, continuously risk being construed as Western hegemonic expansion in disguise" (p. 6). In other words, Beck's approach of methodological cosmopolitanism has been critiqued as cosmopolitanism-from-above—as being elitist, West-centric and hegemonic—since it pays scant attention to the importance of the emotional meanings of the nation-state, especially for postcolonial nations. We believe in Beck's position that we must move beyond the nation-state in terms of identifying, operationalizing and theorizing culture and communication. However, we agree with his detractors as well—as is evident from our largely postcolonial orientation in this book. We take the position that the nation-state still exists and impacts cultural emotions, identities and flows. Therefore, we must act and research with the nation-state still in mind, but in ways that are context-specific and contest archaic assumptions about its influences and nature.

As an alternative, Werbner states that methodological cosmopolitanism must be made vernacular, engaged in by local activists, in a manner that more closely resembles Spivak's call for subaltern advocacy at the local level (rather than Beck's desired cosmopolitan intervention from above). It should be noted here that vernacular cosmopolitanism research does not need to be carried out just by local activists, but can be conducted by any researcher embodying an ethic of advocacy and transformative social justice in and through their work. Further, vernacular cosmopolitanism can be applied to situations of diversity within cities and localities (within nation-states), as well as across nation-states (or translocally). Indeed, Shome and Hegde (2002) specifically problematize how we are used to thinking of space in relation to culture—they note that subaltern groups across nation-states can be more similar to each other than to privileged members of their own nation-state—i.e., "the conditions of subalternity within a particular national site may have more in common with the conditions of subalternity in a different national site, than with other sectors of population in the same national site" (p. 180).

Thus, while methodological cosmopolitanism should not be constrained by rigid nation-state conceptualization, *neither* should it assume that the nation-state has disappeared, which it most certainly has not. Vernacular cosmopolitanism-as-method can be thought of as "discontented cosmopolitanism," or "a form of discursive and practical empowerment [of marginalized populations], a critique of cosmopolitics and a simultaneous, dynamic, decisive engagement with it" (Kirtsoglou & Theodossopoulos, 2010, p. 87). This form of cosmopolitanism-as-method works in a circular or bottom-up, rather than in a linear/unidirectional, or top-down, manner since it is created at the local level, engages larger levels but is enacted at the local level. Further, it critiques traditional social scientific methods which engage in 'Othering' and 'theoretical provincialism,' e.g., when U.S. American scholars mainly cite other U.S. American scholars (Forte, 2008).

While methodological cosmopolitanism has been theorized and critiqued across several disciplines within the social sciences, we are primarily concerned with how cosmopolitanism-as-method might be envisioned for intercultural communication scholarship in particular. We now address this matter.

Cosmopolitanism-as-Method and Intercultural Communication

We take the position that both Beck's version of methodological cosmopolitanism as well as vernacular methodological cosmopolitanism can be useful as cosmopolitanism-as-method for intercultural communication scholarship. Intercultural communication scholars, having arrived later in the established social science scene than sociologists and anthropologists, are in a prime position to embrace cosmopolitanism-as-method (which is capable of engaging multiple paradigmatic as well as disciplinary perspectives). That is, cosmopolitanism-as-method, as a broad and multiscalar framework for research, involves reacting against methodological nationalism that keeps scholars in their 'nation-state' boxes. For example, Shome (2010) calls for the deterritorialization of race and for a transnational movement against conflating race with nationality in critical race communication studies.

Intercultural communication scholarship (and indeed, communication scholarship in general) has already transcended methodological boundaries by publishing, funding and teaching postpositive, interpretive, critical, postmodern and postcolonial ways of knowing (Martin & Nakayama, 2012). These varying paradigmatic approaches each declare their own definition and operationalization of 'culture' and how to go about studying it. Many intercultural communication scholars engage in cross-pollination of scholarship, both through multi-method research within the discipline or through interdisciplinary approaches (see Martin & Nakayama, 1999). Indeed, intercultural communication scholarship draws from, among others, the disciplines of English, history, international relations, psychology, anthropology, sociology, law, feminist/women's studies, cultural studies and performance studies. Given the meta-level ability of intercultural communication scholarship to transcend disciplinary and methodological boundaries, we feel that it is well suited to take on the cosmopolitanism-as-method approach. We propose methodological cosmopolitanism as an epistemology for intercultural communication research, with vernacular cosmopolitanism being particularly suited to the more current critical and postcolonial turn in intercultural communication scholarship. Vernacular methodological cosmopolitanism in intercultural communication should demand "a critical deconstruction of global arenas of exchange" (Shome & Hegde, 2002, p. 182) through the study of the flows, disjunctures and interstices of culture and communication processes across various boundaries, in addition to that of the traditional nation-state.

We now illustrate how cosmopolitanism has been studied and applied across multiple paradigms and disciplines, and from here, explain how intercultural communication scholars might be able to approach cosmopolitanism as a phenomenon for study as well as a method.

COSMOPOLITANISM AS PHENOMENON OF STUDY ACROSS DISCIPLINES AND PARADIGMS

Cosmopolitanism as Variable: Postpositivist Cosmopolitanism

Cosmopolitanism has been studied across various disciplines utilizing varied methods. While it comes as no surprise, given the more recent critical postcolonial turn, that it has been studied from critical/interpretive perspectives, what might not seem quite so obvious is cosmopolitanism studied from a social scientific viewpoint. This would seem possible only if cosmopolitanism is operationalized as a variable that makes up intercultural interactions, similar to the manners in which such constructs as age, race, nationality and travel experience have been operationalized as variables. This form of work has been done. From this paradigmatic perspective, cosmopolitanism has been operationalized as individual personality attributes, as an attitudinal measure, and as an outcome of interpersonal interactions and intercultural experience. Examples of such studies include the work of Mau, Mewes and Zimmerman (2008), who use empirical survey data of the entire German population to analyze the relationship between transnationalism and cosmopolitanism. In this study, the authors hypothesized that transnational experience (independent variable) would lead to an increase in cosmopolitan attitude (dependent variable). In this manner, cosmopolitanism has been measured as an attitude or a shift in attitude towards the world, i.e., cosmopolitanism has been studied as the outcome of multiple variables, leading to a cosmopolitan outlook (see also work by Lammers, 1974; Woodward, Skrbis, & Bean, 2008).

While it is useful to note that cosmopolitanism is being studied in postpositivist research, the most compelling example we found of a quantitative study was one by Furia (2005). In his article "Global citizenship, anyone? Cosmopolitanism, privilege, and public opinion," Furia, from the discipline of political science, uses the World Values Survey and the Inter-University Survey on Allegiance to produce data that refutes the critique that cosmopolitanism is an elitist and Western phenomenon. Curiously, his findings show that these critiques are over exaggerated and in many cases false. He also found that many people who exhibit the characteristics of cosmopolitanism don't identify as such, and that cosmopolitanism exists in many non-Western cultures and among many non-elite individuals. *In fact, Furia calls for the recognition that the very claim that cosmopolitanism is elitist and overly-Western is an elitist, overly-Western claim.* It is important to note here that the evidence of cosmopolitanism Furia finds in his work is more akin to Werbner's (2008) vernacular cosmopolitanism than the cosmopolitanism-from-above of Kant or even early Hannerz. In essence, Furia's work provides a response to critics of cosmopolitanism in a creative and paradigm-bending fashion, and the 'proof' is in the numbers. His findings show that cosmopolitanism "actually exists" (Robbins, 1998) on the ground in cultures outside the West, and in populations that are not considered elite within the West. In this manner, Furia uses quantitative methods to both make and refute critical and even some postcolonial arguments.

In terms of the general use of social scientific methods in the operationalization of cosmopolitanism, we recognize that it is certainly problematic to reduce cosmopolitanism to a variable, and one that is limited to attitudinal measures. Further, most researchers who subscribe to vernacular methodological cosmopolitanism will likely find the postpositivist methods colonizing in and of themselves. As Appiah (2006) states, the deepest problem with positivism is in its starting point (p. 27). That is, meanings, morals, values, agreements and disagreements vary by person, are socially constructed, and cannot be predetermined, unless we want to risk imposing our meanings, morals, values, agreements and disagreements on those we study—which would be a form of epistemic colonization. For a different perspective, we next turn to the interpretivist paradigm for researching cosmopolitanism.

Cosmopolitanism as Socially Constructed: Interpretivism and Cosmopolitanism

Cosmopolitanism lends itself well to an interpretive paradigm since it assumes culture and identity to be dynamic and socially constructed, and focuses on multiple realities and knowledge of many truths. To study cosmopolitanism from an interpretive perspective is to engage pluralism and relativism in a grounded manner—i.e., working in the bottom-up spirit of vernacular cosmopolitanism. This paradigmatic approach to studying cosmopolitanism stands in direct opposition to the views of those who advocate for top-down forms of cosmopolitanism since interpretivism, by its very nature, assumes the existence of multiple realities and ways of knowing and seeing the world, all the while maintaining that no reality (or its interpretation) is more 'real' than another.

Interpretivism and the ethnographic method lend themselves well to research on cosmopolitanism. In interviews and participant/observation research, the researcher co-constructs the reality s/he is studying throughout the research process. This requires researchers to not only filter research through their own bodies as instruments, but to empathetically engage in the research site. Ganga and Scott (2006) describe how the position of the researcher in qualitative research on transnationalism can allow researchers and co-participants to reflexively construct social processes within their own hybrid cultural spaces within the research site itself. Ethnographers can work with their co-participants to create spaces in which the nature of cosmopolitanism, as it is understood and performed within the community being studied, can be accessed by the researcher as an insider within the site. The ethnographic eye allows cosmopolitanism to be experienced within the research, rather than be identified as an externally defined variable to be controlled. Clifford (1986) reminds us that "interpreters constantly construct themselves through the others they study" (p. 11), and further describes the importance of moving beyond Eurocentric and Western texts that privilege the interpreter's voice to a sharing and co-construction of text and voice with co-participants. Indeed, in Clifford and Marcus's (1986) text, *Writing Culture: The Poetics and Politics of Ethnography*, Rabinow describes critical cosmopolitanism as a guiding value for ethics of ethnographers:

> This is an oppositional position, one suspicious of sovereign powers, universal truths, overly relativized preciousness, local authenticity, and moralisms high and low . . . it attempts to be highly attentive to (and respectful of) difference, but is also wary of the tendency to essentialize difference. (p. 258)

This perspective, of the in-betweenness of ethnographers and co-participants, also allows the researcher to practice and engage with cultural empathy in ways that embody cosmopolitan ideals. Further, since cosmopolitanism as phenomenon of ethnographic study can be simultaneously experienced by the researcher and the co-participants, this allows for multiple nuances to emerge. Ethnography as method is, therefore, especially suitable for studying various forms of cosmopolitanisms in their specific contexts.

For example, when Sobré-Denton (2011) studied an international student group at Arizona State University (INTASU), through her interviews with her co-participants she came to a better understanding of how cosmopolitanism emerged within the research site itself (see Chapter 8 for examples and details). As she communicated in greater depth with her site, members found that the notion of cosmopolitanism provided a name for their embodied experiences of being a member of that group. That is, when the members of INTASU read the material from the research and discussed it with Miriam, or were introduced to the construct of cosmopolitanism in interviews or during conversations with the author during participant/observation, they overwhelmingly found that this term of connecting across cultural boundaries based on their own hybridized and displaced identities described their own lived experience. This (unnamed) cosmopolitan phenomenon seemed to assist in the recruitment and retention of new members, and in solidifying the group's mission to assist international students in maintaining their hybrid identities while simultaneously integrating with U.S. American cultures. In this manner, then, the mutually constitutive nature of the culture–communication relationship creates a strong connection between ethnographic methods and cosmopolitanism. That is, in order to learn about this phenomenon on the ground, researchers benefit from being able to engage with the research site in a manner that allows them to embody, as well as socially and dialogically co-construct, a cosmopolitan experience.

The largest body of interpretive work on cosmopolitanism can be found in the discipline of anthropology. Anthropological ethnographic approaches to the study of cosmopolitanism can be instructive to intercultural communication research (see Sobré-Denton, 2011; Theodossopoulos & Kirtsoglou, 2010; Werbner, 2008) since such grounded and immersive research allows for the conceptualization of culture, communication, difference and identity in postmodern and postcolonial ways (Marcus, 1995). Examples include Wardle's (2000) ethnography which explores vernacular cosmopolitanism in the postcolonial and transnational community of Kingston, Jamaica. In this study, Wardle uses his own experiences and that of his neighbors, friends and colleagues in Kingston. While he draws from Kant's cosmopolitanism and Simmel's notion of the stranger (described in Chapter 4), he reaches several illuminating conclusions on the postcolonial transnational networks of citizens of Kingston throughout the northern hemisphere. He describes the openness of Kingston to external cultural influences and describes how cosmopolitan philosophical values have emerged vernacularly within all levels of Kingston society (Wardle, 2000; see also Hannerz, 2007).

In *The Cosmopolitan Canopy: Race and Civility in Everyday Life* (E. Anderson, 2011), sociologist Elijah Anderson ethnographically examines Philadelphia's Center City, where multiple classes and races of people come together to create a cosmopolitan public life. Anderson uses "folk ethnography," or an "intense form of people watching" that makes "cultural sense of strangers in public places" (p. 11). In doing this, he describes what he calls the "cosmopolitan canopy," or a shifting, postmodern civic space where people come together in various representations of race, class and gendered performances of urban life, which is created and recreated throughout the city of Philadelphia. Similarly, Marina Peterson, a performance studies anthropologist, describes the creation of a civic space of musical performance that brings together disparate cultures in Los Angeles's Bunker Hill neighborhood. Through her ethnographic research, Peterson (2012) describes performances of ethnic and cultural identity through hip-hop, Afro-Celtic, Chinese modern dance and other artistic endeavors as hybridized cultural and civic community-building processes that cross cultural and socioeconomic boundaries (these two approaches to cosmopolitan ethnography fit well with Sobré-Denton's work with Hostelling International–Chicago, described later in this chapter, in terms of the creation of postmodern cosmopolitan spaces in urban settings). In these and many other studies, the ethnographic approach illustrates its suitability for studying manifestations of cosmopolitanism in various non-Western and/or non-elitist contexts (it is, of course, suitable for Western and entangled contexts as well).

Ethnographic research focusing on cosmopolitanism is obviously well-suited to studying communities that might self-identify as cosmopolitan or those which seemingly exhibit a cosmopolitan outlook. Examples would include groups participating in translocal social movements (e.g.,

Hodgson, 2008), global–local communal ties (e.g., Sobré-Denton, 2011) or transnational cosmopolitan communities within local environments (e.g., E. Anderson, 2011; Peterson, 2012; Sobré-Denton, 2011). Cosmopolitan social groups and networks, whether they include those working towards indigenous rights in Africa (Hodgson, 2008), the indigenous cosmopolitans of Papa New Guinea (Strathern & Stewart, 2010), or the cosmopolitan monoculturals, biculturals and internationals of Arizona State University's International ASU (INTASU) group (Sobré-Denton, 2011), can all be explored and understood through this method that emphasizes the simultaneous existence of multiple ways of knowing and intellectual and cultural pluralism. The researcher, in such studies, would attempt to understand the specific cosmopolitan experiences of the group members by immersing herself in that cosmopolitan experience.

While we focus specifically on ethnography, other interpretive methods such as focus groups, rhetorical and textual analyses and non-ethnographic interviewing could potentially also be used to study cosmopolitanism. Given space constraints and the amount of information available on cosmopolitan ethnography, we chose to focus primarily on this method. We would like to note here though that while anthropology has sometimes interrogated the relationship between Self/researcher and native/Other, it has also been complicit in the colonizing process of entrenching binaries between Self (researcher) and Other (native) (Clifford, 1986, p. 8). The new anthropology (such as the work done by Werbner and others) makes greater attempts to destabilize and recenter the problematic and colonizing discourses on identity and Self/Other binaries that the discipline itself was in a large part responsible for creating. It should also be noted that these interpretivist approaches to the study of cosmopolitanism often tend towards critical and postcolonial influences. We now turn to this paradigm.

Cosmopolitanism as Social Movement: Critical and Postcolonial/Decolonial Cosmopolitanism

As described in Chapter 1, a growing number of scholars are revisiting cosmopolitanism from the perspectives of the critical paradigm. Delanty (in sociology) and Mignolo (a semiotician specializing on responses to colonialism), have both made substantial arguments for the reimagining of cosmopolitanism from translocal and decolonizing perspectives. They have argued that the critical approach is much more useful when engaging views from the margin, and for the purposes of interrogating the injustices of colonialism and neoliberal globalization. We should also note that, given the range of methods and approaches used in critical research, it is difficult to neatly discuss critical research from the perspective of operationalization. The following suggestions are made with this caveat in mind.

From the critical perspective, cosmopolitanism has been reappropriated as a framework through which to highlight the complexities of an emergent social phenomenon (i.e., vernacular cosmopolitanism) that has major implications for critiques of modernity and social inquiry (Delanty, 2006, p. 28). The traditional top-down Kantian or early Hannerzian (and, some might argue, Beck- and Nussbaum-influenced) approach to cosmopolitanism exists far removed from critical theory's mission to emancipate, revolutionize and illuminate social and global injustices. However (and as we have argued and demonstrated), cosmopolitanism as a philosophical and cultural framework can and has been decolonized (even deterritorialized), reappropriated and made useful in new and transformative ways.

Critical approaches to cosmopolitanism often direct researchers towards a postcolonial or decolonial view. Indeed, all critical cosmopolitanism researchers need to address the difference in focus between traditional top-down views of cosmopolitanism and its postcolonial/decolonial and critical reappropriation. Galinsky, Hugenberg, Groom and Bodenhausen (2003) define reappropriation as taking "possession for oneself that which was once possessed by another" (p. 222), meaning that instead of passively accepting the negative connotations of a contested term, that term is infused with new and empowering meaning.

Critical and postcolonial cosmopolitanism scholars must work with and through the awareness that this 'term' is highly contested and contains a negative and Eurocentric history in its etymology. Kantian cosmopolitanism contains the highly problematic, racist and tacit assumption that world citizenship is only available to those privileged enough to attain citizenship status. Hannerz's (1996) earlier views on cosmopolitanism pertain to privileged, voluntary travelers with access to social and cultural capital as well as finances and time through which to transcend national and cultural borders. These two forms of top-down cosmopolitanism have no use for the dispossessed, the fragmented and the resistant, and has little value for transforming the social world in a way that benefits anybody other than those voluntary and privileged world citizens themselves (Kirtsoglou, 2010). Critical scholars argue that cosmopolitanism must be reimagined to represent and empower the local, the historically oppressed and the marginalized.

Critical and postcolonial researchers of cosmopolitanism tend to look towards larger systemic issues involving the forces of neoliberal globalization, cultural flows and disjunctures, diaspora, processes of hybridity, translocalism and transnationalism. Cosmopolitanism in critical research can be operationalized at multiple levels. First, this can be done at the meta-level of critique (e.g., addressing past critiques of cosmopolitanism through alternative imaginings and approaches). For example, Mignolo (2002) addresses the shortcomings of seemingly cosmopolitan movements and phenomena such as Christianity and 19th century imperialism, or emancipatory-seeming philosophies, such as those advocated by Kant and Karl Marx, and calls for a critical cosmopolitanism, which he describes as "the need to discover other options beyond both benevolent recognition . . . and humanitarian pleas for inclusion" (p. 160).

A second means of operationalizing critical cosmopolitanism is to utilize an interpretive approach to studying cosmopolitanism with critical or postcolonial outcomes of exposing problematic systems or regimes and Eurocentric approaches to knowledge production and experience. Several examples of such studies abound (see Theodossopoulos & Kirtsoglou, 2010). One particularly illustrative study is Valls' (2010) ethnographic description of indigenous notions of cosmopolitanism in rural southern Japan. Valls argues that perspectives on locality, internationalization and national identity cannot be derogated as un-cosmopolitan simply because they don't fulfill Western understandings of globalization and cosmopolitanism. Finally, and this is particularly worthwhile for postcolonial scholarship, cosmopolitanism can be critically operationalized as conceptualizations of large-scale transnational cultural flows and disjunctures (Appadurai, 1996), and through reimaginings of social systems which problematize certain 'known quantities' (such as Orientalism, Edward Said's [1978] argument about the West's colonial representations of the Rest as inferior and exotic, and accompanying assumptions of first-world superiority and elitism) for alternative ways of seeing and knowing the world.

For example, Aihwa Ong (1999), in her book *Flexible Citizenship*, describes diasporic cosmopolitanism through an in-depth analysis of affluent Chinese communities in the U.S. She describes their movement of economic and social capital, focusing on how this creates complex and often misunderstood interrelationships between the U.S. and China as well as a sense of a cosmopolitan third space. Ong calls for a broadened scope of anthropological understanding of power structures through an analysis of the wealthy and privileged to add another dimension to the popular anthropological concentration on the "poor, the downtrodden, the marginalized, and the exploited in the third world" (p. 30). Chinese expatriate communities in San Francisco, for example, have a deep stake in that city's legislation, and they are now inextricably financially tied to the city's economy. They strive for acceptance in San Francisco, but all the while maintain both cultural and economic ties with China, and never intend for full-scale relocation to the U.S. Issues of (in this case, elite) Chinese-American citizenship and the complexity of ties across the two cultures that simultaneously entwines and balks at traditional U.S./Chinese roles (with the Chinese in San Francisco demonstrating the power of affluence while needing U.S. educational and cultural capital to remain elite in China) demonstrate that entrenched ways of understanding power and identity need to be revisited in postcolonial globality. Indeed, the critical paradigm offers a wealth of intersections of epistemology and operationalization to scholars interested in research on cosmopolitanism.

OPERATIONALIZING COSMOPOLITANISM AT DIFFERENT LEVELS OF INTERCULTURAL COMMUNICATION

As is evident from the previous section, cosmopolitanism in research can be operationalized across several paradigms, and this creates a vastly useful pathway for future research. Cosmopolitanism can also be operationalized at the level of the individual (e.g., Hannerz, 2006), social-group (e.g., Sobré-Denton, 2011) and societal/transnational (e.g., Furia, 2005), depending on the nature and purpose of the research. Although we draw examples from multiple disciplines in the previous section, all these examples clearly indicate how they may be translated into the discipline of intercultural communication.

At the individual level, cosmopolitanism can be operationalized as the communication of people who cross multiple cultural boundaries (physical and/or mental) and the kinds of networks they develop and the social connections they make, which they would neither be exposed to nor probably have an interest in if they weren't situated in a cosmopolitan context. This form of operationalization is supported by the work of several scholars such as Kraidy (2002), Bhabha (1994), Kraidy and Murphy (2008), Hannerz (2006) and Shome and Hedge (2002). We extrapolate from such scholarship that hybrid identities, border dwelling experiences and biculturalism are all characteristics of a more cosmopolitan age, in which it is necessary to become more Other- and world-oriented in order to succeed in professional settings and in life and be able to engage with issues of social and global justice. At this level, then, cosmopolitanism can be operationalized as the communicative dimensions of an identity orientation that is always in process (see Chapters 3 and 4) and provides "a perspective, a state of mind, or—to take a more processual view—a mode of managing meaning" (Vertovec & Cohen, 2002, p. 13). This identity orientation is presented through our working definition and assumptions of cosmopolitan peoplehood.

Cosmopolitanism can also be operationalized as a lens through which to move beyond essentializing Self–Other and Us–Them dichotomies during cultural border-crossing communicative experiences. Here, we propose cosmopolitanism be thought of as a lens for understanding and engaging in intercultural processes of transition and change (such as, adaptation or insularism with regard to host cultures or cultural Others during transitions, or creating communicative spaces in transnational situations) in an increasingly globalizing world (see Held, 2002; McEwan & Sobré-Denton, 2011). This level of operationalization involves cosmopolitan communication (see Chapter 2) that can be learned through intercultural interactions. Here, cosmopolitanism is performed at the interpersonal level.

Further, cosmopolitanism can also be operationalized to describe a social network comprising people with cosmopolitan dispositions who negotiate with multiple cultural Others, either through familial and social circumstances, or through travel, work or migration. Belonging to multicultural social support groups (as an alternative to single-culture groups) during transitions can result in many individuals, sharing the same experience of cultural displacement, communicatively engaging their identities in a cosmopolitan manner and spirit. Such cosmopolitan social networks are usually created and maintained in migrant/immigrant communities, as well as online (see Sobré-Denton, 2011). In such cases and situations, cosmopolitanism is operationalized at the social-group level.

Finally, cosmopolitanism can be operationalized at the level of the workings of transnational and translocal cultural flows and networks. At this level, cosmopolitanism becomes a condition through which it is possible to imagine and create multiscalar connections between societies and cultures that supplant the traditional nation-state format (i.e., the 'inter-national' format) of relations and alliances (Vertovec & Cohen, 2002). Several such cosmopolitan connections and communities exist today in various non-Western, Western, postcolonial and entangled contexts (e.g., all of the studies described in Theodossopoulos & Kirtsoglou, 2010; see also E. Anderson, 2011; Hodgson, 2008). Here we would like to emphasize that cosmopolitanism exists as a sociocultural condition (Vertovec & Cohen, 2002) stemming from globalization, which "is to be celebrated for its vibrant cultural creativity as well as its political challenges to various ethnocentric, racialized, gendered and national narratives" (p. 100). Thus, at this macro level, cosmopolitanism can be operationalized as transnational, translocal and multi-societal communication and discourse at supra and subnational levels. Such macro-level communication networks are often studied by intercultural communication researchers.

Thus cosmopolitanism lends itself as a critically-oriented intercultural communication philosophy that can be studied at multiple levels and through various forms of communication and discourse. This, as we noted in Chapter 2, is an important strength since the intercultural communication field, and the discipline of communication in general, needs more theoretical visions that can span and be theorized across various levels and forms of communication and discourse (see Ganesh, Zoller, & Cheney, 2005). Now that we have described how cosmopolitanism as a phenomenon may be studied through multiple paradigmatic perspectives, as well as how it can be operationalized at various levels of intercultural communication, we move on to describe how an intercultural communication study engaging cosmopolitanism might be designed (for more examples of how cosmopolitanism is being researched within the communication discipline today, see Chapter 8).

DESIGNING AN INTERCULTURAL COMMUNICATION STUDY ENGAGING COSMOPOLITANISM

The pragmatic question that follows from our discussion in this chapter so far is: What might an intercultural communication study engaging cosmopolitanism look like? Since space restrictions and the scope of this book does not allow us to get into a full-scale study, we provide here a brief snapshot, if you will, of how such a study might be designed. In this snapshot we address questions an intercultural communication researcher might pose when deciding to design and conduct a study engaging cosmopolitanism. In order to do this, we draw upon a study in progress being conducted by Miriam.

When it comes to accessing cosmopolitan frames for intercultural communication research purposes, we align with Appiah's (2006) perspective that cosmopolitanism is often mundane and requires a focus on negotiating shifting identities and the particular uniqueness of cultural Others through "conversation." According to Appiah (2006):

> Cosmopolitanism shouldn't be seen as some exalted attainment: it begins with the simple idea that in the human community, as in national communities, we need to develop habits of coexistence: *conversation* in its older meaning, of living together, association. (pp. xviii–xix, italics added)

Thus intercultural communication research utilizing cosmopolitanism needs to focus on these everyday (and in some cases special and focused) forms of conversation, whether happening at the individual, interpersonal, intercultural, local, translocal, transnational, global or (as is the case in the example we provide), several levels simultaneously.

In the snapshot example of study design that we now offer, Miriam and her research assistant had to first develop research questions, figure out how best to operationalize cosmopolitanism and learn how to look for "actually existing" cosmopolitanism within the site they are studying.

Research Questions, Site of Study and Role of the Researchers

When Miriam first contemplated designing a research study utilizing cosmopolitanism from below, she was unsure of how and where to 'look for' this phenomenon. At this time, she was already working with Hostelling International–Chicago (HI–Chicago) on helping them fine-tune and promote their mission statement—"to help all, especially the young, gain a better understanding of the world and its people through hostelling" (particularly within their local communities). Hostelling International–USA (HI–USA) is the U.S. American arm of Hostelling International, a federation of over 4,000 hostels in over 80 countries. HI–USA is a non-profit organization which simultaneously fulfills two functions: Engaging in educational programming about intercultural communication and the benefits of travel and hostelling (bringing a non-elite perspective to voluntary travel) to both underserved communities and any potential travelers within their communities; and providing safe, affordable accommodations and local experiences to travelers who stay at their hostels.

Hostelling International–Chicago is the flagship branch for educational programming, and has pioneered multiple educational programs for Chicago's highly segregated neighborhoods. HI–Chicago has been specifically working with Communities in Schools (CIS) and Chicago Public Schools (CPS) to promote intercultural communication competence and engage students in participating in intercultural experiences in underserved communities within the city. HI–Chicago provided an ideal space for Miriam to study vernacular cosmopolitanism in a vein similar to E. Anderson (2011), who focuses on "actually existing" cosmopolitanism in Philadelphia's inner city. This organization and its work provided an ideal site for exploring cosmopolitanism as a communication phenomenon, and how pedagogically 'planting seeds' of cosmopolitanism in the imaginations of youth might create in them a more cosmopolitan perspective of the world and their place in it.

With these goals in mind, Miriam designed the following broad research questions:

> RQ1: How do HI–Chicago staff and volunteers engage in the process of educating for cosmopolitanism in accordance with the HI–USA mission statement?
> RQ2: Does HI–Chicago's educational programming engender a cosmopolitanism outlook and approach to communication in its program participants? If yes, how?

Over a course of 9 months, Miriam and her research assistant used an interpretive/critical framework to design this study. They immersed themselves in the site and worked with co-participants to create shared meanings through ethnographic and qualitative research. They worked with the co-participants after data collection was completed to utilize the results to illuminate existing power structures, including how race, history and intercultural communication are taught within Chicago Public Schools, as well as how the City of Chicago can work to desegregate its inner-city youth. In particular, Miriam and her research assistant are working with HI–USA as consultants to illuminate the importance of and bringing more funding to intercultural education for public schools in Chicago (Chicago, like the rest of the country, is currently suffering from budget cuts and reallocations).

The research, once completed, will go directly back to Hostelling International and Chicago Public Schools in ways Miriam hopes will assist with lobbying for the continuation of these educational programs (which are currently in jeopardy due to both organizational restructuring and diminishing grant funding) and help the organization find out how to improve these programs from the perspectives of both academic scholarship and the students' voices and input. In this manner, the research was engaged in from a participatory action framework that involves participants in the entire research process and returns the research to those participants through its conclusions and potential actions arising from the research.

For example, Miriam and her assistant have returned their final research report to HI–USA, where it is being circulated as a means of advocating for pedagogical practices such as experiential and reflective learning in the non-profit's policy-making (Tanno & Jandt, 1993).

Miriam and her research assistant observed 9 programming events at HI–Chicago: Four Cultural Kitchens (CK), three Exchange Neighborhoods (ENS) and two Community Walls (CW; see Chapter 8 for detailed descriptions of each of these programs) as well as orientations for the teachers and classroom visits by HI–Chicago programming staff. Each of the programs included an overnight stay at the hostel, and the opportunity for the CPS students to engage and interact with both domestic and international travelers staying there. Fifty-eight interviewed participants ranged in age from 14 to 58 years old, and embodied multiple and hybrid ethnicities, races, religions, socioeconomic statuses and life experiences. Roughly 65% of the interviewees (35 participants) were students in CPS schools, ranging from freshmen to seniors. All of the students identified as belonging to lower socioeconomic classes, with the racial and ethnic make-up (also self-identified) being 45% African American, 45% Latino, 5% Asian and 5% White (of whom, all were first-generation, generally Polish or Italian immigrants). Fifty-eight students, teachers, volunteers and programming staff were interviewed. They were asked questions designed to illuminate the impact of the three kinds of educational programming on the students (and staff) who take part in them. Finally, Miriam and her assistant perused over a 100 documents generated by the students throughout the programs, including reflection exercises, post-program surveys and debriefing sessions. While their role as researchers was to serve primarily as observers and interviewers, they did pitch in with the programs whenever they were able to help (in this way, they were, at times, participant-observers).

How Cosmopolitanism Can Be 'Looked For'?

Although she knew she wanted to study how cosmopolitanism "actually exists" and/or may be cultivated through interactions between CPS students, travelers and programming materials, Miriam had to carefully decide where to start. She didn't want to impose an *a priori* assumption of cosmopolitanism on the site and its members. Further, she wanted to engage with the site using a grounded approach, letting the data draw out the conclusions (i.e., an emic, rather than etic, approach). Therefore, she had to understand how to 'look for' aspects of cosmopolitanism without leading the research. In creating the interview protocol, she wanted to design questions that would elicit students' experiences regarding cosmopolitanism, and debated how to best go about this. It became imperative to first define what she meant by cosmopolitanism in the context of this particular study.

Miriam knew she wanted to study vernacular cosmopolitanism from the perspective that there do exist cosmopolitan practices, spaces and ideas outside of the West which are non-Eurocentric, and within underserved (read: non-elite) communities within the West as well. She chose to work with the notion of inclusive cosmopolitanism, what Pollock (cited in Bhambra, 2011) calls "provincial cosmopolitanism," through which we can:

> . . . learn from others when we recognize that what they contribute is *not a confirmation of what we already know*, but the bringing into being of new understandings relevant to the worlds we inhabit together. These new understandings both reconfigure our existing perceptions *of the world*, as well as inform the ways in which we live *in the world*. (p. 323, italics added)

She developed several themes that she thought might be indicative of this sort of provincial cosmopolitanism within the chosen site. These included: empathy; learning together as a means of sharing knowledge (rather than mono-directional, teacher-to-student knowledge transfer); global/local ties; interest in social and global justice issues; understanding the value of valuing; recognition of ethical obligation to cultural Others; cultural self-awareness (being able to describe one's own culture); cultural curiosity; interest in communicating across difference; and the ability to imagine communities beyond one's own neighborhood/locality. She worked these themes into the interview protocols for both students and staff, and made the protocols semi-structured, since different co-participants, types of programming and experiences would elicit different responses and require different questions.

After collecting about half of the data, Miriam began to abductively develop a codebook that examined emergent themes. The initial coding schema includes 18 open codes (or lower-order themes) that have emerged from the data. Of these, six seem to be directly related to cosmopolitanism as it was operationalized for this study. These are: cultural curiosity; awareness of multiple perspectives/cultural relativity; respect and value for difference; a sense of unity and global belonging (connection to a larger world); cultural self-awareness; and ethical obligations to cultural Others. The next steps involved completing data coding, analyzing the data, the creation of higher-order codes, and eventually developing larger thematic issues emergent from the data. Some of these are described below.

What Makes This Study One About Cosmopolitanism and Intercultural Communication?

For Miriam, cosmopolitanism as studied through this research project focused on the argument that actual national boundary crossing is not necessary in today's globalizing world for one to communicatively experience and engage in cosmopolitanism and to open up one's imagination towards the world. That is, by studying HI–USA's educational programs in Chicago, the researchers could see how cosmopolitanism is being taught and experienced at a local level, and attempt to understand how these values and ideals may be both pedagogically cultivated in underserved youth and may manifest over time through further intercultural experience (both experiential and didactic). The researchers could also examine how cosmopolitanism exists in one diverse city, in non-elite populations who engage with cultural difference on a day-to-day basis. This study is an example of an intercultural communication study of cosmopolitanism using ethnography and qualitative research as a method, as well as an example of an ethnography that is attempting to explore what cosmopolitanism may 'look like' in a non-elite setting, at the vernacular level, and in an entangled (Western and non-Western) context. The study also strives to understand what makes this sort of cosmopolitanism communicative, and whether or not cosmopolitanism can be communicated through pedagogy.

For this project, Miriam and her research assistant found that, from a critical/interpretive perspective that is cognizant of power structures impacting the underserved communities of young adults served by these programs, aspects of cosmopolitan communication (see Chapter 2) and cosmopolitan peoplehood (see Chapter 4) are both present at this site. To return to our seven assumptions of cosmopolitan communication, after careful analysis of the large body of data collected over 9 months, the researchers found that each assumption can be illustrated through the findings. That is, at varying points across all three programs, the communication between the students and teachers, the students themselves, and the students and hostellers (all three of which were analyzed) exhibited characteristics of cosmopolitan communication and its various assumptions.

Cosmopolitan communication within the context of the educational programming was found to be world-oriented (Assumption 1), in that students are encouraged to view culture as dialogic and to see themselves as citizens of the world as well as ambassadors of their local neighborhoods and city for travelers as well as other students. Students are encouraged to view their identities from the perspective of their own neighborhoods (such as in Community Walls) as well as through the lenses of being first generation immigrants, members of dominant as well as non-dominant groups within their neighborhoods, the city of Chicago, the U.S. and the world.

The programming encourages mutuality (Assumption 2) as the hostel itself and the experiential learning accomplished there exists as an in-between space, in which students and travelers are still in Chicago, but engage in dialogues with culturally different Others (either other students, travelers or even their own teachers, all of whom are seen outside their usual context within school grounds). Facilitated activities and reflections allow for possibilities of change and the creation of new meanings at student–student, student–traveler and student–teacher levels. Further, in some situations, teachers reported students returning with these new lessons and meanings to their neighborhoods and schools, and attempting to create new spaces for dialogue among their peers based on what they had learned. This is also evidence of internalization of Assumption 6 (critical self-transformation) which entails self-reflexivity as well as openness to interruptions of prior held assumptions about culture, identity, Self and cultural Other.

Assumption 3, which states that cosmopolitan communication is attentive to power, can be seen in several aspects of these programs. Students are taught to engage in empathetic behavior, to imagine communities of students like them (similar in age) in places nearby (such as in ENS, where they visit other communities of students in their city) or places far away (such as in CK, where they are asked to picture a day in the life of a teenager in another country, which cannot be one that is represented by their own community). For example, students from Pilsen, a largely Mexican American community, cannot choose the country of Mexico for their cultural study. This helps them to develop understandings that while they may feel marginalized for various reasons in their own lives (due to poverty, violence, race/ethnicity or other reasons), they should understand that they are not the only people to experience these kinds of setbacks—and that they can push back against such injustices through education and critical self-reflexivity. It also promotes pride in local communities and the desire to return their experiences to their own communities. For example, two students involved in HI–Chicago's educational programs have won municipal World Citizen awards for service to their communities; additionally, several students involved with the CK program also serve in such global-oriented non-profit groups as Buildon.org and the International Baccalaureate program.

In terms of Assumption 4 (actively engaging borders), this is probably the most easily-recognizable aspect of cosmopolitan communication in the work done at HI–Chicago. Cultural borders are crossed in all three programs: All students spend the night at the hostel, often leaving the borders of their neighborhoods for the first or second time in their lives. They also cross borders when engaging with the travelers at the hostel (particularly in CW and CK), and as they introduce the travelers to aspects of the city of Chicago the travelers might otherwise never have access to, simultaneously changing their own perspectives on cultural Others as well as changing the ways cultural Others view the U.S. in general, and the city of Chicago in particular. ENS students cross the border of their neighborhood and experience other neighborhoods that, while only 30 minutes by bus or six miles away from their homes, feels "like traveling to a different country" (in the words of a participant interviewed during the study). Students learn that neighborhoods like the South Side of Chicago, which they had stereotypical views of, can be accessible and spaces of learning when they are shown around by members of that community. In this way, students also exhibit the desire and ability to engage positively with difference and do not feel the need to resist ambiguities and the emergence of new relational meanings at the intersections of multiple cultural differences (Assumption 5).

Assumption 7, that cosmopolitan communication is hopeful and deliberate, is the driving force behind the educational programming taking place at HI–Chicago. When studying these programs, the researchers found that all three utilized Hansen et al.'s (2009) three arts of cosmopolitan learning: hope (particularly present in CK), memory (particularly present in CW) and dialogue (particularly present in ENS; for more on these three arts see Chapter 8). The programs engage these arts through deliberate combinations of pedagogical tools, including didactic classroom-based lessons and presentational assignments on culture, norms, mores and other intercultural lessons; experiential learning including going to the hostels, playing intercultural games with the travelers and playing training games (such as Brief Encounters) in their classrooms; and deliberative reflection in facilitated sessions on the last day of each program, where students are asked to recap and reflect on the lessons they had learned about themselves, hostelling, travel, culture and the world.

As described in Chapter 4, cosmopolitan communication and cosmopolitan peoplehood are mutually constitutive. Our notion of peoplehood describes critical self-transformation in relation to cultural Others as a lifelong process of continually engaging in dialogue with Others through cosmopolitan communication. The research found that HI–Chicago's educational programming students have been oriented into the first stages of this process. While this is by no means a guarantee that all of these students will go on to a life devoted to critical self-transformation and the decentering of the Self, the data certainly did exhibit a focus on hope and dialogue that did, in certain situations, lead towards opening the door to the process of becoming more Other- and world-oriented, reflective and culturally aware. Since cosmopolitan peoplehood is a process, and not a concrete outcome (can it really ever be 'achieved' or concretely 'measured'?), we believe that these three HI programs make possible important first steps towards learning cosmopolitan communication in order to work towards cosmopolitan peoplehood.

CONCLUSION

Intercultural communication as a discipline has shifted over the course of its existence, moving through the decades from postpositivistic to interpretive to critical and postcolonial paradigms, thereby widening its scope through various approaches to scholarship. Cosmopolitanism-as-method provides opportunities to connect and traverse paradigmatic boundaries in our research. We are indeed comparing cosmopolitan approaches to intercultural communication scholarship to Martin and Nakayama's (1999) call for a dialectic approach to intercultural communication paradigms. Like them, we are advocating for cross-pollination of our work rather than remaining in water-tight boxes, separated from one another by our paradigms, our specific epistemological leanings and our specific conceptualizations of culture, communication, identity and difference.

In this chapter we have described cosmopolitanism from two methodological perspectives: cosmopolitanism as *method* of study and cosmopolitanism as *phenomenon* of study. Our conclusion is that questions of method as they relate to cosmopolitanism are complex and multifaceted, and highly applicable to intercultural communication scholarship. The example of the study we have briefly discussed is only one example of a cosmopolitanism research study in intercultural communication, and it is still a work in progress. In the next chapter, we provide detailed examples of completed research on cosmopolitanism, i.e., recent studies that are utilizing cosmopolitanism within the discipline of communication.

7 Communication Studies and Cosmopolitanism

In the current debate of transnational mobility, cosmopolitanism has become the privileged, prime term of analysis for characterizing qualities in people and their identities. Transnational groups are figured as the bearers of deterritorialized cosmopolitanism, as 'always already cosmopolitan,' which goes beyond the grip of any individual state. Their cultures are characterized as worldly, productive sites of crossing. . . . (Kim, 2011, p. 280)

I propose the idea of a rhetorical cosmopolitanism because rhetoric as 'world disclosure' is shown in constitutive interactions between the global and the local that are manifested in and through everyday experiences. (Petre, 2010, p. 8)

Throughout this book, we have described and referenced empirical and theoretical research that utilizes cosmopolitanism in multiple different ways and across several disciplines. As we have shown, cosmopolitanism has been widely approached across the social sciences and humanities, and has a rich history of being applicable to various fields in varied ways. This chapter focuses on recent studies that illustrate how cosmopolitanism is currently being utilized within the discipline of communication studies. While we had originally planned to describe studies specific to intercultural communication, our search yielded few results—thus further illustrating the need for this book. For this reason, we chose to focus on studies from across the field of communication studies, and made sure that the ones selected included a prominent intercultural dimension.

What follows is a brief analysis of seven research articles, representing both empirical and theoretical approaches, which utilize cosmopolitanism in some way that link them to intercultural communication. As this chapter functions as a sort of informal review of these works, we begin by describing how we found the studies we did and why we decided to include them. Next, for each work included, we provide the abstract in the author's words, provide a genre or subdisciplinary home for the work (e.g., rhetoric, interpersonal communication, pedagogy, etc.), describe how the authors define cosmopolitanism and provide a sense of the theoretical underpinnings (i.e., where the authors draw their influences from), describe how cosmopolitanism is applied in the work (including operationalization, if applicable), and discuss implications of the work for the communication discipline. We conclude with a larger set of implications about how cosmopolitanism can—and we feel, should—be incorporated into the field of intercultural communication and the communication discipline as a whole.

THE PROCESS OF SELECTING STUDIES

One of the primary reasons we feel our book is appropriate and necessary for our discipline is because both of us have thoroughly searched for
cosmopolitanism research within communication studies (and specifically
intercultural communication) for the past several years and have found very
little. While sociology, anthropology, political science, global and international studies, linguistics, education, cultural and media studies, peace
studies, English, history and philosophy abound with research that engages
cosmopolitanism, in communication studies there is surprisingly little work
being done. Furthermore, the majority of the limited work in communication studies focuses primarily on the Stoics of ancient Greece within the
area of rhetoric (see, for example, the 2011 special issue of *Advances on the
History of Rhetoric* entitled "Rhetorics of reason & restraint: Stoic rhetoric from antiquity to the present" [Haskins, 2011]). Indeed, when doing a
Google Scholar search on 'cosmopolitanism and communication,' the vast
majority of research that emerges resides in disciplines outside of communication studies. Roberts and Arnett's edited volume *Communication Ethics:
Between Cosmopolitanism and Provinciality* (2008) is, to our knowledge,
the only book that has been published on this subject in the communication field, and in many ways it engages cosmopolitanism obliquely, as a
jumping-off-point for discussions on other topics related to globalization
and ethics.

In order to locate the research included in this chapter, we used several
search engines, primarily Google Scholar, EBSCOhost, Communication &
Mass Media Complete, and Comm Search. We then searched specific communication journals, including all of those listed on the National Communication Association (NCA) website, as well as *Communication Studies*;
Communication Theory; *Howard Journal of Communications*; *Communication, Culture & Critique*; and the *Journal of Intercultural Communication Research*. We did not specifically search many regional journals as
we assumed that relevant studies would appear in our larger searches. In
order for research to be included, it had to be conducted by individuals who
identify/affiliate as communication scholars, and preferably (although not
required) appearing in discipline-specific journals. We also did not include
mass communication and media studies within our parameters; nor did
we include specific critiques of cosmopolitanism that make no attempt to
further the notion within the discipline.

Key words utilized in our search process included: cosmopol*, cosmopolitan* comm*, cosmopol* intercult*, cosmopol* intercult* comm*, cosmopolitanism and communication, cosmopolitanism and communica*,
cosmopolitanism and intercultural communication, cosmopolitanism and
intercultural. In addition, we also sent a call out on NCA's listserv CrtNet,
and received materials through networking at the NCA conferences, Central States Communication Association conferences and The Eighth Annual

Congress of Qualitative Inquiry. We have included two unpublished conference publications which we found through such networking. Finally, we included an article presented at the NCA meeting in November 2012. This article is currently in press at the *International Journal of Sociology of Language*.

Through this search process we located 33 articles and conference papers that fit all of our parameters. From these articles, we sifted through to find seven that we thought to be appropriate and multifaceted illustrations of cosmopolitanism in communication research, with regard to the ways we have engaged with cosmopolitanism throughout this book. While we understand that there are many worthy articles that we have not included by choice or accident, we are constrained by time and space requirements. Indeed, at this point it would be worthwhile, we feel, to put together an anthology of cosmopolitanism as it is treated in communication research. With this in mind, at the end of this chapter, we provide a brief reading list of additional communication studies which utilize cosmopolitanism in the hope that it will be useful to our readers.

ANALYSIS OF STUDIES SELECTED

Transnational and Critical Cosmopolitanism

The first two studies describe the cosmopolitanism experiences of transnational populations living and working in non-home culture environments. These authors critique cosmopolitanism and situate it within critical and postcolonial contexts.

Study 1: Female cosmopolitanism? Media talk and identity of transnational Asian women (Y. Kim, 2011)

Abstract. *Based on empirical research on transnational Asian women in London, this study interrogates the notion of cosmopolitanism and challenges the general assumptions of cosmopolitan identity formation as it intersects with the media. Are these women becoming cosmopolitan subjects? Can they afford a cosmopolitan identity? The author argues that the possibility of becoming cosmopolitan subjects is contingent upon discursive encounters with Others and upon relational experience. She finds that no cosmopolitan yearning, and a situated but characteristically "thin cosmopolitanism," arises from the experience of the actual conditions of transnational lives, unequal relations of power, and discourses of exclusion and inclusion. Instead, a cosmopolitan sense of style, eager exploration of global Others, and heightened motivations emerged through the increasing experience of the media imaginary among women while inhabiting in their homeland, embracing the world at a reflexive distance.* (Y. Kim, 2011, p. 279)

Context of the Work

Y. Kim is a professor of global communications at the American University in Paris. In this empirical study, she examines transnational Asian women (whom she calls "transnational Asian women on the move" [p. 280]) voluntarily sojourning to London for study abroad. The stated purpose of Kim's study is to "interrogate the notion of cosmopolitanism and challenge the general assumptions of cosmopolitan identity formation as intersected with the media" (p. 280). The study takes a qualitative, interview-based approach, and Kim interviewed 60 Korean, Japanese and Chinese women in their late 20s and early 30s, studying abroad in the "world city" of London for 3 to 7 years. She also collected e-mail journals from her participants. Cosmopolitanism here works as (a) the transnational and mediated flow of cultural messages that influence the decision of study participants to study abroad and affects their sojourning experience, and (b) as a social movement of acceptance of difference and understanding of the importance of communicating with strangers.

Definition of Cosmopolitanism/Theoretical Influences

Y. Kim derives her use and application of cosmopolitanism largely from more traditional sources, including Appiah, Nussbaum, Appadurai, the early Hannerz and Beck. She defines cosmopolitanism as transcending local ties to achieve a sense of cosmopolitan universalism, where "extensive learning of human diversity will lead to a finding of common human qualities and purposes" (p. 281). While she utilizes the theorists described above in her definitions, she critiques the authors as advocating for cosmopolitanism from above, which she finds problematic. After critiquing cosmopolitanism for being a West-centric and Eurocentric construct, as well as for being more of a normative philosophy, Kim uses work from Robbins (1998) and Pichler (2008) to offer up a discrepant, postcolonial approach to cosmopolitanism or cosmopolitan from below. She describes the cosmopolitanism engaged in by her participants as a "thin cosmopolitanism," which she claims emerges from the non-dominant voices of her participants as a reaction to globalization and cultural imperialism of the West (in this case, London) over the East (in this case, the Korean, Japanese and Chinese women living there).

How Cosmopolitanism is Applied

This study interprets "cosmopolitan subjects" to be those who exist in a state of privilege within uneven global power structures, particularly the "hierarchically defined world of the West, where Asian women strive to negotiate their status transnationally" (p. 282). Cosmopolitanism represents an orientation to the world that has a direct impact on social relationships, belonging and differentiation of the Other (in this case, Asian women studying in London) from the more mainstream society. The imagined cosmopolitanism of these Korean, Japanese and Chinese women provides "a rare condition of everyday reflexivity and possible transformation in the light of revised self-understandings" (p. 295), offering an identity-restructuring process that accepts and promotes both personal difference and communicating with Others as it emphasizes the importance of dual-level strangerhood (i.e., the host locals seem strange to the sojourners; the sojourners seem strange to the host locals; the negotiation of this 'strangeness' can be better accomplished through the framework of cosmopolitan understanding).

Implications for the Field

Y. Kim finds that her Asian female participants read cosmopolitanism as a largely Western construct, one which they cannot participate in due to their inherent difference or Asian-ness. These findings fit the views of the critics of Beck (e.g., Bhambra, 2011; Chernilo, 2006) who describe cosmopolitanism as Eurocentric. Specifically, the sense of displacement of these women— neither fitting in with the "homeland" nor with the host culture (London), illustrates the postcolonial and hybrid identities that vernacular cosmopolitanism seeks to uncover. Transnational media representations of cosmopolitan ideals (Westernized ideals promoted through pop culture in Japan; *Sex and the City* and *Cosmopolitan* magazine's influences in Korea; and negative Western impressions of Chinese culture) serve to highlight the sense of dual alienation experienced by these Asian female expats in both their home and host cultures. In their case, cosmopolitan identification comes not by choice, but by "mutual understanding and validation . . . recognition of otherness as equally worthy of respect, if not always necessarily desirable" (p. 294). That is, cosmopolitanism must be something that is attributed to the individual by others, not avowed by the individual herself.

Further, Kim asserts that—and this is contrary to what we have argued earlier—the idea of cosmopolitanism is largely under-applied and indeed not known in East Asian cultures such as Korea, China and Japan. However, Kim does note that the notion of imagined cosmopolitanism (similar to B. Anderson's [1991] "imagined communities") is widespread throughout the world (particularly in female communities) through globalized media as a cultural force. In short, Kim's study illustrates cosmopolitan influences through media cultural flows and life experiences of (voluntary) transnational movement and simultaneously problematizes the acceptance of the 'stranger' as a cosmopolitan being existing in a cosmopolitan space (such as Asian female students living in London).

Y. Kim herself is a good example of a communication scholar who is interested in moving away from top-down cosmopolitanism, but who may find it useful to integrate notions described and applied in our book, such as vernacular cosmopolitanism, and ways in which cosmopolitanism may enable intercultural bridgework. Indeed, if Kim chooses to use the notion of vernacular cosmopolitanism—or our concepts of cosmopolitan communication and peoplehood—as a framework and works to move away from West vs. Rest perspectives on cosmopolitanism (which echo typical critiques of cosmopolitanism addressed throughout this book), she could make an important contribution to intercultural communication—that of a feminist cosmopolitanism. It could be argued that the use of transnational media and pop culture creates in the imaginary a strong sense of cosmopolitanism in the female participants of her study, of ties to the global that present themselves in the local in ways that are strong enough to empower her participants to travel thousands of miles from home in order to learn and live. The resultant hybridization of identity (neither fitting in at home nor abroad) characterizes the plight of many migrants, such as, for example, pink collar workers. This work could provide important implications for utilizing feminist cosmopolitanism (certainly a form of cosmopolitanism that arises from below; see Werbner, 2008) as a means of reconceptualizing intercultural transitions and their impacts while moving beyond a West vs. Rest dichotomy.

Study 2: Transmigrant families: Intercultural and bilingual competencies development (Barea, Torrico, Lepe, Garzón, Llorente, & Dietz, 2010)

Abstract. *This article presents the results of a research project concerned with analysing and identifying the discourses and related strategies used by Spanish–German transmigrant families to support and develop bilingual and intercultural competences stemming from their transmigratory experiences. Using the biographical-narrative approach, we reconstruct the families' migratory phases, emphasising shifting parental discourses on bilingual practices and intercultural competences in the home. After presenting the analysed empirical data, the results obtained are grouped into four broader interpretive frameworks: bilingual practice, life-world intercultural theories, social networks and "cosmopolitanism."* (Barea et al., 2010, p. 429)

Context of the Work

This particular study emerged through collaboration of scholars primarily in Spain (with one author being from Veracruz, Mexico). These authors come together across disciplines, spanning sociology, international education, religion and the humanities. We included this article because regardless of (and to a certain extent, due to) the multidisciplinary backgrounds of the authors, the topic of this study lies squarely within the realm of intercultural communication. Indeed, the authors focus on "intercultural competencies," or "the ability to communicate, perform and interact in diverse and heterogeneous situations with people from different cultural, social, ethnic and national contexts" (p. 432). The purpose of the article is to report the findings of an empirical study that identifies and analyzes intercultural communication strategies (and multilingual strategies) developed by transnational and transmigratory families. The researchers employ a multi-method approach, utilizing ethnographic methods to explore transnational families in Granada, as well as quantitative data collected in Hamburg.

Definition of Cosmopolitanism/Theoretical Influences

The authors take a primarily transnational approach. They discuss spatial transmigration, in which mobility (in a spatial and economic sense) and hybridized life-worlds are "the norm." However, it should be noted here that this research does not take a critical perspective—that is, the "norm" of these transmigratory and hybridized life-worlds is that of voluntary migration, privilege, and indeed, Eurocentrism, in that the researchers are primarily investigating Spanish-German families' voluntary cultural movements within the European Union. Cosmopolitanism, while not the primary focus of the study, emerges clearly from the data, and is framed as a form of discourse. That is, Barea et al. define the cosmopolitan discourse which emerged from their data as containing "highly positive values and attitudes towards travel, pendulum migrations, cultural enrichment, knowledge of different languages and universal values, independent of whether or not the interviewed person participates in these practices" (p. 438). The authors take their theoretical cues primarily from Appiah, Hannerz and Beck.

How Cosmopolitanism is Applied

Cosmopolitanism is applied as one of four analytical categories through which participants linguistically and interculturally adapt to the host (receiving) culture and language. It exists as both a framework that celebrates intercultural experience and as a means of addressing displacement that may come from hybridization of identity and family. Indeed, to a certain extent, participants' ownership of cosmopolitan discourse determines whether they are likely to embrace cultural hybridity as a positive or negative attribute.

Implications for the Field

Although this study originates from disciplines outside of intercultural communication, it is a useful example of the manner through which individual conceptions of cosmopolitanism are more likely to be considered potentially valuable in an increasingly intercultural and hybridizing world. In conceptualizing cosmopolitanism as a discursive strategy, the authors locate it firmly within the field of communication, and particularly as a useful motivational technique for intercultural competency and understanding of hybridized life-worlds in which individuals may find themselves. In other words, those who identify as being part of a cosmopolitan discourse (and consider this to be a positive thing) are more likely to communicate effectively, both linguistically and self-reflexively, in their hybridized cultural positions.

For the field of intercultural communication, this work is an example of applying cosmopolitanism as a framework that impacts hybridized identity negotiation. It works at intersections of cosmopolitanism, discourse, language and identity, as well as provides a solid example of innovative interpretive methods that lead to the emergence of cosmopolitanism as a characteristic of communication and identity-building. Intercultural communication scholars could potentially learn much through carrying out similar research across several linguistic transmigratory groups, adding cosmopolitanism (or in this case, cosmopolitan discourse) to the front end of the study based on Barea et al.'s findings. Further, taking a more critical and postcolonial approach to this topic, for example through studying groups that may have experienced linguistic colonization and how this impacts hybridized identities and resulting cosmopolitan discourses, could open up doors for integrating interpretive and postcolonial scholarship.

Classical Intercultural Communication Studies

The following three studies focus on cosmopolitanism in intercultural interactions through study abroad or international student experiences and linguistic landscapes. These studies take generally interpretive/ethnographic perspectives, and utilize cosmopolitanism in less critical manners and as descriptions of varying communicative experiences of sojourners and expatriates.

Study 3: Cultivating cosmopolitan, intercultural citizenship through critical reflection and international, experiential learning (J. Jackson, 2011)

Abstract. *This paper explores the notion of cosmopolitan intercultural citizenship in relation to intercultural education and study abroad. As part of a larger investigation of the second language sojourn, the individual developmental trajectories of more than 100 Chinese university students were examined to better understand their language and intercultural learning and identity expansion. This paper presents an illustrative case study of a young woman who took significant steps toward a more sophisticated, cosmopolitan self through deep reflection and intercultural interaction in localized, global spaces. Critical cultural awareness and experiential learning (both at home and abroad) were key elements in her journey toward intercultural, global citizenship, intercultural communicative competence, and a broader, more balanced, sense of self.* (J. Jackson, 2011, p. 80)

Context of the Work

Representing another non-U.S. American study, this particular research was carried out by a professor in the Department of English at The Chinese University of Hong Kong. We included this work because out of all of the studies we found linking cosmopolitanism and intercultural communication, this was the only one that addressed critical reflection and experiential learning as tools for the development of cosmopolitan citizenship, and further linked that development to adaptation across cultures (in this case that of a Chinese woman acclimating to life in the U.K., and describing her own intercultural progress and hybridized identity through journals, interviews and personal narratives).

Definition of Cosmopolitanism/Theoretical Influences

J. Jackson doesn't specifically define cosmopolitanism per se, but she utilizes the work of Guilherme (2007) and Starkey (2007), who approach cosmopolitanism primarily through language study as a vehicle for intercultural citizenship. From her theoretical review, we can derive that cosmopolitanism is essentially the final step on the path of intercultural citizenship "which favors multiculturalism and equality, requires awareness and respect of self and other, the desire to interact across cultures, and the acquisition of the knowledge and skills that facilitate constructive, active participation in today's complex society" (J. Jackson, 2011, p. 82).

How Cosmopolitanism is Applied

The author takes a primarily qualitative and interpretive approach to the data, building an in-depth case study of one young woman (Mira) out of 100 Chinese university students studying in the U.K. J. Jackson discusses "critical reflection," which in this case acts as a pedagogical tool that guides ethical intercultural communication. Indeed, Mira is considered an ideal subject for cosmopolitan citizenship due primarily to her self-reflexivity, humility and willingness to spend significant time interacting with and reflecting upon host locals through work and extracurricular activities. In this study, cosmopolitanism is largely conflated with intercultural communication competence through five *savoirs* or areas of knowledge and skills: intercultural attitudes of curiosity and openness; knowledge of social practices in the host culture; skills of interpreting events within one's own cultural context; skills of discovering new information about a culture; and critical cultural awareness—in this case, the ability to evaluate intercultural interactions and events across cultural milieu. Similar to Sobré-Denton (2011; see later), J. Jackson draws several comparisons between cosmopolitan citizenship and Y. Y. Kim's (2008) stress–adaptation–growth model of acculturation. It is Mira's willingness to engage in risky and potentially stressful interactions with the host culture and her critical evaluation of her own progress that creates the personal growth she experiences during her sojourn.

Implications for the Field

This article provides much useful information by linking cosmopolitanism to pedagogy, acculturation and identity transformation. It weaves together aspects of acculturation literature, communication pedagogy and cosmopolitanism in ways similar to Sobré-Denton's (2011) work to highlight the importance of future research tying these related areas together. Further, it does so squarely within the realm of intercultural communication scholarship (differing from most work on cosmopolitan education housed largely in the philosophy of education discipline, coming out of Columbia Teacher's College). Indeed, out of all the studies visited for this chapter, J. Jackson's work is certainly the most classically intercultural, even with its language–education framework. The work could draw from more nuanced cosmopolitanism theory (Appiah and Nussbaum are both completely absent from the references) and problematize the differences between cosmopolitan identity orientation and intercultural citizenship; however, as a preliminary case study, the work raises interesting possibilities for linking cosmopolitanism, intercultural communication and cross-cultural adaptation.

Communication scholars who endeavor to include cosmopolitan pedagogy into their own work, particularly as it intersects with postcolonialism and intercultural communication, can benefit from tying J. Jackson's discussion of critical reflexivity and experiential learning to Hansen and colleagues' (2009) arts of hope, memory and dialogue. In Miriam's work on Hostelling International (see Chapters 6 and 8), for example, J. Jackson's work can serve to emphasize the emergent links that she found between the importance of experiential learning and reflection as part of the cosmopolitan pedagogical process, and how these processes situate cosmopolitan pedagogical practices within the intercultural communication discipline.

Study 4: The emergence of cosmopolitan group cultures and its implications for cultural transition: A case study of an international student group (Sobré-Denton, 2011)

Abstract. *The purpose of this study was to discover how cosmopolitanism impacts cross-cultural adaptation when groups of international students build social support networks that are not divided along home and host cultural lines. Using a social constructivist approach and qualitative methods such as participant observation and interviewing, a two-and-a-half year ethnography is described that elucidates the formation and activities of an international student group at Arizona State University in Phoenix, and the impact this group has on the adaptation processes of its members. The results reconceptualize the construct of cosmopolitanism, indicating that such a framework provides an accurate description of a multinational, multicultural social support network for international students.* (Sobré-Denton, 2011, p. 79)

Context of the Work

This research project was completed by Sobré-Denton as her dissertation research. It situates cosmopolitanism (drawing largely from the disciplines of anthropology and sociology) firmly within the context of intercultural communication scholarship. In this study, cosmopolitanism works as a descriptor of an identity-state or orientation achieved through membership and active communicative engagement in a group that embodies multiple global perspectives.

Definition of Cosmopolitanism/Theoretical Influences

Sobré-Denton defines cosmopolitanism mainly using Hannerz in anthropology, Beck in sociology and Shome and Hegde for postcolonial intercultural communication with a focus on cultural hybridity. Cosmopolitanism, in this study, is conceptualized as a state of identity tension between global and local ties, and as being reinforced through membership in a group largely made up of others who identify and place their interests and experiences in cosmopolitan values e.g., through attending cultural events of both the host culture (Phoenix) and multiple other cultures (for instance, the Lebanese Festival and Matsuri, the Japanese lantern festival), and by critically consuming media, popular culture and world events/news, and discussing them with other group members. Cosmopolitanism here is achieved during voluntary transitions, and through thoughtful engagement and intercultural interaction. Members of the international student group (INTASU) who do not identify as world citizens and don't exhibit cosmopolitan openness and cultural curiosity are largely not accepted by their peers, and tend to limit membership and activities.

How Cosmopolitanism is Applied

Sobré-Denton studied cosmopolitanism in a class on global and transnational ethnography, and utilized the philosophy as one of several to describe intercultural transitions and identity work accomplished by members of INTASU. She specifically asks what a cosmopolitan cultural group looks like, and defines it through the following qualities: cultural competency (being able to understand and apply cultural rules to appropriate contexts, across a wide variety of cultural groups and situations); world citizenship (the sense that group members identify first as global citizens and then by specific national, ethnic or religious ties); and openness and cultural curiosity (an active interest in learning about multiple cultures, and in critically reflecting on how various cultural groups interact and impact one another). Again, members who don't demonstrate these qualities or interest in pursuing this kind of world citizenship don't generally last long in the group; those who wish to only engage socially with other members of their own home culture, for example, lose interest in the group rapidly, and therefore don't take on larger membership roles within the organization.

Implications for the Feld

Sobré-Denton's work has several practical and theoretical applications. It provides rich qualitative data tying cosmopolitanism to adaptation, and describes how identifying as cosmopolitan can both assist and hinder host-culture adaptation. Further, it situates cosmopolitanism as a communicative phenomenon, created and maintained through interaction and engagement with other members of the group over an extended period of time. However, the author stops short of engaging critical cosmopolitanism, and tends to locate cosmopolitanism as a voluntary, privileged status embodied by educated sojourners. This implies that more concerted effort should be made to studying vernacular cosmopolitanism and to understanding some of the key factors that lead to different forms of embodied cosmopolitan identity (e.g., how those who sojourn due to involuntary causes might experience a different form of cosmopolitanism than those who choose to study and live abroad). What this study does accomplish is that it draws direct ties between cosmopolitanism, acculturation and intercultural communication, and provides implications for the future of the cosmopolitan vision within our discipline.

Study 5: Mapping cosmopolitanisms in Taipei: Toward a theorization of cosmopolitanism in linguistic landscape research (Curtin, in press).

Abstract: *While frequently referenced in linguistic landscape (LL) research, the notion of "cosmopolitanism" has generally been under theorized in the field. This study, in keeping with the call for an ethnographically grounded, multicentric understanding of different varieties of cosmopolitanism, traces the emergence of a "bona fide cosmopolitanism" in the LL of Taipei, Taiwan. This overarching cosmopolitanism is cumulatively indexed via orthographies employed in several domains of the LL: (i) traditional Mandarin Chinese characters and Romanization systems thereof, (ii) non-Chinese scripts in official and unofficial domains, and (iii) graffiti. Furthermore, each domain contributes to several varieties of cosmopolitanism. Drawing upon theorizations of social indexicality, distinction, and transgressive semiotics, these varieties have been given the working labels of "presumptive, distinctive, and transgressive cosmopolitanisms." This study thus demonstrates that cosmopolitanism in the LL is best apprehended as multicentric and recursive, as well as highly situated.* (Curtin, in press)

Context of the Work

Curtin has a Ph.D. in intercultural communication from the University of New Mexico, and has taught intercultural communication at Southern Illinois University–Carbondale. She is currently teaching and conducting research in the linguistics department at the University of California at Santa Barbara. Her work focuses on the intersections of language and intercultural communication, which is where she locates her current work on cosmopolitanism. In this article, Curtin utilizes cosmopolitanism to add to the notion of linguistic landscape in two different manners: A diachronic study of how urban/rural landscapes in Taipei have changed over recent decades; and integrating what she calls "bona fide cosmopolitanism" with theorizations of identity and space in the linguistic landscape of Taipei.

Definition of Cosmopolitanism/Theoretical Influences

Curtin draws from anthropological and sociological traditions in her theorizing of cosmopolitanism, citing Vertovec and Cohen (2002) and Hannerz (2006) in her review of relevant literature. In particular, Curtin dwells on the difference between political and cultural cosmopolitanism, describing both but situating her analysis in the cultural, which she defines as "'post-identity politics of overlapping interests and heterogeneous or hybrid publics'" (as cited in Vertovec & Cohen, 2002, p. 1). Indeed, Curtin focuses primarily on Vertovec and Cohen's (2002) notion of cosmopolitanism as a sociocultural condition that creates and recreates linguistic landscapes that reflect globalization's influences as people become more consciously (and consumptively) cosmopolitan.

How Cosmopolitanism is Applied

From this perspective, Curtin utilizes cosmopolitanism to analyze linguistic landscapes through cosmopolitan consumers of capitalist messages. She positions cosmopolitanism as a sociocultural condition (see Vertovec & Cohen, 2002) as seen through postmodern linguistic landscapes which serve as exemplars of a "socially and culturally interpenetrated world that *enriches* the cultural repertoires of many people, thus contributing to a vibrant level of cultural creativity" (Curtin, in press, italics in original). She uses this framework to ethnographically map visual examples of cosmopolitanism in Taipei, through which she argues for cosmopolitanism from below, or banal cosmopolitanism. These forms of cosmopolitanism use words, semiotics/symbols and images from multiple cultural milieus as cultural cues and markers of cosmopolitan identity and influences, including logos on T-shirts, shop windows and clothing ads—as well as the transgressive act of graffiti art where English, French and Japanese languages and symbols may be deliberately misspelled or otherwise reappropriated in manners that differ from their original intended uses. The very acts of encoding and decoding, as well as interpolating such messages create a nuanced, liminal cosmopolitanism in the identities and shared but locally-situated conceptualizations of the consumers as well as their acts of consumption (which can exist throughout varying socioeconomic status levels).

Implications for the Field

Curtin's analysis illustrates how cosmopolitanism and semiotics (as well as other aspects of linguistic theory) can provide nuance for the (visual) ethnographic study of linguistic ingroups, cultural and sociocultural identity constructions and local/global communication practices. Specifically, and of much interest to us here, Curtin demonstrates conceptualizations of intercultural communication and linguistic practices in a non-Western, translocal and bottom-up context of cosmopolitanism, illustrated in everyday messages throughout one specific linguistic landscape. This work is a rich example of ethnographic and linguistic analysis of cosmopolitan practices, particularly in the visual sphere. The study also provides useful evidence of the dialectic nature of cosmopolitanism (which Curtin terms "polemical"), and illustrates how cosmopolitan semiotic practices can act as sites of protestation, resistance and subversion of dominant cultural norms and visual linguistic messages.

Cosmopolitanism in Rhetorical Studies

Rhetorical studies is the area of communication studies in which we found the most active research on cosmopolitanism. We include here two examples of this scholarship. These two works were included because they were part of a panel on cosmopolitanism at the 2010 Central States Communication Association conference, and they represent two of the major approaches of rhetoricians to cosmopolitanism: The first provides an overview of how we can situate cosmopolitanism within rhetoric, while the second is an example of what kind of research can emerge at the intersections of rhetorical studies, cosmopolitanism and communication.

Study 6: Cosmopolitanism and "the space of communicative praxis" (Petre, 2010)

Abstract. *Cosmopolitanism is variously understood as the translation of different histories across identities that lend to transnational sites of political action; a post-universalistic political concept; and an obligation to others stretching beyond political relations. Extensive discussion exists concerning how worlds are constituted in-between the global and the local. Absent from this discussion is consideration of how rhetorical communication participates in this process, leading to the following question: How does a constitutive rhetorical orientation toward cosmopolitanism contribute to understanding how transnational political action emerges within a process of world disclosure between the local and global? In this paper, I argue that cosmopolitanism can be perceived as a rhetorical process, constituted in everyday action that creates a way of understanding the ethical relations between the self and other. I am specifically interested in how an orientation towards cosmopolitanism rooted in conceptions of rhetoric as a constitutive process locates cosmopolitanism within human communication.* (Petre, 2010, p. 1)

Context of the Work

Petre is an assistant professor of communication with a specialization in rhetoric, currently teaching at McKendree College in Illinois. We find his work to be particularly useful as it applies cosmopolitanism to rhetoric in a way that is similar to our approach in this book. That is, Petre directly applies cosmopolitanism as a construct to rhetorical studies in communication. The stated purpose of this article is to understand "how a rhetorical understanding of cosmopolitanism locates it within the realm of human communication, and can be a useful addition to current scholarship on cosmopolitanism" (Petre, 2010, pp. 1–2).

Definition of Cosmopolitanism/Theoretical Influences

This article draws primarily from Delanty's (2006) discussions of critical, non-universalizing cosmopolitanism. Petre defines cosmopolitanism as a rhetorical process "constituted in everyday speech and action that open up a way of understanding the ethical relation between self and other" (p. 1). He draws parallels between rhetoric and cosmopolitanism, in that both find a grounding in dialogue and translation, constitute the negotiation of shared realities and provide a space of communicative praxis. However, Petre takes special care to differentiate rhetoric from cosmopolitanism, proposing instead a "rhetorical cosmopolitanism" that negotiates dialogue between the global and the local through everyday communicative experiences.

How Cosmopolitanism is Applied

Petre engages in a critique of cosmopolitan universalism. This top-down approach to cosmopolitanism is usually the focus of scholarship among rhetorical scholars (see Roberts & Arnett, 2008), who tend to define cosmopolitanism through Kant, Nussbaum and the Stoics (much research on cosmopolitanism within rhetoric focuses, not surprisingly, on the ancient Greek and Stoic understandings of global citizenship). Petre argues against this, describing rhetorical cosmopolitanism as critical, locally situated and transformative. Specifically, he draws connections between rhetoric as "world disclosure" in everyday experiences of a global public, and cosmopolitanism as providing a means to engage this praxis at local levels in self-reflexive, ethical and communicative ways through activities such as recognizing cultural flows of goods, commodities, media and individuals across boundaries and in liminal and translatable spaces. Indeed, Petre's rhetorical cosmopolitanism is not much different from Werbner's vernacular cosmopolitanism, except that it adds a more communicative and interactive element—that of "engaging with one another and co-constituting shared ways of understanding the world" (Petre, 2010, p. 11).

Implications for the Field

The implications of this work are compelling for the discipline of communication in that it situates cosmopolitanism firmly within the scope of communicative praxis, community and interactive engagement. It describes ways that rhetoric and communication scholarship can be informed by vernacular cosmopolitanism, as well as provides a case study (the author shopping for food in a small town in the U.S. Midwest) that is an illustrative example of localized application of theory. Just as Petre seeks to "bring cosmopolitanism into the realm of human communication by focusing attention on how negotiations of local and global ways of being are implicated by rhetoric's constitutive character" (p. 13), we too intend to do this for the field of intercultural communication.

Study 7: The dialogic appearance of the cosmo-polis (Brower, 2010)

Abstract. *Within contemporary debates concerning global human rights, much scholarship focuses on the problematic character of universal social and political rights. Theoretical and practical insights suggest two paths: The first portrays human rights as a paradigmatic constellation of ideas fundamentally inclined toward Eurocentric philosophic culture. The second understands human rights as an incomplete project in need of expansion towards the protection of economic, social, and cultural rights. The latter path is best understood as a cosmopolitan approach to human rights, asserting that some forms of universalism are not mutually exclusive with culturally specific practices. This paper addresses prospects for a cosmopolitan ethics of judgment in the context of human rights practice with particular consideration of the tensions between the global and local. I focus on the need for a perspective grounded in consensus-building that attends to the diversity of communicative phenomena that participate in the constitution of a common world.* (Brower, 2010, p. 1)

Context of the Work

Brower, a visiting assistant professor of communication at Western Connecticut State University, draws some connections between cosmopolitanism and rhetorical studies, focusing specifically on the "cosmopolitical" which, according to Arendt, means living in a *polis*, or space of freedom. The context of this work highlights some linkages between communication studies and political philosophy, particularly through the use of Mignolo's (2010) dialogic cosmopolitanism. In this sense, Brower is more overtly critical of traditional, Kantian (Enlightenment) and Cynic-driven cosmopolitan thought, utilizing instead critical and dialogic cosmopolitanism as a viable alternative through which to understand differences and similarities across cultures and political spheres.

Definition of Cosmopolitanism/Theoretical Influences

Brower begins with definitions of cosmopolitanism that heavily highlight universalism, with the vague centralizing feature of "human beings sharing a common world" (p. 1). He describes cosmopolitan universalism through its grammatical and philosophical origins with the Greek Cynics, including the notions of *cosmos* (meaning universe or world) and *polis* (meaning city-state and thereby citizen). Brower then discusses Kantian cosmopolitan rationalism and its bigoted categories of citizenship (i.e., all white, privileged Europeans should be considered citizens of the world), and creates a space of contrast through which he introduces dialogical cosmopolitanism (or Mignolo's critical cosmopolitanism). He then makes the case that dialogic cosmopolitanism exists within a model of intersubjective relationality, and that this is how it can be contextualized within the subdiscipline of rhetoric. Here relationality, in essence, is a space of relational speech and action that recognizes cosmopolitanism's universal commitment to difference across politics and citizenships in ways that move towards post-national considerations of identity through dialogue.

How Cosmopolitanism is Applied

Brower's work sets up a useful postcolonial critique of ancient Greek and Enlightenment cosmopolitanism, but does so in ways that create spaces for forays into politics, political philosophy and political identity. The cosmopolitanism he champions calls for "a universal commitment to difference as an essential element of cooperation and investment across polities in a way that embraces a post-national conception of citizenship" (p. 11). Cosmopolitanism here is a space of inquiry through which local–global tensions are addressed and negotiated in and through dialogue of human beings, who are all essentially strangers to one another before engaging in this dialogic relationality.

Implications for the Field

The primary usefulness of this study for the field of communication, and intercultural communication specifically, is that it describes manners through which cosmopolitanism can be operationalized as a space for both dialogue and critique. Further, this work moves beyond notions of cultural identity as confined to citizenship within the nation-state, and does this in ways that draw parallels between rhetoric and intercultural communication. That is, in studying the ways through which people are defined by and through political entities such as belief systems and national or racial citizenship, and how these can be reconstituted through dialogue that embraces tensions and recenters identity outside of nation-state boundaries, Brower shows how cosmopolitanism can be reappropriated in postcolonial and intercultural ways.

COSMOPOLITAN COMMUNICATION AND PEOPLEHOOD

Cumulatively, these studies address cosmopolitanism in various ways, many of which reflect aspects of our concepts of cosmopolitan communication and peoplehood. Specifically, all of the authors utilize cosmopolitanism to explore notions of difference in several ways (e.g., cultural differences, linguistic differences, identity negotiation differences, etc.). Petre, Brower, Barea et al. and (to a lesser extent) Y. Kim all address the notion of cosmopolitanism as critically implicating power struggles with a focus on social and global justice. Sobré-Denton, Curtin and J. Jackson, on the other hand, address cosmopolitanism through a descriptive and interpretive lens, and are concerned with mutuality and ongoing understanding but are less focused on social and global justice goals and emerging power inequities (J. Jackson particularly focuses on critical self-transformation, while Curtin discusses cosmopolitanism as a site of consumer transgression and resistance towards the economic norms and cultural flows of globalization).

In terms of cosmopolitan peoplehood, several interesting points can be made with regard to the trends present in these seven representative articles. Clearly, all of the articles perceive cosmopolitan identity orientation to be open-ended, Other-oriented, in-between and dialogic. However, it should be noted that three out of the seven studies (Sobré-Denton, Y. Kim and J. Jackson) concentrate on cosmopolitanism as an identity orientation of a group of people who *voluntarily* migrate to another location, more often than not in order to study abroad. This certainly highlights entanglement between Self and cultural Others, but does not necessarily complicate notions of strangerhood, or address the power dynamics of voluntary and non-elite transmigratory cultural flows (which are addressed in Barea et al., but only within the context of the European Union) and involuntary and/or non-elite postcolonial migration. Sobré-Denton, Curtin and J. Jackson all discuss critical approaches, but speak to a much less paradigmatic definition of 'critical,' i.e., they speak more in terms of being self-critical or critical of the media, rather than pointing towards social and global justice goals and illuminating unjust power systems.

While all the authors work against Cartesian dualism, several of the articles still assume culture to be equal to the nation-state (e.g., Y. Kim, Sobré-Denton, Barea et al. and J. Jackson), thereby maintaining methodological nationalism. Furthermore, the notion of difference itself and how it is communicatively produced is not the primary focus in these studies (with the possible exception of Curtin). Finally, while all of these studies make at least oblique references to global–local (and other) dialectics (particularly Curtin), none of them focus heavily on the Self–Other dialectic which is a primary focus of our concepts of cosmopolitan communication and peoplehood.

Regarding implications for intercultural communication, we find that thus far, scholarship tends to oversimplify cosmopolitanism and under apply the critical and postcolonial turn in the debate on cosmopolitanism (unless they are critiquing or responding to Kantian or ancient Greek cosmopolitanism). We feel that in order to adequately absorb cosmopolitanism into intercultural communication scholarship, our concepts of cosmopolitan communication and peoplehood provide a framework for a more dialectic, dialogical, critical, postcolonial and Other- and world-oriented approach to empirical and theory-based research. In our vernacular approach, we advocate for more sustained emphasis on intercultural bridgework, positive engagement with difference, kindness to the stranger, empathy and implicature. In other words, in combining hope with a critical approach, we particularly emphasize critical self-transformation through dialogue with the cultural Other, and hope that our contribution will have heuristic value for future of work on cosmopolitanism within the discipline of intercultural communication.

A FUTURE FOR COSMOPOLITANISM ACROSS THE COMMUNICATION DISCIPLINE

Overall, the seven studies analyzed in this chapter provide varied illustrations of how cosmopolitanism is currently being researched within the discipline of communication studies and related fields. We have attempted to represent multiple ways through which cosmopolitanism can be defined and operationalized. Y. Kim (2011), Curtin (in press) and Sobré-Denton (2011) use ethnographic methods; Barea et al. (2010) use narrative strategies; J. Jackson (2011) provides an illustrative personal case study; Petre (2010) combines a theoretical piece with personal narrative; and Brower (2010) takes a conceptual, theoretical approach. All of the authors (with the exception of Sobré-Denton and J. Jackson) address the problematic of cosmopolitan universalism, and explore ways in which this notion can be somewhat retained while still conceptualizing identities and communication as dynamic and border-oriented (such as those of sojourners, transmigrant families and U.S. American citizens making consumptive decisions in rural localities).

Some of the studies operationalize cosmopolitanism as an identity-state of hybrid citizenship (e.g., Sobré-Denton, J. Jackson and Y. Kim), and several of the authors understand cosmopolitanism as a space for dialogue across difference (e.g., Barea et al., Sobré-Denton, Curtin, Y. Kim and Brower). Barea et al., Petre and Brower all describe cosmopolitanism as a discursive praxis that is grounded in human communication. Y. Kim, Barea et al., Petre and Brower all critique various forms (specifically ancient Greek and Kantian) of cosmopolitanism as oversimplified, homogenizing and universalizing, and re-envision ways to transform its use in and through communication research. All of the authors emphasize the usefulness of cosmopolitanism in understanding intercultural encounters and conceptualizing dialogue with strangers, and doing the kind of identity work that may be effected through such dialogue.

As mentioned in our introduction to this chapter, we were surprised at the paucity of published studies engaging cosmopolitanism by intercultural communication scholars in intercultural communication journals. As we wanted to keep our concentration on studies that utilize varying methods and frameworks through which to conceptualize cosmopolitanism, we drew out seven studies that we felt fit within the discipline of communication; even out of those, only three (Y. Kim's, Curtin's and Sobré-Denton's) were carried out by intercultural communication scholars publishing in communication discipline journals. We were heartened, however, to find several conference papers, master's theses and doctoral dissertations in the discipline which did address cosmopolitanism, several of which we have included in the additional reading list that follows this chapter. What we make of this is that there is a yawning gap between the amount of conference papers addressing cosmopolitanism and the amount of published articles available. We anticipate that cosmopolitanism as a topic of research—beyond rhetoric and media studies—will proliferate rapidly in the field of intercultural communication. However, we believe this will happen only if cosmopolitanism research can find welcoming publication homes and reviewers who are amenable to the notion that this term can be reappropriated from its problematic, colonial roots.

Below, we provide an additional reading list of articles that we found to be useful and applicable for integrating cosmopolitanism and intercultural communication, but which did not quite fit with our own criteria for in-depth inclusion in this chapter. We hope our readers will find these additional resources both useful and inspiring for developing further research grounding cosmopolitanism within intercultural communication scholarship.

ADDITIONAL READING LIST

Arizzi, E. (2008, November). *Toward a 'rooted cosmopolitanism:' Reading in the shadow of no towers as a call for local community.* Paper presented at the National Communication Association Conference, San Diego, CA.

Arnett, R. C. (2011). Civic rhetoric—meeting the communal interplay of the provincial and the cosmopolitan: Barack Obama's Notre Dame speech, May 17, 2009. *Rhetoric and Public Affairs, 14*(4), 631–671.

Atay, A. (2010, April). *Shifting identities: Cyber cosmopolitanism.* Paper presented at Central States Communication Association Conference, Cincinnati, OH.

Bean, H., Keranen, L., & Durfy, M. (2011). 'This is London:' Cosmopolitan nationalism and the discourse of resilience in the case of the 7/7 terrorist attacks. *Rhetoric and Public Affairs, 14*(3), 427–464.

Bishop, P. (2011). Eating in the contact zone: Singapore foodscape and cosmopolitan timespace. *Journal of Media and Cultural Studies, 25*(5), 637–652.

Bracken, C. C., Jeffres, L., Neuendorf, K., Kopfman, J., & Moulla, F. (2006). How cosmopolites react to messages: America under attack. *Communication Research Reports, 22*(1), 47–58.

Bunker, J. C. (2012). *Cosmopolitan foreign policy: Obama's new era of American leadership.* Manuscript submitted for publication.

Callahan, C. (2011). Negotiating adaptation: Perceptions of culture and communication among sojourners. *Communication, Culture & Critique, 4*(3), 314–332.

Chalaby, J. K. (2007). Beyond nation-centrism: Thinking international communication from a cosmopolitan perspective. *Studies in Communication Sciences, 7*(1), 61–83.

Elsayed, H. (2010, May). *I'm Egyptian, I'm Muslim, but I'm also cosmopolitan: The unlikely young cosmopolitans of Cairo.* Paper presented at the International Communication Association Conference, Boston, MA.

Fincher, R. (2011). Cosmopolitan or ethnically defined selves? Institutional expectations and the negotiated identities of international students. *Social and Cultural Geography, 12*(8), 905–927.

Frank, D. A. (2011). Obama's rhetorical signature: Cosmopolitan civil religion in the Presidential Inaugural Address, January 20, 2009. *Rhetoric and Public Affairs, 14*(4), 605–630.

Gavriely-Nuri, D., & Lachover, E. (2012). Reframing the past as a cosmopolitan memory: Obituaries in the Israeli *Daily Haaretz*. *Communication Theory, 22*(1), 48–65.

Hier, S. P. (2008). Transformative democracy in the age of second modernity: Cosmopolitanization, communicative agency and the reflexive subject. *New Media & Society, 10*(1), 27–44.

Kanouse, B. (2007, November). *Between cosmopolitan self-choice and tribal determinism: The self and the possibilities of a communication ethics.* Paper presented at National Communication Association Conference, Chicago, IL.

Lam, S. K. S. (2009, May). *Networked risk or cosmopolitan society as the top social agenda of global governance and communication?* Paper presented at International Communication Association Conference, Chicago, IL.

McEwan, B., & Sobré-Denton, M. S. (2011). Virtual third cultures: Social media, cultural capital, and the creation of cultural spaces. *Journal of International and Intercultural Communication, 4,* 252–258.

Pason, A. (2008, November). *Towards a feminist cosmopolitan theory: A corrective to nationalism, fear and war.* Paper presented at the National Communication Association Conference, San Diego, CA.

Polsen, E. (2011). Belonging to the network society: Social media and the production of a new global middle class. *Communication, Culture & Critique, 4*(2), 144–163.

Roberts, K. G. (2011). 'Brand America:' Media and framing of cosmopolitan identities. *Critical Studies in Media Communication, 28*(1), 68–84.

Sarigollu, B. (2011). The possibility of a transnational public sphere and new cosmopolitanism within the networked times: Understanding a digital global utopia. *Online Journal of Communication and Media Technologies, 1*(4), 150–170.

8 Towards a Cosmopolitan Pedagogy in Intercultural Communication

> Through cosmopolitan education, we learn more about ourselves. . . .
> By looking at ourselves through the lens of the other, we come to see
> what in our practices is local and nonessential, what is more broadly
> or deeply shared. Our nation is appallingly ignorant of most of the
> rest of the world. I think this means that it also, in many crucial ways,
> is ignorant of itself. (Nussbaum, 1996, p. 11)

In addition to being scholars of intercultural communication—we are also, and maybe more importantly, teachers of intercultural communication. Therefore, in this last chapter, we focus on pedagogy. As both of us have struggled to make intercultural communication theory from a postcolonial perspective engaging and accessible time and again in the classroom, we realize the necessity of addressing the intersections of cosmopolitanism and pedagogy.

Cosmopolitanism and pedagogy have been linked by many scholars, one of the earliest ones being Martha Nussbaum (1994, 2002). Within studies of cosmopolitanism, pedagogy has been addressed mainly in the discipline of education (see particularly the work of David T. Hansen and colleagues at Columbia University Teachers College, 2010; Banks, 2004; Waks, 2009); more obliquely, notions similar to cosmopolitanism, such as educating for global citizenship (Gibson et al., 2008; Reimers, 2010) and intercultural communication competence (Woodin, 2010), have also been addressed. And while Woodin notes that intercultural communication should be both a subject taught and an approach to teaching and learning, cosmopolitan pedagogy is largely neglected in intercultural communication research (for notable exceptions see J. Jackson, 2011; Rodriguez & Chawla, 2010).

With this in mind, in this chapter we discuss how cosmopolitanism can be used in intercultural communication pedagogy. We begin by defining and situating pedagogy within the realms of intercultural communication and cosmopolitanism. We then briefly outline current research on cosmopolitanism and pedagogy. Next, we address how cosmopolitanism and pedagogy intersect with intercultural communication, focusing on two main domains. First, we examine cosmopolitanism as a framework for pedagogy. By this we mean teaching communication skills and perspectives that would ideally lead to a more cosmopolitan outlook for moving through the world—this is similar to but not the same as educating for global competency. In this domain, we also address critiques of cosmopolitan elitism, and how cosmopolitan outlooks can be pedagogically communicated to those who might not fit the description of being elitist and privileged. In order to do this, we draw from research currently being carried out by Miriam, which explores how cosmo-politan values can be taught and shared with underserved communities of students in Chicago, Illinois.

Second, we describe how cosmopolitanism can be taught as a subject to an advanced intercultural communication class at the university level. Here we draw from Miriam's experience of teaching such a class to upper division undergraduates, master's and doctoral students. This class used a Freirean pedagogical approach (i.e., the class was co-facilitated by the professor and the students using a discussion and brainstorming-based approach), through which the instructor and students jointly created an evolving definition of cosmopolitanism for intercultural communication, i.e., they moved from a novice to a more sophisticated understanding of the literature on cosmopoli-tanism through the course of the semester. We conclude the chapter with an outline for a program of cosmopolitan pedagogy for intercultural communi-cation which can be utilized not as a lesson plan but rather as a pedagogy for postcolonial and Freirean approaches to the shared ownership of knowledge, experiential learning and educational outcomes involving empathy, connec-tion with others and ethical responsibilities for the global and the local. We also link our concepts of cosmopolitan communication and peoplehood with the cosmopolitan pedagogy we are suggesting.

PEDAGOGY, GLOBAL CITIZENSHIP AND COSMOPOLITANISM

We approach pedagogy through Freire's (2004) discussion of hope, shared responsibility for learning, and giving voice to those silenced by forced assimila-tion to norms and values of dominant groups within and outside the classroom. We further focus our discussion on postcolonial pedagogy, which exhibits a deep level of concern for sociocultural and historical-political constructions of reality which are marked by Eurocentrism and forces of colonialism, and deconstruct how assimilationist philosophies can influence and interfere with emancipatory pedagogy. Through both these approaches, the 'classroom' (in a physical or metaphorical sense) becomes a site for transformation.

Intercultural communication pedagogy often focuses on outcomes such as teaching individuals to become global citizens, generally through concen-trations on intercultural communication competence, dialogic approaches and cultural identity (Woodin, 2010). Such intercultural pedagogy is defined as "a pedagogy of change within the person" through experien-tial learning and "the need for a supported process-oriented approach to intercultural development" (Woodin, 2010, p. 234). To entwine this peda-gogical approach with cosmopolitanism, experiential learning (as well as service learning opportunities and movement beyond the classroom) may be best combined with reflective and ethical engagement. Reardon and Snauwaert (2011) suggest that cosmopolitan pedagogy should include three types of reflection: critical/analytical, moral/ethical, and contemplative/

ruminative—all of which focus on the importance of active and experiential learning followed by internalized reflection: "Reflective inquiry is not only a means to the actualization of cosmopolitanism; reflective inquiry is an *ethical requirement*, and thus a *constitutive element*, of cosmopolitanism" (Reardon & Snauwaert, 2011, p. 4, italics added).

A key question that arises here is: What is the difference between cosmopolitan pedagogy and educating for global citizenship? Educating for global citizenship, as defined by Reimers (2010), involves the mastering of three competencies: first—attitudes, values and skills that reflect openness to difference (leading to cultural flexibility and empathy); second—foreign language acquisition and nonverbal communication skills; and third—disciplinary knowledge and engagement in comparative fields, as well as an understanding of culture, history and politics. In short, global citizenship pedagogy involves training future citizens of the world. This is quite similar to Nussbaum's idea of "cosmopolitan universalist education" (Waks, 2009, p. 589), which envisions a universal curriculum that challenges students to question their narrow and local attachments through relating to ideas and people from cultures (racial, religious, national, socioeconomic, etc.) outside of their own.

Cosmopolitan pedagogy, on the other hand, involves teaching the value of valuing (Hansen et al., 2009), or encouraging an orientation to the world that values humanity and ethically obliges those who adopt this orientation to work for social justice in their communities first, and then at national and global levels—this is a more relativist approach influenced by the works of scholars and philosophers such as Appiah. Rather than competencies, this approach focuses on interests and orientations: " . . . deep personal interests, intercultural contacts, and openness to intercultural exchange" (Waks, 2009, p. 595). From our perspective, cosmopolitan pedagogy becomes not simply a matter of teaching communication competence (although such training is, indeed, important), but rather about creating a learning experience at both local and global levels in order to provide critique and hope, an ethical orientation towards and recognition of difference and a space through which to engage in critical self-reflection and cultural humility (Tervalon & Murray-García, 1997). In this way, cosmopolitan pedagogy becomes much more about lifelong learning processes of critical self-transformation rather than about the specific 'outcome' of global citizenship.

Cosmopolitanism and pedagogy also intersect in the idea of challenging traditional and assimilationist notions of citizenship, as well as critiquing elitism and ethical disengagement. This pedagogical stance, however, must also offer hope through which to engage and answer such critiques (Freire, 1997). Thus, we put forth a cosmopolitan pedagogical framework that engages cosmopolitan values in the very framework of constructing and creating an intercultural communication classroom. We address questions such as: How can the global and local intersect in a classroom space? What kinds of pedagogical approaches lead to cosmopolitan identification, and how can they imbue in students the ability to value communication across difference, ethical obligations to others in the classroom, and the willingness to change and engage in other- and world-oriented communication? What kinds of combinations of memory, critique, cultural curiosity, values, experience, service and reflections create cosmopolitan pedagogical experiences and teach cosmopolitanism to students? We detail below a combination of approaches to pedagogy, including works by Nussbaum, Freire, Ricoeur and Hansen and colleagues, which we believe can help create pedagogical spaces that would enable both thinking about cosmopolitanism and cosmopolitan communication and peoplehood to flourish.

CURRENT APPROACHES TO COSMOPOLITAN PEDAGOGY

Research on cosmopolitan pedagogy spans disciplines from anthropology (Rapport, 2007), English (J. Jackson, 2011), linguistics (Guilherme, 2007) and history (Papastephanou, 2002) to philosophy of education (Hansen et al., 2009; Waks, 2009). As described above, this research does overlap with intercultural and "multicultural" education research (Banks, 2004); however, rarely is cosmopolitanism as pedagogy studied *within* the intercultural communication discipline. Most discussions of cosmopolitan pedagogy stem from one of two camps: the viewpoints of Nussbaum and those of Appiah and Werbner (Waks, 2009). Cosmopolitan education from a Nussbaumian perspective calls for a politics of universalism, justly critiquing U.S. American solipsism and emphasizing good, civic, Stoic educational values that require learning about the world beyond local borders. This form of cosmopolitan pedagogy emphasizes ethical obligations to the global community, the self-awareness imperative (Martin & Nakayama, 2012)—which states that the journey into another culture leads to a journey into the Self, and what Nussbaum (1996) describes as Stoic values: " . . . respect for human dignity and the opportunity for each person to pursue happiness" (p. 13).

This universalist, cosmopolitanism-from-above perspective makes salient important points regarding ethical obligations to others, empathetic responses to difference and global justice. However, it has been critiqued as evoking Western, liberal values as the only possible antidote for overly nationalist tendencies (Papastephanou, 2002, p. 81). An alternative to this view is provided by Appiah (2006) and Werbner (2008), who focus on a rooted, vernacular cosmopolitanism. This ground-up perspective, which focuses on local ties and translocal connections, provides for cosmopolitan pedagogy a more postmodern and postcolonial framework. It speaks to the decolonization of knowledge and education, asks where knowledge is centered, how it relates to authority and addresses the in-between complexities of postcolonial spaces and identities (Diversi & Moreira, 2009). This form of cosmopolitan pedagogy engages knowledge as a socially constructed phenomenon, in which 'teacher' and 'learner' become fused positions in and of themselves, allowing for all to share in the learning experience and focus on values such as translation, shared memory, forgiveness (Papastephanou, 2004) and imagination (Norton, 2001).

So how do we use these two perspectives in creating a framework for cosmopolitan pedagogy for intercultural communication? The key, we believe, is to examine the values discussed by several authors across disciplines in order to ascertain what cosmopolitan pedagogy strives to accomplish. An important thing to remember here is that the intersections of cosmopolitanism with pedagogy can be applied in several ways: First, cosmopolitanism can be the object of the lesson or class (i.e., teaching students what cosmopolitanism is—cosmopolitanism as *object* of lesson); second, cosmopolitan values can be taught or imparted to students (e.g., using activities, service learning and experiential learning to teach students about empathy, cultural self-awareness, local–global ties, etc.); and third, cosmopolitanism can provide a framework (or pedagogical approach) for teaching other subjects in a manner similar to critical communication pedagogy.

In order to illustrate these intersections of cosmopolitanism and pedagogy, we first distill the values of cosmopolitan pedagogy found in the extant literature; then we address how these values can be applied to cosmopolitan pedagogy at all three levels (i.e., teaching the concept of cosmopolitanism, teaching cosmopolitan values, teaching a class through a cosmopolitan framework) by using case studies for the first two and providing a framework for cosmopolitan pedagogy for the third.

VALUES THROUGH, AROUND AND WITHIN COSMOPOLITAN PEDAGOGY

Of all the scholars working on cosmopolitan pedagogy across various disciplines, David T. Hansen of Columbia Teachers College arguably has created the widest body of work in terms of the links between values, valuing and cosmopolitan orientations towards education. Focusing primarily on cultural and moral cosmopolitanism (as separate from but related to political and economic cosmopolitanism), Hansen et al. (2009) describe values as being "bound up with people's sense of reality" in ways that focus "not just on the values people hold but on their ways or modes of valuing" (p. 589). In this manner, values exist at a deeper level which speaks more to moral and cultural attitudes, behaviors and orientations than competencies or skills more prevalent in some educational approaches for global citizenship. Further, Hansen et al. (2009) describe how two background meta-values—or values about valuing— underlie a cosmopolitan orientation: the value of valuing itself, and the value of reflecting on what it means to value. In these larger orientations, we see that people can hold entirely different values near and dear to themselves but share the idea that it is important to have values and to reflect on those values.

Hansen and colleagues list three arts through which to understand what it means to value: hope, memory and dialogue. Interestingly, these arts closely mirror Martin and Nakayama's (1999) history/past–present/ future dialectic for understanding and practicing intercultural communication (see Chapter 2). Hope, defined as valuing the future *within* the present—or an awareness of a future that holds promise rather than accident or threat—is in front of our eyes if we are aware enough to perceive it. Memory, on the other hand, must be understood through "critical receptivity," in which we are mindful of how we construct, question and judge the past. In this manner, it becomes imperative to critically reflect on the manner in which the past influences the present and the future. Finally, dialogue ties together the work of hope and memory through communication—that is, dialogue is the connecting tissue in the dialectic tension between hope for the future and memory of the past. The art of dialogue can be, according to Hansen et al. (2009), cultivated through education. In short, then, the goal of cosmopolitan pedagogy is not the outcome of a cosmopolitan orientation that can be learned as a concrete competency, but rather the striving for an orientation to the world that constantly calls into question and renegotiates the complex relationship between memory (history/past) and hope (future) through dialogue across and through difference in the present.

Papastephanou (2002) provides an insightful critique of Nussbaum's values regarding cosmopolitan pedagogy. Rather than simply pointing out the flaws, she points to the work of educational philosopher Paul Ricoeur as being useful for enhancing Nussbaum's views of cosmopolitan pedagogy. In particular, Papastephanou recommends the joining of Nussbaum's call for critical self-examination with Ricoeur's models of translation, exchange of memories and forgiveness. These values overlap somewhat with those of Hansen et al., but also bring a postcolonial perspective to cosmopolitan pedagogy that requires grappling with colonizing global and local forces in a manner that recalls, remembers and recompenses for the violences of the past in the present and the future.

For Ricoeur, Papastephanou points out, translation becomes a key space for cultural hospitality. Translation, from Ricoeur's perspective, is a communicative phenomenon that surrounds all linguistic and cultural exchanges, and must engage memory and future in the present space as a means of interpreting culture. But translation must be seen as socially constructed through a dialogic exchange of memories—that is, as a pedagogical space in which the past is reconstructed and critiqued as a product of multiple, sometimes overlapping and sometimes contradictory interpretations. This exchange of memories "contributes to better understanding of cross-cultural encounters," (Papastephanou, 2002, p. 82) and does not allow for the glossing over of past violences and exploitations of colonialism. However, Papastephanou points out that in order for this circle to be complete, Ricoeur calls for not a forgetting of the past, but a forgiveness of it. This notion of forgiveness, Papastepanou claims, "is crucial to a theory of cosmopolitan education aiming to rehabilitate the cosmopolitan significance of teaching history" (p. 82).

In his insightful chapter on educating for global citizenship in his book on the same topic, Schattle (2008) provides a survey of several educational programs in the U.S. at the elementary, secondary and collegiate levels that practice cosmopolitan pedagogy (we note here that his conceptualization of global citizenship is much closer to the cosmopolitan and process-oriented view of this form of citizenship than the bulk of the outcome-oriented literature on global citizenship education). Most of these programs take a non-West-centric, liberal values approach to their pedagogy while simultaneously emphasizing Nussbaum's critical self-examination and reflection. Schattle describes the skills of academic achievement, moral responsibility and cross-cultural empathy, which are concrete, pragmatic indicators of values of courage, wisdom, compassionate imaginative empathy and dialogue.

Students of such programs are encouraged to move beyond using the U.S. or Western liberal arts education as a normalizing standard, and instead are encouraged to learn multiple histories, philosophical pluralism and to take an activist stance on policy and political perspectives. Students are also often pushed to imagine communities of difference and to explore worlds beyond their own. Furthermore, they are expected to engage in cross-cultural dialogue in order to decenter their position from one of patriotic nationalism (a move often criticized by advocates of civic educational policies). *This approach to educating for global citizenship, we must emphasize, is described not as a set of competencies to be learned but rather as an idealized cosmopolitan goal that students are continuously striving towards.* Finally, a strong link between local activism and global justice is emphasized, so that students learn that local acts and service are interconnected with global change.

Another aspect of cosmopolitan pedagogy that is not classified as such is the notion of cultural humility, described by Tervalon and Murray-García (1997). First, Tervalon and Murray-García's (who work out of training in the field of healthcare) focus, similar to Nussbaum, is on critical self-reflexivity as a site of transformation. Critical self-reflexivity, for them, entails the humility to both examine and critique cultural predispositions and stereotyping behaviors towards cultural Others. They also describe cosmopolitan pedagogy (or in their case, cultural humility) as a lifelong learning practice, similar to Schattle's and Hansen and colleagues' notion that cosmopolitanism is not a concrete end-state but rather an open-ended ideal that exists as a process. In their words, it is "a commitment and active engagement in a lifelong process that individuals enter into on an ongoing basis with patients, communities, colleagues, and with themselves" (Tervalon & Murray-García, 1997, p. 118). This dialogic process negotiates a space between humility (through self-reflexivity and critique) and concern with power imbalances across diverse communities.

To summarize, the values emphasized in cosmopolitan pedagogy which are useful for our purposes focus primarily on process rather than outcome, i.e., cosmopolitanism is an open-ended ideal to continuously strive for rather than a concrete competency to be mastered. These processes change over time and emphasize the interconnectedness of the past, present and future. These interconnections are described and understood through socially and dialogically constructed notions of memory, translation, compassion, critical self-reflexivity, hope and community engagement. In order for such pedagogical values to be embraced, a combination of didactic and experiential learning—as well as (we believe), service learning, followed by opportunities for individual and shared critical reflection, must be presented. We further elucidate these values and techniques through our discussion of two case studies of cosmopolitan pedagogy, presented next.

CASE STUDY 1: HOSTELLING INTERNATIONAL— OPENING DOORS, OPENING MINDS

In Chapter 6, we used Miriam's research with Hostelling International–USA (HI–USA) to illustrate how one may design a study using cosmopolitanism-as-method and to study cosmopolitanism as an intercultural communication phenomenon. Here, we return to HI–USA as a site to provide insights into cosmopolitan pedagogy. HI–USA is the U.S.-American arm of Hostelling International, a federation of over 4,000 hostels in over 80 countries. A non-profit organization, HI–USA operates a network of 60 hostels in the U.S. in its effort to realize its mission: "To help all, especially the young, gain a greater understanding of the world and its people through hostelling." Like all youth hostels, HI–USA facilitates intercultural encounters and understanding by making the travel experience accessible, affordable and communal. However, while most hostels provide a space for intercultural contact, they are not necessarily equipped for or interested in providing actual tools for cosmopolitan pedagogy.

Most youth hostels provide dorms, common rooms, kitchens, and occasionally outings that are designed to attract budget travelers who are often from multiple cultures. But once the travelers arrive, it is up to them to engage in intercultural contact, and how they process these experiences is neither facilitated nor monitored. Hostelling International seeks to create and facilitate mindful and reflexive intercultural experiences beyond simply providing the space in which intercultural encounters may occur. Only a fraction of the population engages in hostelling, and international education is still in many cases considered the realm of the privileged. HI–USA is working to change that.

Through didactic (i.e., classroom exercises and lesson plans), experiential, project-based and service learning (Gibson, Rimmington, & Landwehr-Brown, 2008, p. 12), HI–USA creates cosmopolitan pedagogical opportunities for individuals who often have not left the four-block radius of their home city neighborhoods. Examples of this programming include Cultural Kitchen, where high school students spend 10 sessions learning about another culture, then go to the hostel and cook a meal for hostellers that represents that culture. Another program, Exchange Neighborhoods, "pairs two high schools to host the other school in an exploration of each other's cultures," and through this process, teaches high school students in inner city schools to "build pride around their own culture, while opening their minds to learn about a new neighborhood and culture of their peers" ("Hostelling International–Chicago: Exchange Neighborhoods," 2012). Another example of this programming is Community Walls, which asks its participants to create artwork depicting their own neighborhoods and cultural identities for travelers and tourists; this artwork is displayed throughout the cities in which the hostels and students reside: "The program uses original artwork to help young people gain greater cultural understanding, define their community, express what it is like to live there, and build pride in their culture" ("Hostelling International–Chicago: Community Walls," 2012).

At the time of writing, these three programs are being studied by Miriam and her research assistant through ethnographic and participant/observation methods. They have observed 10 programs that took place throughout the academic year 2011–2012 at HI–Chicago and various local schools. The research process included overnight stays at the hostel with the students participating, trips to schools for introductions to the programs, participating in programming activities such as choosing countries for Cultural Kitchen, helping with artwork creation for Community Walls, touring neighborhoods with Exchange Neighborhoods, taking part in classroom visits to some of Chicago's most underserved communities, observing post-program reflection sessions and interviewing students, hostellers/participants, chaperones, teachers and volunteer facilitators.

The communities served by these programs include communities such as Chicago's Pilsen, South Shore and Gage Park neighborhoods, which often contain relatively homogenous non-dominant majorities (Pilsen, for example, is inhabited by 97% Mexican immigrants), have high crime rates, high instances of participation in school lunch programs (a barometer for lower socioeconomic position), high levels of gang violence and low high school matriculation rates. The main research question of this research project is: How does the educational programming at Hostelling International–Chicago create pedagogical opportunities to inspire cosmopolitan values among students who may not otherwise be exposed to environments and people outside the four-block radius of their home and school?

At the time of this writing, the first research report has been completed, describing the first of emergent patterns that make HI–Chicago a useful and encouraging site for understanding cosmopolitan pedagogy designed to impart specific cosmopolitan values. Each of the programs studied emphasizes—and thus far appears to result in—differing values for their students; however, all of these values fall under the umbrella of cosmopolitan pedagogy. Cultural Kitchen (CK), which focuses on specific cultural learning (visualizing culture-as-nation-state), leads students to increased cultural curiosity, to engage in dialogue with others who are different from them and to work through the simultaneous plays of differences and similarities (Martin & Nakayama, 1999)—through which they recognize that they are both different from and similar to the culture they are studying. In the process of learning to speak with others who are different from them—and communicate and engage across difference—CK students seem to discover the notion of translation, and to learn that through certain practices, they can take emotional risks and move beyond their cultural comfort zones.

Exchange Neighborhoods (ENS) teaches students not only higher levels of self-awareness (they have to express their own culture as well as learn about how different a culture can be that exists only blocks from their own homes), but also to engage in intercultural empathy and perspective-taking—i.e., be able to put themselves in the shoes of others whom they may have stereotyped in the past. The privilege-disadvantage dialectic (Martin & Nakayama, 1999) is also emphasized—students learn that although the students from another school and neighborhood may seem more or less privileged than they are, they all have some privileges and some disadvantages relative to one another. Community Walls (CW) focuses primarily on cultural self-awareness in that students are required to articulate their own cultural identities through art, in a manner in which they can share, explain and promote their communities to those who have no idea where they come from.

All of the programs engage participants in learning cosmopolitan values and the process of imagining communities beyond their own. Although each of these programs focuses on different specific issues, all of these issues can be related directly to the values and competencies/arts of inspiring a cosmopolitan outlook. We should emphasize here that none of these programs is emerging as a 'how to' guide for teaching students how to become cosmopolitan and outwardly-oriented in their outlook. As discussed above, cosmopolitanism should not be understood as a concrete outcome, but rather as a facilitating philosophy for an ongoing process of being and becoming, a way of orienting oneself to the world that has no finite endpoint. Further, these programs constitute just a small amount of time—ranging from 2 to roughly 10 weeks—in the adolescent (11 to 18 years old) participants' lives and school careers. The hope here is not that students will learn everything they need to become 'global citizens' through these experiences; rather, the goal of this kind of programming is to plant a seed in a participant's imagination that will hopefully lead to growth in a certain direction, and increase the chances of educational, personal and professional opportunities in the future. The programs assist students in learning to imagine communities that are both different from and similar to theirs, and aspire to pique their cultural curiosity and sense of empathy with members of these communities in ways that may lead them to explore and engage in cultural spaces, both real and imagined, beyond the limited spaces they have grown up experiencing.

While Miriam does not have a large amount of longitudinal data other than interviews with teachers and a few former participants who volunteer or act as chaperones for current programs, she has thus far found several strong indications that such programs do increase the imagination of possibilities and potentials for participants. Students participating in the hostel's programs are far more likely to be involved in such cosmopolitan and global competency programs as International Baccalaureate (see Schattle, 2008) and Buildon.org, both of which are programs that emphasize intercultural communication competence, service to larger local and global communities, dialogic approaches to difference and ethical obligation to cultural Others. Furthermore, students engaged in these programs are more likely to attend college, travel and engage in youth hostelling. Reflections on the experiential learning aspects of the programs—which all participants must engage in—indicate that after taking part in these programs, participants are more willing to explore relationships with those different from them in terms of language, nationality, age, religion, race and other markers of difference. In terms of straightforward intercultural communication pedagogy, she is finding that hostellers staying at the hostel from around the country and the world, who rarely get the opportunity to interact with local youth in an 'authentic' manner, also receive benefits from interactions with the participants in these programs.

In all three programs, students stay overnight in the hostel, and in CK and CW, cook dinner for travelers staying at the hostel, who are invited to join the free meal with the proviso that they interact with the program participants. They sit with the participants at dinner, answer their questions and simply engage in dialogue with them; they play games with the students such as cultural bingo (students get travelers to sign boxes in a bingo card of things they have done and tell stories about them); and in the case of CK, the travelers attend a presentation of a chosen country put on by the students and talk with them about it afterwards. While the students interviewed described the interactions with travelers to be some of the most rewarding aspects of the programs, the travelers interviewed emphasized appreciating the unique opportunity to engage with the communities they were visiting at a truly local level—a level that they might ordinarily not have access to. In several cases, relationships have begun that have lasted long after the facilitated experience is over.

The most compelling aspect of HI's educational programs is that they provide a good example of vernacular cosmopolitanism—cosmopolitanism from below. These programs provide facilitated travel and intercultural communication experiences for youth who may not otherwise have any opportunity to travel. The majority of its participants (in Chicago) are either Latino/a, African American, Southeast Asian, Middle Eastern or Polish American; most of them are first generation immigrants, and many are 'at-risk' youth. Quite often—over 50% of the time—these students have rarely, if ever, been to downtown Chicago. Yet these experiences give the students the opportunity to experience and reflect on intercultural communication from a cosmopolitan perspective. They help them see that they have options in a world beyond their neighborhoods, and that a world beyond their neighborhoods not only exists, but awaits them with opportunities for personal growth.

Cosmopolitan Communication and Peoplehood

Some of the connections between HI–Chicago's programs and cosmopolitan communication and personhood were already made in Chapter 6; however, in this chapter we are focusing primarily on the pedagogical practices that take place at HI–Chicago. The pedagogical style of HI–USA's educational programs focuses on a shared, experiential model, in which students learn curriculum material in the classroom, followed by experiential learning at the hostel and engagement in a reflection session. It should be noted here that while Cultural Kitchen participants do examine culture from a nation-state perspective, students from all three programs are also taught that the nation-state is not the natural container for culture.

HI–Chicago's educational programs speak to cosmopolitan communication's Assumption 5 (see Chapter 2), that cosmopolitan communication entails a dialogical, emancipatory and non-oppositional view of cultural difference. Students learn, through their experiences of interacting with travelers and reflecting after the hostel overnight, that difference is communicatively constructed, and that dialogue with culturally different Others can change their perspectives on their own cultural identities as well as what makes them different from and similar to travelers from all over the country and the world. In these programs, culture is articulated to participants in terms of intersections: It can be found in one's community, one's city, one's religion and so on. Indeed, culture for many of these students exists at the intersections and hybrid spaces between the locations their families are originally from, the identities their migrations have created in them, with whom and what they identify in their schools and neighborhoods, and the salience of their various group memberships, norms and mores. Often, these kinds of intersections are engaged with and negotiated through presentations and dialogues that take place during the hostel overnight, and the reflections that take place afterward.

In this pedagogical lesson, then, students also learn how to begin creating a dialectic/dialogical relationship with cultural Others (Assumption 2 of cosmopolitan peoplehood). Cosmopolitan peoplehood engages notions of the stranger, the imagination, empathy and implicature, and through these programs these students begin to engage in a process of being and becoming more Other- and world-oriented. Through this process, they learn to critically engage in intercultural bridgework between their own cultural identities and neighborhoods and culturally different Others who are visiting their 'home' location. In so doing, they learn that they themselves can be viewed as 'strangers,' and that people they see as 'strangers'—be they from another neighborhood, part of the country, or part of the world—are often more similar in terms of values to them than they initially realized. They learn that not only do they have multiple cultural identities, but that those they encounter who may seem incredibly culturally different from them also have multiple cultural identities. This realization emphasizes to them the open-endedness of the cultural identity process (see Assumption 1 of cosmopolitan peoplehood).

The overall mission of these HI programs is to inculcate within students cosmopolitan values such as empathy, cultural curiosity, cultural and critical self-awareness, openness and engagement across difference and the willingness to change. The intention is to begin the creation of a sense of cosmopolitan peoplehood as a long-term goal to work towards, both through experiential learning and through expanding the horizon of the imagination. This is a different pedagogical model compared to teaching a specific course about cosmopolitanism. The latter, and its benefits, are described in the next case study.

CASE STUDY 2: TEACHING COSMOPOLITANISM AS A COURSE

In autumn of 2011, Miriam developed and taught a course entitled "Cosmopolitanism." This was a hybrid undergraduate/graduate level course. The syllabus described the course as one that would "explore cosmopolitan ideology and how this can be applied to intercultural communication from a postcolonial perspective . . . [and] trace cosmopolitanism's philosophical roots to its current uses, debate its controversial definition and applications, and create a coherent postcolonial framework for operationalizing cosmopolitanism in intercultural scholarship." The course used the following texts: Appiah's (2006) *Cosmopolitanism: Ethics in a World of Strangers*; Breckenridge, Pollock, Bhabha and Chakrabarty's (2002) *Cosmopolitanism*; Theodossopolous and Kirtsoglou's (2010) *United in Discontent: Local Responses to Cosmopolitanism and Globalization*; and Werbner's (2008) *Anthropology and the New Cosmopolitanism*, as well as additional articles spanning intercultural communication, philosophy, sociology, anthropology, political science, education and peace studies. The course was divided into three units: defining terms, critiquing and operationalizing. There were eight students in total in this class (five undergraduates, two master's students and one doctoral student); all but one was a communication student.

Over the course of the semester, students were asked to define cosmopolitanism four times, once at the beginning before they delved into the readings and once after each unit. Additionally, students were required to submit three papers (one defining, one critiquing and one operationalizing cosmopolitanism). Each student led class on either one reading (for under-graduates) or the entire topic covered for the day (graduate students); they participated in a debate on the pros and cons of applying cosmopolitanism to intercultural communication scholarship; and they engaged in discussions on defining postcolonialism and globalization in order to address the ethics of a cosmopolitan world, and to address notions of imagined communities and virtual cosmopolitanism. The course was taught in a Freirean pedagogical style, with the learning process shared and co-created among the students and the instructor in a dialogic fashion, rather than in a top-down, unidi-rectional, banking model style. The class was student-run for 10 days out of the semester out of a total of 30 meetings. Additionally, the class was almost always discussion-based, with ideas framed by the readings but generated through interaction and dialogue that included personal stories (shared by everyone, including the instructor), theoretical ideas from other courses (such as Critical Race Theory) and spontaneous experiential learning.

Students came to the course with varying levels of knowledge about cosmopolitanism and postcolonial theory, but all had some background in intercultural communication. Many of the students had never heard of cosmopolitanism before, and came to this class with the knowledge that they would be learning an entirely new 'language' with which to address intercultural communication. Most students went from little to no knowl-edge of cosmopolitanism or postcolonial theory to an ability to engage in sophisticated dialogue utilizing these terms, theories and paradigms with one another and at a scholarly level, and to apply cosmopolitan values, outlooks and perspectives to their own lives and the worlds they experience every day.

In particular, the working definition of cosmopolitanism, which was cre-ated as a collaborative project by all class members, developed sophistica-tion and depth as the students and instructor worked through the material. Class members would write a definition in a couple of sentences and bring it to class; as a class they would share the definitions while one student wrote them on a white board. These would then be posted electronically on Blackboard. After each unit, the students brought new definitions to class and repeated the process. At the final class meeting, with final definitions in hand, the class used a democratic facilitation process in which students voted on their favorite definitions, then rewrote them, narrowing the defini-tions and terms down to one working definition of cosmopolitanism that they agreed fit the materials covered throughout the semester.

The first set of definitions tended towards the following: "Cosmopoli-tanism is the theory that people are part of a global community based on a shared morality, in which individuals have responsibilities towards each other" (Milica Obrĕtkovich, August 30, 2011). This was offered with little or no background/context of cosmopolitanism beyond the first day's discussion. After the first unit, the class had moved towards defining cosmopolitanism as a philosophy, concept or attitude through which to "educate others and the world to embrace differences *not* as boundaries but as building blocks towards the 'utopia' we are all looking for" (Ryan Trone, September 29, 2011, italics added). By this point the class had begun to view cosmopolitanism as a somewhat vague outlook, an ideal to be strived for but possibly unachievable. After the second unit, on critiquing cosmopolitanism, several perspectives were refined and in some cases even inverted. Interestingly, this set of definitions embraced a much more active position, rather than a passive ideal. One example is Nathan Columbo's definition: "Cosmopolitanism is conceptualized as the actions that lead to the greater good of the community and an understanding of that community through the cosmopolitan body. These actions include, but are not limited to, love, respect, ethical engagement, acceptance, and appreciation for all cultures where the cosmopolitan body resides" (November 29, 2011). At this point, for the first time, critical terms such as oppression, social justice and ethical obligation to others became salient.

The final working definition, collaboratively conceived and voted on unanimously by all class members at the final class meeting, was: "Cosmopolitanism is a state of consciousness, empathy and understanding that humanity is a community both real and imagined, which must be engaged with through ethical accountability to others globally and locally, and with space for personal development" (conceived of by David Whitfield and Ryan Trone with the assistance of the rest of the class, December 13, 2011). It was in the aspects of community and engagement where the students found the intersections of cosmopolitanism and intercultural communication. The acts of creating and maintaining community, of showing empathy and ethical obligations towards humanity and being reflective are constitutive of both communication and culture.

For their final papers, the students created a definition for and operationalized cosmopolitanism across multiple perspectives and applications. For example, Jana Simonis used cosmopolitanism as a framework through which to study home, belonging and hybridization of identities for international students on a U.S. university campus. David Whitfield used cosmopolitanism— and its related notion of counter-cosmopolitanism (Appiah, 2006)—to study how the deaf community takes a counter-cosmopolitan stance to create a space of empowerment when confronted with the dominant, non-hearing-impaired world. Ryan Trone examined the relationship between religious fanaticism and cosmopolitanism, posing the question of whether organized religion makes one less apt to be cosmopolitan. Milica Obretkovich operationalized cosmopolitanism through asking whether or not and how cosmopolitanism can be taught to children, focusing her research on the Boys and Girls Club. Each of these research papers utilized cosmopolitanism in a different way— some pragmatically (i.e., how can it be broken down and taught to children?), and some theoretically (i.e., how cosmopolitanism as an approach to values and valuing is similar to and different from religious orientations).

The noteworthy thing about all of this is that all but two of these students had rarely, if ever, been introduced to the term cosmopolitanism before the semester began. By the end of the semester they were able to apply the very same term and a set of related concepts to intercultural communication scholarship and research at sophisticated levels, often embodying self-reflexivity and critique within their treatment. Further, through teaching this course, Miriam found herself coming away with a more multifaceted knowledge and understanding of cosmopolitanism, somewhat derived from critical thinking and discussion of the readings, but mainly due to the multidimensional perspectives professed to and engaged in by the students in the class.

Cosmopolitan Communication and Peoplehood

The local knowledge of the students and the global knowledge of scholarship on cosmopolitanism from scholars around the world melded to create an environment in which all 9 of the course's participants taught and learned about cosmopolitanism as a framework, an identity orientation, a utopian goal and a lens through which to view the world. Particularly compelling was the critical self-transformation Miriam was able to observe the students engage in over the course of the semester. Through the open pedagogical form of the course, students became more self-reflexive and problematized their own positionalities. They problematized their positionality as white university students in the U.S.; their own assumptions about race, space, culture and identity; and how they might listen to one another's experiences to learn about empathy and the value of valuing beyond surface-level impressions and assumptions (e.g., one student's coming out to the class he taught; another student's identity development as a Serbian-born woman in southern Illinois; a third student's struggles as a military veteran trying to readjust to life in the rural Midwest after touring Iraq and Afghanistan). Most importantly, these students engaged with the notion of hope even as they delved deep into critiques of Westernization, elitism and their own potential roles as both oppressors and oppressed. In short, through their learning community, these students learned to embody the critical self-transformation imperative of cosmopolitan communication (Assumption 6).

Indeed, through engagement with hope, social justice and the imagination, students in this class not only increased their concern with describing and working with cosmopolitanism as a space of transformative critical engagement (as can be seen in the evolution of their definitions over the course of the semester), they also became more active in advocacy in their lives at the university. This was illustrated particularly and powerfully when the class was substituted for during the university's strike in November of 2011. On the first day, Miriam, who was on strike, did not 'teach' class, and the students chose to attend and open up a dialogue with the substitute teacher (whose spouse was in administration and who was unfamiliar with the topic of cosmopolitanism). They empathized with her own politi-cal experiences of crossing the picket line as well as informed her of their informed, pro-labor position on the strike itself (this was not advocated by Miriam and the students made this decision on their own).

On the second day of the strike, they all intentionally picketed with their professors, standing up for our rights as educators and participating in the process of advocacy and collaborative support with their teachers and their peers. This social justice advocacy move (while picketing we actually discussed strike issues and how they related to cosmopolitanism) provides some support for Assumption 5 of cosmopolitan peoplehood: These stu-dents, many of whom had never in the past been involved with a protest or social justice movement, made their own informed decision to engage in dialogue, solidarity and hopeful advocacy for their rights as students and our rights as educators. Such an Other-oriented positionality and willing-ness to both engage in dialogue with the substitute teacher and align with border perspectives by picketing for justice for their teachers illustrates their commitment to social justice goals entailed in cosmopolitan peoplehood.

In the conclusion of this chapter we outline several suggestions for a cos-mopolitan pedagogy for intercultural communication. These suggestions advocate engaging cosmopolitan values not only to embody cosmopoli-tan ideals and teach about cosmopolitanism, but also as a means to share knowledge in a ground-up rather than in a top-down manner.

Towards a Program of Cosmopolitan Pedagogy

Cosmopolitan pedagogy does not necessarily need to involve teaching about cosmopolitanism as a topic, or teaching students how to embody cosmopolitan dispositions (although it is obviously well-positioned to accomplish either, or both, goals). Rather, cosmopolitan pedagogy is an embodied, socially conscious and egalitarian form of education, which, in our view, keeps the following in mind:

- In cosmopolitan pedagogy, similar to Freire's pedagogy of the oppressed, learning is dialogic, with knowledge being created in a ground-up, rather than top-down, manner.
- A cosmopolitan pedagogical framework teaches the value of valuing (Hansen et al., 2009) through engaging in multiple learning styles with an emphasis on experiential learning, dialogue and reflection.
- Cosmopolitan pedagogy is also a postcolonial pedagogy, and as such works to decolonize knowledge in education (Diversi & Moreira, 2009).
- Cosmopolitan pedagogy works to give alternative voices a central position and to translate voice and culture. This can be achieved through readings and activities for participation including and beyond dialogue and experiential learning.

- Cosmopolitan pedagogy, whenever possible, should engage in learning with—not teaching to or at—underserved communities.
- Cosmopolitan pedagogy focuses not just on the global, but also on the interconnectedness of the local with the global, and the use of the labor of the imagination to create links between the two.
- Cosmopolitan pedagogy calls for education that emphasizes ethical obligations to others both at home and at a global level—which should, if possible, include a service learning component.
- Cosmopolitan pedagogy focuses on an egalitarian educational structure in which all have the same rights and responsibilities to knowledge, although some may have more experience or scholarly knowledge in some areas than in others. Thus, education becomes a melded and collaborative process of teaching and learning in which multiple roles are often played out simultaneously. Students should have the opportunity to teach class and teachers should be willing to act as—and learn from—students.
- Cosmopolitan pedagogy emphasizes engagement with the cultural Other as well as critical self-reflexivity. Multiple perspective-taking should be stressed to inculcate the value of empathy.
- Cosmopolitan pedagogy questions the notion of tolerance, attempting, whenever possible, to subvert this notion with that of acceptance and, moreover, appreciation and the willingness to change.
- Cosmopolitan pedagogy challenges the notion of 'normalcy' and instead embraces the notion of 'stranger' (Appiah, 2006). In this process, cosmopolitan pedagogy should teach multiple viewpoints through storytelling, move beyond oversimplified West/Rest dichotomies, recenter alternative histories and emphasize the power of socially constructed memory and narrative (Norton, 2001; Papastephanou, 2004).

These suggestions should be seen as open-ended to allow for such issues as access, funding, age and education level of students and subjects taught. However, they can be widely incorporated into a pedagogical framework that emphasizes the following values: melded teacher/student relationships, shared ownership of knowledge, experiential learning, service learning, social justice, decolonizing knowledge, critiquing and deconstructing 'normalcy,' giving voice to the voiceless and critical self-reflexivity and transformation. Through practicing these values, participants involved in cosmopolitan pedagogies could learn to place dual emphasis on the global and local, learn the value of valuing and the importance of questioning grand narratives and dominant social structures and understand the interrelated nature of hope, dialogue and memory in the production and consumption of knowledge. In this manner, a cosmopolitan pedagogical framework can prepare students to engage in transformative research and social action at the local and global levels of teaching, learning, being and becoming.

Conclusion

As we moved through the writing of this book, gradually developed our concepts of cosmopolitan communication and peoplehood and transformed ourselves, we found ourselves becoming more and more involved with the concepts of the cultural Other as stranger and strangerhood. The spiritual practices of many religions, such as Judaism, Islam, Buddhism, Christianity and Hinduism, have for thousands of years advocated openness towards strangers. The Quran specifically notes the importance of kindness to strangers, and Jews, derogatorily considered the original rootless cosmopolitans, have been narrated as engaging in empathy, charity and hospitality towards strangers due to the ability to see the stranger within (see Kristeva, 1991). The spiritual practices of these cultural groups teach that we must extend hospitality beyond our own communities.

These approaches towards the stranger and strangerhood—encouraging kindness, hospitality, recalling that we are all strangers—extend well beyond monotheistic religions and spiritual teachings. They permeate various forms of literary and artistic discourses. For example, they are addressed by Victor Hugo (1862/1987) in *Les Misérables,* when the bishop shows kindness to the stranger Jean Valjean by taking him in and giving him silver candlesticks, which he had attempted to steal from the bishop, in this way making it possible for Jean Valjean to rebuild his life. In *Crime and Punishment*, Fyodor Dostoyevsky (1866/2003) writes that "we sometimes encounter people, even perfect strangers, who begin to interest us at first sight, somehow suddenly, all at once, before a word has even been spoken" (p. 10). Donald Blum, from the indie-rock band the Von Bondies, describes how "we are born anew within every stranger's eye." Japanese cellist Yo Yo Ma has been quoted as saying that "good things happen when you meet strangers." Enlightenment philosopher Francis Bacon also had a perspective on strangers, although we are slightly altering his words here: "If a [wo/man] be gracious and courteous to strangers, it shows [s/he] is a citizen of the world." In our own larger discipline of communication studies, John Durham Peters (1999) in *Speaking Into the Air: A History of the Idea of Communication* writes:

The problem of communication is not language's slipperiness, it is the unfixable difference between the self and the other. The challenge of communication is not to be true to our own interiority, but to have mercy on others for never seeing ourselves as we do. (pp. 266–267)

And of course there is the famous quote by Tennessee Williams' Blanche Dubois in *Cat on a Hot Tin Roof*: "I've always depended on the kindness of strangers."

We find hope and comfort in such widespread support for kindness to strangers. It indicates to us that the idea of peoplehood is considered an important cultural value across multiple cultures, countries, religious groups, artists, musicians, scholars and philosophers. While the prevailing despair inherent in the critical perspective on neoliberal globalization leads many of us to rightly worry about how some cultures and groups stand on the backs of others, and how gaps between the dominant and the marginalized widen every day, cosmopolitan peoplehood and its enduring concept of kindness to strangers is also widespread and has been for centuries. Just as people inherently want to build walls and potentially tribalize and dominate, it seems that people across generations and cultural boundaries can also empathize with what it means to be a stranger—an experience which we believe will grow in this age of postcolonial and postmodern globality. It is quite possible that only once we have experienced strangerhood, have felt what it is to be different and be perceived as the Other, can we learn that difference is not to be feared but to be embraced for its creative and emancipatory potential (Lorde, 1984/2007). This notion encourages us to widen intercultural communication scholarship's focus from learning how to simply overcome difference (or worse, to minimize it) to understanding that difference is an inherent human and communicative experience that needs to be normalized and positively engaged with.

HOPE FOR THE FUTURE: IMPLICATIONS FOR INTERCULTURAL COMMUNICATION AND BEYOND

We find, in the writing of this book, that our optimism about critical and postcolonial cosmopolitanism as an ethical vision for engaging in communication across difference has continued to grow. It has hardly been difficult to uncover everyday instances where cosmopolitanism's notion of kindness to strangers has positively impacted notions of mutuality, empathy and critical self-transformation. Acts of kindness from a cosmopolitan perspective can range from a small gesture like purchasing a breakfast and coffee for the driver behind you at the Starbucks drive-through for no particular reason, through imagining and then engaging in intercultural bridgework with communities across oceans. In hearing stories and reading articles, finding case studies and analyzing classrooms and research projects, we have found our hopes solidifying and growing stronger.

According to Werbner (2012), cosmopolitan hope for our planet is threatened mainly on two fronts: " . . . on one front is xenophobia, a fear and rejection of strangers; on the other, hegemonic cultural universalisation which is homogenising and intolerant of difference" (p. 154). She emphasizes that we must move forward and push back against these threats, and that in so doing we must avoid seeing cosmopolitanism "as a hidden form of westernization," "engage with global inequalities" and reject "any association with former imperial colonisers or moralizing elites" (p. 154). In our work, we have tried to follow this advice, and following are some implications we hope will be taken from this book and applied to intercultural communication scholarship, research and pedagogy, and indeed to areas beyond our discipline.

- We must commit ourselves as critical and ethical global citizens to intercultural communication praxis and research that serves social justice at local and global levels. In so doing, we must strive not to gloss over past and emerging problems and colonialisms, but rather to incorporate them into our visions for the future. These visions must not privilege assumptions of Western modernity as the 'correct' way of doing things.
- As Falk (1996) notes: "A credible cosmopolitanism has to be combined with a critique of the ethically deficient globalism embodied in neoliberal modes of thought and the globalism that is being enacted in a manner that minimizes the ethical and visionary content of conceiving the world as a whole" (p. 57). Critical/postcolonial cosmopolitanism, when joined with intercultural communication, promises hope for interrupting the hegemony of neoliberal globalization.
- As several postcolonial scholars such as Said (1994) have argued, we need to move creatively beyond West vs. Rest binaries of intercultural communication, and particularly cosmopolitanism. We must trouble the notion that cosmopolitanism is elitist and Western, because when we make this argument, we support the dominant narrative of cosmopolitanism and help further reify problematic dichotomies. We believe that intercultural communication scholars utilizing cosmopolitanism need to imagine the world as multipolar and marked by multiple modernities, rather than one that privileges the West as the center. In so doing, we will develop the vision to see exemplars of cosmopolitanism in our localities and throughout the world, regardless of socioeconomic status or geographical location.
- We must conceptualize difference through a dialectic and dialogic process, in which we can recognize that we are all both strangers and community members. We need to write, teach and research with this in mind. This will hopefully lead to less of a top-down approach to

scholarship and pedagogy, and encourage more of a holistic and vernacular approach to research and teaching within the conditions of postcolonial globality. Taking this approach encourages intercultural communication scholars to remember that the Self–Other dialectic and engagement is a constant state of in-betweenness.

- We must remember that cosmopolitanism does not have to always exist across nation-state borders, and that a culture-as-nation focus can lead us to neglect cosmopolitanism within nation-state borders. We must move away from methodological nationalism through turning the gaze inward (through critical self-transformation and humility) as well as outward, engaging our imaginations and ontologically and pragmatically interrupting divisive boundaries and borders.
- We must recognize that the discipline of intercultural communication is inextricably linked to morality. The ways through which we as intercultural communication scholars, teachers and students engage with and perform difference and kindness to strangers should constantly and consistently work with the world stage in mind. It is our responsibility to engage in cosmopolitan communication to create our own identities within the frame of cosmopolitan peoplehood. We must not expect others to do this until we have attempted to walk this walk ourselves.

In other words, cosmopolitanism's values should be made locally relevant, even as they are performed on a world stage: "In short, in order to flourish, we must see ourselves at the same time as members of a particular community of particular meaning and as members of the larger community of human beings. This is certainly quite difficult" (Commissiong, 2012, p. 187). But it is not impossible. Intercultural communication scholar Stella Ting-Toomey (2005) observes that too much cultural rootedness results in ethnocentrism and too much rootlessness results in lack of direction and chaos. A balance between the two ways of being, combined with a high tolerance for ambiguity, can help us appreciate and learn from "strangers" and engage cultural borders without fear and with respect (see also Gudykunst & Y.Y. Kim, 2003). Cosmopolitanism, when combined with intercultural communication, can guide us to this state of relating, being and becoming.

In their concluding chapter of *The Handbook of Critical Intercultural Communication*, editors Nakayama and Halualani (2010) write:

> We live in a world with increased opportunities to interact with people around the globe. Communication has played a key role in both making the global economy possible, as well as emerged as a vital part of resistance to it. This dialectic tension opens up enormous challenges for critical intercultural communication scholars, as well as all of us who

live in this new global world. There is no turning back, only the facing of what has been, what is, and what will become. (p. 599)

We feel that we have taken up this call for critically engaging with the world by building a bridge between cosmopolitanism and intercultural communication. Critical intercultural communication scholars must find ways to ethically engage with cultural Others, both near and far, because, as Anzaldúa (2002) reminds us, "the complexities of our age demand that we develop a perspective that takes into the account the whole planet" (p. 3). While cosmopolitanism may be superficially, and even imperialistically, deployed to support the goals of neoliberal globalization, it may also be "salvaged" as an ethical perspective "to illuminate different images of humanity" (Lu, 2000, p. 253). In this book we have taken the latter path, and we are indebted to all the scholars and philosophers whose works have made it possible for us to do so. Just as Kraidy (2005) makes the compelling argument that hybridity is the cultural logic of contemporary globalization, we make the argument that cosmopolitanism is a moral imperative for communicatively engaging with the proliferating spaces of interculturality within contemporary globalization.

Our final few words of caution are that as we participate in cosmopolitan communication and peoplehood in our own lives as much as possible and teach it and support it however we can, we must not make any attempts to force cosmopolitanism on others. Nor should we marshal it simply as an academic fashion, or inadvertently position cosmopolitanism as the path towards some sort of 'evolved' identity in which the cultural Other is objectified as a serviceable Other for the Self's use. Hope becomes hope because it sees the potential in what can be achieved, not because it forces people to achieve that potential. Our hopes have been laid out in this book. We strongly believe that as critical intercultural communication scholars, we must not give up hope since hope can lead to empowerment. It is our hope that we can inspire our students and ourselves to humbly embrace our own inner stranger, inspire others to do the same and collectively move outward from a local to a global embrace. Only then can we make another world possible . . .

Glossary

Classical cosmopolitanism—Cosmopolitanism of ancient Greece, specifically attributed to the Cynics and the Stoics, who advocated for a moral cosmopolitanism in which citizenship should extend beyond the borders of the local/polis/city-state.

Cosmopolitan communication—A world- and Other-oriented practice of engaging in deliberate, dialogic, critical, non-coercive and ethical communication. Through the play of context-specific dialectics, cosmopolitan communication works with and through cultural differences and historical and emerging power inequities to achieve ongoing understanding, intercultural growth, mutuality, collaboration and social and global justice goals through critical self-transformation.

Cosmopolitan pedagogy—An embodied and egalitarian pedagogical program that teaches the value of valuing, encourages an orientation to the world that values humanity and ethically obliges teachers and students to work for social and global justice through the reflective arts of hope, memory and dialogue.

Cosmopolitan peoplehood—An open-ended, Other- and world-oriented and dialogic ('in-between') identity orientation that is morally committed to addressing social and global injustices in their many forms. It is an embodied way of being in the world that engages views from the margins, celebrates the powers of empathy and the imagination to connect the local/national with the global and sees ambiguity as opportunity for intercultural growth and learning. Through non-violent entanglement between Self and cultural Others (near and far), it entails differential belonging, intercultural bridgework, kindness to strangers and continuous engagement in critical self-transformation through cosmopolitan communication.

Cosmopolitanism-as-method—A method of inquiry and epistemology that takes a postcolonial, social constructionist, critical and transformative approach towards culture, communication, difference, power and identity. This approach does not intend to throw the notion of the nation-state out altogether, but strives to understand how nation-states are transformed in the cosmopolitan constellation and how new structures and cultural politics arise from the blurring and transcending of nation-state boundaries.

Cosmopolitanism-as-phenomenon of analysis—Ways through which cosmopolitanism as a phenomenon can be studied (within intercultural communication scholarship).

Critical cosmopolitanism—Mainly associated with the work of sociologist Gerard Delanty, critical cosmopolitanism is a dialogic and reflexive orientation to the world that involves openness to critical self-transformation, and the ability to hear and see the cultural Other with empathy and respect.

Cultural cosmopolitanism—An ethical and philosophical framework through which we may envision human and mediated intercultural communication for a more humane world.

Decolonial cosmopolitanism—Mainly attributed to the work of Walter Mignolo, decolonial cosmopolitanism approaches the world from multiple trajectories, aims to empower the marginalized and undo the workings of colonizing powers, and move towards pluriversality (or cosmopolitan localism based in colonial and postcolonial difference).

Despotic cosmopolitanism—Forced top-down cosmopolitanism.

Discrepant cosmopolitanism—Attributed to historian James Clifford, this form of cosmopolitanism entails multiple articulations of cosmopolitanism that are not necessarily just Western or elite in nature.

Elite cosmopolitanism—This form of cosmopolitanism is engaged in by global elites (usually white male) who hop from country to country and sample cultures as they go. The conceptualization of cosmopolitanism in the earlier works of Ulf Hannerz is typical of elite cosmopolitanism.

Emancipatory cosmopolitanism—Called for by globalization scholar Jan Nederveen Pieterse, this orientation to cosmopolitanism critiques Western domination and champions goals of emancipation for the postcolonial and marginalized peoples of the world (see postcolonial cosmopolitanism)

Kantian cosmopolitanism (and top-down universalism)—An Enlightenment form of cosmopolitanism, championed by Immanuel Kant, that describes a normative ethical political order limited to those elite enough to attain 'global citizenship' status. Kantian cosmopolitanism is based in an absolute Western modernist and rationalist universalism, and advocates for a world modeled after Europe.

Methodological cosmopolitanism (and methodological nationalism)—Ulrich Beck and colleagues' response to the assumption that the nation-state is the natural unit of analysis for society and culture (methodological nationalism); methodological cosmopolitanism requires a reconceptualization of nation-state-centric cultural definitions and methodologies and advocates for an epistemology that makes the study and production of knowledge about culture and society a transnational phenomenon in itself.

Political cosmopolitanism—A systemic and structural approach to cosmopolitanism adopted by political activists and philosophers, as well as by rhetoricians in the discipline of communication studies; it often advocates for a centralizing World State that protects human rights.

Postcolonial cosmopolitanism—An approach to cosmopolitanism that stresses its relational and dialogical contexts, and entails understanding the Self and the cultural Other through historical and geopolitical location and other postcolonial power dynamics.

Postuniversal cosmopolitanism—Attributed to Gerard Delanty, this approach to cosmopolitanism does not stress the top-down, one-size-fits-all universalistic aspects of Kantian cosmopolitanism, but rather recognizes the multiplicity of varying forms of cosmopolitan projects which emerge transnationally and translocally.

Rooted cosmopolitanism—Attributed to philosopher Kwame Anthony Appiah, this perspective on cosmopolitanism entails a dialectical tension between the global and the local, and requires an understanding that local allegiances and struggles determine who we are as much as global ones do. Rooted cosmopolitanism states that all cosmopolitanisms are ultimately rooted in localities where the local and the global intersect.

Traditional cosmopolitanism—A term presented as a foil to rooted, vernacular, translocal, postuniversal, postcolonial and decolonial cosmopolitanism, traditional cosmopolitanism takes its influences from classical and Kantian approaches (as well as the early works of Ulf Hannerz) and speaks to Eurocentric, top-down, elitist and even despotic cosmopolitanism.

Translocal cosmopolitanism—Cosmopolitanism emphasizing subnational, local-to-local connections, often advocated for by scholars of cosmopolitanism for ground-up alliance-building for social and global justice purposes.

Transnational cosmopolitanism—This form of cosmopolitanism draws upon the work of cultural anthropologist Arjun Appadurai and acts against neoliberal globalization ideologies. It pays attention to global flows (of people, media, technologies, capital and ideologies) and disjunctures, heterogeneity, diversity and empowerment at local levels.

Vernacular cosmopolitanism (also ordinary, mundane, banal cosmopolitanism)—This term is attributed to postcolonial studies scholar Homi Bhabha. It joins the oxymoronic notion of global enlightenment with local specificity, encompasses non-elitist and non-Western cosmopolitanisms, and advocates for a cosmopolitanism-from-below approach that directly incorporates Appiah's rooted cosmopolitanism while critiquing top-down Kantian approaches.

References

Aboulafia, M. (2010). *Transcendence: On self-determination and cosmopolitanism.* Stanford, CA: Stanford University Press.

Abu-Lughod, J. (1989). *Before European hegemony: The world system A.D. 1250–1350.* New York: Oxford University Press.

Adler, P. (1977). Beyond cultural identity: Reflections upon cultural and multicultural man. In R. Brislin (Ed.), *Culture learning: Concepts, applications, and research* (pp. 24–41). Honolulu, HI: University Press of Hawaii.

Allen, D. (1997). Social constructions of self: Some Asian, Marxist, and feminist critiques of dominant western views of self. In D. Allen (Ed.), *Culture and self: Philosophical and religious perspectives, East and West* (pp. 3–26). Boulder, CO: Westview Press.

Althusser, L. (1971). *Lenin and philosophy and other essays.* London: New Left Books.

Anderson, B. (1991). *Imagined communities.* London: Verso.

Anderson, E. (2011). *The cosmopolitan canopy: Race and civility in everyday life.* New York: W. W. Norton and Co.

Anderson, L. E. (1994). A new look at an old construct: Cross-cultural adaptation. *International Journal of Intercultural Relations, 18*(3), 293–328.

Andreotti, V. (2006). Soft versus critical global citizenship education. *Policy & Practice: A Development Education Review, 3,* 40–51.

Anthias, F. (2001). New hybridities, old concepts: The limits of 'culture.' *Ethnic and Racial Studies, 24*(4), 619–641.

Anzaldúa, G. (1990). Bridge, drawbridge, sandbar, or island: Lesbians of color Haciendo Alianzas. In L. Albrecht & R. M. Brewer (Eds.), *Bridges of power: Women's multicultural alliances* (pp. 216–231). Philadelphia, PA: New Society Publishers.

Anzaldúa, G. (2002). (Un)natural bridges, (un)safe spaces. In G. Anzaldúa & A. Keating (Eds.), *This bridge we call home: Radical visions for transformation* (pp. 1–5). New York: Routledge.

Appadurai, A. (1996). *Modernity at large: Cultural dimensions of globalization.* Minneapolis, MN: University of Minnesota Press.

Appadurai, A. (2000). Grassroots globalization and the research imagination. *Public Culture, 12*(1), 1–19.

Appiah, K. A. (1996). Cosmopolitan patriots. In J. Cohen (Ed.), *For love of country: Debating the limits of patriotism* (pp. 21–29). Boston, MA: Beacon Press.

Appiah, K. A. (2006). *Cosmopolitanism: Ethics in a world of strangers.* London: Penguin Books.

Asante, M. K. (1980). Intercultural communication: An inquiry into research direction. *Communication Yearbook, 4,* 401–410.

Asante, M. K. (2011). Maat and human communication: Supporting identity, culture, and history without global domination. *Intercultural Communication Studies, 20*(1), 49–56.

Bakhtin, M. (1981). *The dialogic imagination* (M. Holquist, Ed.; C. Emerson & M. Holquist, Trans.). Austin, TX: University of Texas Press.

Banks, J. A. (2004). Teaching for social justice, diversity and citizenship in a global world. *The Educational Forum, 68*, 289–298.

Bardhan, N. (2011). *Slumdog Millionaire* meets 'India Shining': (Trans)national narrations of identity in south Asian diaspora. *Journal of International and Intercultural Communication, 4*(1), 42–61.

Bardhan, N. (2012). Postcolonial migrant identities and the case for strategic hybridity: Toward 'inter'cultural bridgework. In N. Bardhan & M. P. Orbe (Eds.), *Identity research in intercultural communication: Reflections and future directions* (pp. 149–164). Lanham, MD: Lexington Books.

Bardhan, N., & Orbe, M. P. (2012). Introduction. In N. Bardhan & M. P. Orbe (Eds.), *Identity research in intercultural communication: Reflections and future directions* (pp. viii–xxv). Lanham, MD: Lexington Books.

Barea, E. G., Torrico, M. G., Lepe, E. M., Garzón, F. R., Llorente, M. T. P., & Dietz, G. (2010). Transmigrant families: Intercultural and bilingual competencies development. *Globalisation, Societies and Education, 8*(3), 429–442.

Bauman, Z. (1997). *Postmodernity and its discontents.* Cambridge, UK: Polity Press.

Baxter, L. (2006). Dialogue. In G. Shepherd, J. St. John, & T. Striphas (Eds.), *Communication as . . . Perspectives on theory* (pp. 101–109). Thousand Oaks, CA: Sage Publications.

Baxter, L., & Montgomery, B. (1996). *Relating: Dialogues and dialectics.* New York: The Guilford Press.

Beck, U. (2000). The cosmopolitan perspective. On the sociology of the second age of modernity. *British Journal of Sociology, 51*, 79–106.

Beck, U. (2006). *The cosmopolitan vision.* Cambridge, UK: Polity Press.

Beck, U. (2007). Cosmopolitanism: A critical theory for the twenty-first century. In G. Ritzer (Ed.), *The Blackwell companion to globalization* (pp. 162–176). Malden, MA: Blackwell Publishing.

Beck, U. (2009). Foreword. In M. Nowicka & M. Rovisco (Eds.), *Cosmopolitanism in practice* (pp. xi–xiii). Surrey, UK: Ashgate Publishing.

Beck, U., & Sznaider, H. (2006). Unpacking cosmopolitanism for the social sciences: A research agenda. *The British Journal of Sociology, 57*(1), 1–23.

Benhabib, S. (2002). *The claims of culture: Equality and diversity in the global era.* Princeton, NJ: Princeton University Press.

Bennett, J. M., & Bennett, M. J. (2004). Developing intercultural sensitivity: An integrative approach to global and domestic diversity. In D. Landis, J. M. Bennett, & M. J. Bennett (Eds.), *Handbook of intercultural training* (3rd ed.; pp. 147–164). Thousand Oaks, CA: Sage Publications.

Bennett, M. J. (1993). Towards ethnorelativism: A developmental model of intercultural sensitivity. In R. M. Paige (Ed.), *Education for the intercultural experience* (2nd ed.; pp. 21–71). Yarmouth, ME: Intercultural Press.

Berman, G., & Paradies, Y. (2008). Racism, disadvantage and multiculturalism: Towards effective anti-racism praxis. *Ethnic and Racial Studies, 33*(2), 214–232.

Bhabha, H. (1989). Location, intervention, incommensurability: A conversation with Homi Bhabha. *Emergences, 1*(1), 63–88.

Bhabha, H. (1990). Interview with Homi Bhabha: The third space. In J. Rutherford (Ed.), *Identity: Community, culture, difference* (pp. 207–221). London: Lawrence & Wishart.

Bhabha, H. (1994). *The location of culture*. New York: Routledge.

Bhabha, H. (1996a). Culture's in-between. In S. Hall & P. du Gay (Eds.), *Questions of cultural identity* (pp. 53–60). London: Sage Publications.

Bhabha, H. (1996b). Unsatisfied: Notes on vernacular cosmopolitanism. In L. García-Moreno & P. C. Pfeifer (Eds.), *Text and nation: Cross-disciplinary essays on cultural and national identities* (pp. 191–207). Columbia, SC: Camden House.

Bhambra, G. K. (2011). Cosmopolitanism and the postcolonial condition. In M. Nowicka & M. Rovisco (Eds.), *The Ashgate research companion to cosmopolitanism* (pp. 313–328). Aldershot: Ashgate.

Brah, A., & Coombes, A. (Eds.) (2000). *Hybridity and its discontents*. London: Routledge.

Breckenridge, C., Pollock, S., Bhabha, H., & Chakrabarty, D. (Eds.). (2002). *Cosmopolitanism*. Durham, NC: Duke University Press.

Brennan, T. (1997). *At home in the world: Cosmopolitanism now*. Cambridge, MA: Harvard University Press.

Brennan, T. (2001). Cosmopolitanism and internationalism. *New Left Review, 7*, 75–84.

Broome, B. J. (1991). Building shared meaning: Implications of a relational approach to empathy for teaching intercultural communication. *Communication Education, 40*, 231–249.

Brower, J. (2010, April). *The dialogic appearance of the cosmo-polis*. Paper presented at Central States Communication Association Conference, Cincinnati, OH.

Buber, M. (1970). *I and thou* (W. Kauffman, Trans.). New York: Simon & Schuster.

Calhoun, C. (2002). The class consciousness of frequent travelers: Towards a critique of actually existing cosmopolitanism. In S. Vertovec & R. Cohen (Eds.), *Conceiving cosmopolitanism* (pp. 86–109). Oxford: Oxford University Press.

Calloway-Thomas, C. (2010). *Empathy in the global world: An intercultural perspective*. Los Angeles: Sage Publications.

Canagarajah, A. S. (1999). On EFL teachers, awareness and agency. *ELT Journal, 53*(3), 207–214.

Canclini, N. G. (2005). *Hybrid cultures: Strategies for entering and leaving modernity* (C. Chiappari & S. Lopez, Trans.). Minneapolis, MN: University of Minnesota Press.

Cargyle, A. (2005). Describing culture dialectically. In W. J. Starosta & G.-M. Chen (Eds.), *Taking stock in intercultural communication: Where to now? International and Intercultural Communication Annual, XXVIII* (pp. 99–123). Washington, DC: National Communication Association.

Carrillo Rowe, A. (2005). Be longing: Toward a feminist politics of relation. *NWSA Journal, 17*(2), 15–46.

Carrillo Rowe, A. (2008). *Power lines: On the subject of feminist alliances*. Durham, NC: Duke University Press.

Carrillo Rowe, A. (2010). Entering the inter: Power lines in intercultural communication. In T. K. Nakayama & R. T. Halualani (Eds.), *The handbook of critical intercultural communication* (pp. 216–226). Malden, MA: Wiley-Blackwell.

Casmir, F. (1993). Third-culture building: A paradigm shift for international and intercultural communication. *Communication Yearbook, 16*, 407–428.

Casmir, F. L. (1997). *Ethics in intercultural and international communication*. Mahwah, NJ: Lawrence Erlbaum Associates.

Cavallaro, D. (2001). *Critical and cultural theory: Thematic variations*. New Brunswick, NJ: The Athlone Press.

Chakrabarty, D. (2007). *Provincializing Europe: Postcolonial thought and historical difference* (2nd ed.). Princeton, NJ: Princeton University Press.

Chávez, K. (2012). Doing intersectionality: Power, privilege and identities in political activist communities. In N. Bardhan & M. P. Orbe (Eds.), *Identity research in intercultural communication: Reflections and future directions* (pp. 21–32). Lanham, MD: Lexington Books.

Chawla, D. (2012). Performing home/storying selves: Home and/as identity in oral histories of refugees in India's Partition. In N. Bardhan & M. P. Orbe (Eds.), *Identity research in intercultural communication: Reflections and future directions* (pp. 87–99). Lanham, MD: Lexington Books.

Cheah, P. (1998). Introduction Part II: The cosmopolitical—today. In P. Cheah & B. Robbins (Eds.), *Cosmopolitics: Thinking and feeling beyond the nation* (pp. 20–41). Minneapolis, MN: University of Minnesota Press.

Chernilo, D. (2006). Social theory's methodological nationalism: Myth and reality. *European Journal of Social Theory, 9*(1), 5–22.

Cleveland, H., Mangone, G. J., & Adams, J. C. (1960). *The overseas Americans.* New York: McGraw-Hill.

Clifford, J. (1986). Introduction: Partial truths. In J. Clifford & G. E. Marcus (Eds.), *Writing culture: The politics and poetics of ethnography* (pp. 1–26). Berkeley, CA: University of California Press.

Clifford, J. (1992). Traveling cultures. In L. Grossberg, C. Nelson, & P. Treichler (Eds.), *Cultural studies* (pp. 96–116). New York: Routledge.

Clifford, J. (1994). Diasporas. *Cultural Anthropology, 9*(3), 302–338.

Clifford, J. (1998). Mixed feelings. In P. Cheah & B. Robbins (Eds.), *Cosmopolitics: Thinking and feeling beyond the nation* (pp. 362–370). Minneapolis, MN: University of Minnesota Press.

Clifford, J., & Marcus, G. E. (Eds.). (1986). *Writing culture: The politics and poetics of ethnography.* Berkeley, CA: University of California Press.

Collier, M. J. (1988). A comparison of conversations among and between domestic culture groups: How intra- and intercultural competencies vary. *Communication Quarterly, 36*(2), 122–144.

Collier, M. J. (1998). Researching cultural identity: Reconciling interpretive and postcolonial perspectives. In D. Tanno & A. González (Eds.), *Communication and identity across cultures, International and Intercultural Communication Annual, XXI* (pp. 122–147). Thousand Oaks, CA: Sage Publications.

Collier, M. J. (2003). Negotiating intercultural alliance relationships. In M. J. Collier (Ed.), *Intercultural communication competence, International and Intercultural Communication Annual, XXV* (pp. 1–16). Thousand Oaks, CA: Sage Publications.

Collier, M. J. (2005). Theorizing cultural identification: Critical updates and continuing evolution. In W. B. Gudykunst (Ed.), *Theorizing about intercultural communication* (pp. 235–256). Thousand Oaks, CA: Sage Publications.

Commisiong, A. B. (2012). *Cosmopolitanism in modernity: Human dignity in a global age.* Lanham, MD: Lexington Books.

Conquergood, D. (1991). Rethinking ethnography: Towards a critical cultural politics. *Communication Monographs, 58,* 179–194.

Cooks, L. (2001). From distance and uncertainty to research and pedagogy in the borderlands: Implications for the future of intercultural communication. *Communication Theory, 11*(3), 339–351.

Cooks, L. (2010). Revisiting the borderlands of critical intercultural communication. In T. K. Nakayama & R. T. Halualani (Eds.), *The handbook of critical intercultural communication* (pp. 112–129). Malden, MA: Wiley-Blackwell.

Cooper, A., & Rumford, C. (2011). Cosmopolitan borders: Bordering as connectivity. In M. Rovisco & M. Nowicka (Eds.), *The Ashgate research companion to cosmopolitanism* (pp. 261–276). Farnham, UK: Ashgate Publishing Limited.

Crenshaw, K. (1991). Mapping the margins: Intersectionality, identity politics and violence against women of color. *Stanford Law Review, 43,* 1241–1299.

Cross, W. (1991). *Shades of black: Diversity in African-American identity*. Philadelphia, PA: Temple University Press.

Cupach, W. R., & Imahori, T. T. (1993). Identity management theory: Communication competence in intercultural episodes and relationships. In R. L. Wiseman & J. Koester (Eds.), *Intercultural communication competence, International and Intercultural Communication Annual, XVII* (pp. 112–131). Newbury Park, CA: Sage Publications.

Curtin, M. (in press). Mapping cosmopolitanisms in Taipei: Toward a theorization of cosmopolitanism in linguistic landscape research. *International Journal of Sociology of Language*.

Dace, K. L., & McPhail, M. L. (2002). Crossing the color line: From empathy to implicature in intercultural communication. In J. N. Martin, T. K. Nakayama, & L. A. Flores (Eds.), *Readings in intercultural communication: Experiences and contexts* (2nd ed.; pp. 344–351). New York: McGraw-Hill.

Davies, L. (2006). Global citizenship: Abstraction or framework for action? *Educational Review, 58*(1), 5–25.

de Certeau, M. (1984). *The practice of everyday life*. Berkeley, CA: University of California Press.

Delanty, G. (2006). The cosmopolitan imagination: Critical cosmopolitanism and social theory. *The British Journal of Sociology, 57*(1), 25–47.

Delanty, G. (2009). *The cosmopolitan imagination: The renewal of critical social theory*. Cambridge, UK: Cambridge University Press.

Delanty, G. (2012). Introduction. In G. Delanty (Ed.), *Routledge handbook of cosmopolitanism studies* (pp. 1–8). Abingdon, Oxon: Routledge.

Dempsey, S. (2011). Theorizing difference from transnational feminism. In D. Mumby (Ed.), *Reframing difference in organizational communication studies: Research, pedagogy, practice* (pp. 55–75). Los Angeles: Sage Publications.

Dempsey, S., Parker, P., & Krone, K. (2011). Navigating socio-spatial difference, constructing counter space: Insights from transnational feminist praxis. *Journal of International and Intercultural Communication, 4*(3), 201–220.

Derrida, J. (1981). *Positions*. Chicago: University of Chicago Press.

Derrida, J. (1997). *Cosmopolites de tous les pays, encore un effort!* Paris: Galilée.

de Turk, S. (2006). The power of dialogue: Consequences of intergroup dialogue and their implications for agency and alliance building. *Communication Quarterly, 54*(1), 33–51.

Diversi, M., & Moreira, C. (2009). *Betweener talk: Decolonizing production, pedagogy and practice*. Walnut Creek, CA: Left Coast Press.

Dostoyevsky, F. (2003). *Crime and punishment*. New York: Bantam Dell. (Original work published 1866)

Drzewiecka, J. A., & Halualani, R. T. (2002). The structural–cultural dialectic of diasporic politics. *Communication Theory, 12*, 340–366.

Eagleton, T. (1990). *The ideology of the aesthetic*. Oxford: Basil Blackwell.

Evanoff, R. (2006). Ethics in intercultural dialogue. *International Journal of Intercultural Relations, 30*(4), 421–437.

Eze, E. C. (2001). *Achieving our humanity*. New York: Routledge.

Fabian, J. (2002). *Time and the Other: How anthropology makes its object*. New York: Columbia University Press. (Original work published 1983)

Falk, R. (1996). Revisioning cosmopolitanism. In J. Cohen (Ed.), *For love of country: debating the limits of patriotism* (pp. 53–60). Boston, MA: Beacon Press.

Falkheimer, J. (2007). Anthony Giddens and public relations: A third way perspective. *Public Relations Review, 33*(3), 287–293.

Featherstone, M. (1995). *Undoing culture: Globalization, postmodernism and identity*. London: Sage Publications.

Fine, R., & Cohen, R. (2002). Four cosmopolitan moments. In S. Vertovec & R. Cohen (Eds.), *Conceiving cosmopolitanism* (pp. 137–162). Oxford: Oxford University Press.

Fisher, W. (2008). Glimpses of hope: Rhetorical and dialogical discourse promoting cosmopolitanism. In K. Glenister Roberts & R. Arnett (Eds.), *Communication ethics: Between cosmopolitanism and provinciality* (pp. 47–68). New York: Peter Lang.

Forte, M. (2008). Methodological cosmopolitanism and anthropology. Retrieved April 14, 2012, from http://zeroanthropology.net/2008/10/20/methodological-cosmopolitanism-in-anthropology/

Forte, M. (2010). Introduction: Indigeneities and cosmopolitanisms. In M. Forte (Ed.), *Indigenous cosmopolitanisms: Transnational and transcultural indigeneity in the twenty-first century* (pp. 1–16). New York: Peter Lang.

Freire, P. (1997). Mentoring the mentor: A critical dialogue with Paulo Freire. In P. Freire, J. Fraser, D. Macedo, T. McKinnon, & W. T. Stokes (Eds.), *Mentoring the mentor: A critical dialogue with Paulo Freire* (pp. 308–329). New York: Peter Lang.

Freire, P. (2004). *Pedagogy of the oppressed* (30th anniversary ed.). New York: Continuum.

Friedman, J. (1999). Hybridization of roots and the abhorrence of the bush. In M. Featherstone & S. Lash (Eds.), *Spaces of culture: City–nation–world* (pp. 235–255). London: Sage Publications.

Furia, P. (2005). Global citizenship, anyone? Cosmopolitanism, privilege and public opinion. *Global Society, 19*(4), 231–259.

Galinsky, A. D., Hugenberg, K., Groom, C., & Bodenhausen, G. V. (2003). The reappropriation of stigmatizing labels: Implications for social identity. In J. Polzer, M. Neale, & E. Mannix (Eds.), *Identity issues in groups* (pp. 221–256). Greenwich, CT: Elsevier Science Press.

Ganesh, S. (Ed.). (2011). Intercultural dialogue [Special Issue]. *Journal of International and Intercultural Communication*, 4(2).

Ganesh, S., Zoller, H., & Cheney, G. (2005).Transforming resistance, broadening our boundaries: Critical organization communication meets globalization from below. *Communication Monographs, 72*(2), 169–191.

Ganga, D., & Scott, S. (2006). Cultural 'insiders' and the issue of positionality in qualitative migration research: Moving 'across' and moving 'along' researcher–participant divides. *Forum: Qualitative Social Research* [online]. Retrieved April 4, 2012, from http://www.qualitative-research.net/fqs-texte/3–06/06–3-7-e.htm

George, S. (2004). *Another world is possible if . . .* London: Verso.

Ghosh, A. (1994). *In an antique land.* New York: Vintage Books.

Gibson, K. L., Rimmington, G. M., & Landwher-Brown, M. (2008). Developing global awareness and responsible world citizenship with global learning. *Roeper Review, 30*, 11–23.

Giddens, A. (1990). *The consequences of modernity.* Cambridge, UK: Polity Press.

Giri, A. K. (2006). Cosmopolitanism and beyond: Towards a multiverse of transformations. *Development and Change, 37*(6), 1277–1292.

Giri, A. K. (2009). A new global humanity and the calling of a post-colonial cosmopolis: Self-development, inclusion of the other and planetary realizations. *Journal of Human Values, 15*(1), 1–14.

Gómez-Peña, G. (1996). *The new world border.* San Francisco, CA: City Lights.

Gouldner, A. W. (1957). Cosmopolitans and locals: Toward an analysis of latent social roles—I. *Administrative Science Quarterly, 2*, 281–306.

Gouldner, A. W. (1958). Cosmopolitans and locals: Toward an analysis of latent social roles—II. *Administrative Science Quarterly, 2*, 444–480.

Grossberg, L. (1996). Identity and cultural studies—Is that all there is? In S. Hall & P. du Gay (Eds.), *Questions of cultural identity* (pp. 87–107). London: Sage Publications.

Grossberg, L. (2002). Postscript. *Communication Theory, 12*(3), 367–370.

Gudykunst, W., & Kim, Y. Y. (2003). *Communicating with strangers: An approach to intercultural communication* (4th ed.). New York: McGraw-Hill.

Guilherme, M. (2007). English as a global language and education for cosmopolitan citizenship. *Language and Intercultural Communication, 7*, 72–90.

Gupta, A., & Ferguson, J. (1992). Beyond 'culture': Space, identity, and the politics of difference. *Cultural Anthropology, 7*(1), 6–23.

Hall, S. (1990). Cultural identity and diaspora. In J. Rutherford (Ed.), *Identity: Community, culture and difference* (pp. 222–237). London: Lawrence & Wishart.

Hall, S. (1996). Introduction: Who needs identity? In S. Hall & P. du Gay (Eds.), *Questions of cultural identity* (pp. 1–17). London: Sage.

Hall, S. (1997). The local and the global: Globalization and ethnicity. In A. King (Ed.), *Culture, globalization and the world-system* (pp. 19–39). Minneapolis, MN: University of Minnesota Press.

Hall, S. (2008). Cosmopolitanism, globalization and diaspora. In P. Werbner (Ed.), *Anthropology and the new cosmopolitanism: Rooted, feminist, and vernacular perspectives* (pp. 345–360). New York: Berg.

Halualani, R. T. (2008). 'Where exactly is the Pacific?': Global migrations, diasporic movements, and intercultural communication. *Journal of International and Intercultural Communication, 1*(1), 3–22.

Halualani, R. T., Mendoza, S. L., & Drzewiecka, J. (2009). 'Critical' junctures in intercultural communication studies: A review. *The Review of Communication, 9*(1), 17–35.

Hannerz, U. (1990). Cosmopolitans and locals in world culture. *Theory, Culture & Society, 7*, 237–251.

Hannerz, U. (1996). *Transnational connections: Culture, people, places*. London: Routledge.

Hannerz, U. (2006). Two faces of cosmopolitanism: Culture and politics. *Documentos CIDOB, Dinámicas Interculturales, 7*, 3–29.

Hannerz, U. (2007). Cosmopolitanism. In D. Nugent & J. Vincent (Eds.), *A companion to the anthropology of politics* (pp. 69–85). Malden, MA: Blackwell.

Hansen, D. T. (2010). Cosmopolitanism and education: A view from the ground. *Teachers College Record, 112*(1), 1–30.

Hansen, D. T., Burdick-Shepherd, S., Cammarano, C., & Obelliero, G. (2009). Education, values, and valuing in cosmopolitan perspective. *Curriculum Inquiry, 39*, 587–612.

Harjo, J. (2011). *Soul talk, soul language*. Middletown, CT: Wesleyan University Press.

Harvey, D. (1989). *The condition of postmodernity*. Cambridge, UK: Blackwell.

Haskins, E. (Ed.). (2011). Rhetorics of reason & restraint: Stoic rhetoric from antiquity to the present [Special Issue]. *Advances in the History of Rhetoric, 14*(1).

Hawley, J. C. (Ed.). (2008). *India in Africa, Africa in India: Indian Ocean cosmopolitanisms*. Bloomington, IN: Indiana University Press.

He, B., & Brown, K. (2012). An empirical world of cosmopolitan Asia. In G. Delanty (Ed.), *Routledge handbook of cosmopolitanism studies* (pp. 427–442). Abingdon, Oxon: Routledge.

Hecht, M. L. (1993). A research odyssey: Towards the development of a communication theory of identity. *Communication Monographs, 60*, 76–82.

Hecht, M. L., Collier, M. J., & Ribeau, S. (1993). *African-American communication: Ethnic identity and cultural interpretation*. Newbury Park, CA: Sage Publications.

Hecht, M. L., Warren, J. R., Jung, E., & Krieger, J. L. (2005). The communication theory of identity: Development, theoretical perspective, and future directions.

In W. B. Gudykunst (Ed.), *Theorizing about intercultural communication* (pp. 257–278). Thousand Oaks, CA: Sage Publications.

Hegde, R. S. (1998). Swinging the trapeze: The negotiation of identity among Asian Indian immigrant women in the United States. In D. Tanno & A. González (Eds.), *Communication and identity across cultures, International and Intercultural Communication Annual, XXI* (pp. 34–55). Thousand Oaks, CA: Sage Publications.

Held, D. (2002). Cosmopolitanism and globalization. *Logos: A Journal of Modern Society and Culture, 1*(3), 1–17.

Heyman, J., & Campbell, H. (2009). The anthropology of global flows: A critical reading of Appadurai's 'Disjuncture and difference in the global cultural economy.' *Anthropological Theory, 9*(2), 131–148.

Hodgson, D. L. (2008). Cosmopolitics, neoliberalism, and the state: The indigenous rights movement in Africa. In P. Werbner (Ed.), *Anthropology and the new cosmopolitanism* (pp. 215–232). New York: Berg.

Hofstede, G. (1980). *Culture's consequences: International differences in work related issues.* Beverly Hills, CA: Sage Publications.

Hogan, P. C., & Pandit, L. (Eds.). (2003). *Rabindranath Tagore: Universality and tradition.* Cranbury, NJ: Rosemont Publishing.

Holland, D., Lachicotte, W., Skinner, D., & Cain, C. (1998). *Identity and agency in cultural worlds.* Cambridge, MA: Harvard University Press.

Holliday, A. (2009). The role of culture in English language education: Key challenges. *Language and Intercultural Communication, 9*(3), 144–155.

Holling, M. A., & Calafell, B. (2007). Identities on stage and staging identities: ChicanoBrujo performances as emancipatory practices. *Text and Performance Quarterly, 27*(1), 58–83.

Holton, R. J. (2009). *Cosmopolitanisms: New thinking and new directions.* Houndmills, Basingstoke, Hampshire: Palgrave MacMillan.

Hostelling International–Chicago: Community Walls. Retrieved April 4, 2012, from http://www.hichicago.org/community_cw.shtml

Hostelling International–Chicago: Exchange Neighborhoods. Retrieved April 4, 2012, from http://www.hichicago.org/community_ens.shtml

How and why people move. (n.d.). Retrieved June 5, 2012, from http://hdr.undp.org/en/statistics/data/mobility/people/

Hugo, V. (1987). *Les misérables.* New York: Signet Classic. (Original work published 1862)

Inglis, D. (2012). Alternative histories of cosmopolitanism: Reconfiguring classical legacies. In G. Delanty (Ed.), *Routledge handbook of cosmopolitanism studies* (pp. 11–24). Abingdon, Oxon: Routledge.

Inglis, D., & Robertson, R. (2011). From cosmos to globe: Relating cosmopolitanism, globalization and globality. In M. Rovisco & M. Nowicka (Eds.), *The Ashgate research companion to cosmopolitanism* (pp. 295–311). Burlington, VT: Ashgate Publishing Company.

International gay rights movement. (2012). Retrieved on September 18, 2012, from http://www.globalpost.com/international-gay-rights-movement

Jackson, J. (2011). Cultivating cosmopolitan, intercultural citizenship through critical reflection and international, experiential learning. *Language and Intercultural Communication, 11*(2), 80–96.

Jackson II, R. L. (1999). *The negotiation of cultural identity.* Westport, CT: Praeger.

Jackson II, R. L. (2002). Cultural contracts theory: Toward an understanding of identity negotiation. *Communication Quarterly, 50*(3 & 4), 359–367.

Jackson II, R. L. (2006). *Scripting the black masculine body: Identity, discourse, and racial politics in popular media.* Albany, NY: SUNY Press.

Jackson II, R. L., & Dangerfield, C. (2002). Defining Black masculinity as cultural property: An identity negotiation paradigm. In L. Samovar & R. Porter (Eds.), *Intercultural communication: A reader* (10ᵗʰ ed.; pp. 120–130). Belmont, CA: Wadsworth.

Johnson, J. R., & Bhatt, A. J. (2003). Gendered and racialized identities and alliances in the classroom: Formations in/of resistive space. *Communication Education, 52*(3 & 4), 230–244.

Kaplan, C. (1996). *Questions of travel.* Durham, NC: Duke University Press.

Kendall, G., Skrbis, Z., & Woodward, I. (2008). Cosmopolitanism, the nation-state and imaginative realism. *Journal of Sociology, 44*(4), 401–417.

Kendall, G., Woodward, I., & Skrbis, Z. (2009). *The sociology of cosmopolitanism: Globalization, identity, culture and government.* Houndmills, Basingstoke, Hampshire: Palgrave MacMillan.

Kim, M.-S. (2002). *Non-western perspective on human communication.* Thousand Oaks, CA: Sage Publications.

Kim, Y. (2011). Female cosmopolitanism? Media talk and identity of transnational Asian women. *Communication Theory, 21*(3), 279–298.

Kim, Y. Y. (2007). Ideology, identity, and intercultural communication: An analysis of differing academic conceptions of cultural identity. *Journal of Intercultural Communication Research, 36*(3), 237–253.

Kim, Y. Y. (2008). Intercultural personhood: Globalization and a way of being. *International Journal of Intercultural Relations, 32,* 359–368.

Kirtsoglou, E. (2010). Conclusion: United in discontent. In D. Theodossopoulos & E. Kirtsoglou (Eds.), *United in discontent: Local responses to cosmopolitanism and globalization* (pp. 168–180). New York: Berghahn Books.

Kirtsoglou, E., & Theodossopoulos, D. (2010). Intimacies of anti-globalization: Imagining unhappy others as oneself in Greece. In D. Theodossopoulos & E. Kirtsoglou (Eds.), *United in discontent: Local responses to cosmopolitanism and globalization* (pp. 83–102). New York: Berghahn Books.

Kleingeld, P. (2003). Cosmopolitanism. *Stanford encyclopedia of philosophy.* Retrieved November 9, 2012, from http://plato.stanford.edu/entries/cosmopolitanism/

Kögler, H.-H. (2011). Hermeneutic cosmopolitanism, or: Toward a cosmopolitan public sphere. In M. Rovisco & M. Nowicka (Eds.), *The Ashgate research companion to cosmopolitanism* (pp. 225–242). Farnham, UK: Ashgate Publishing Limited.

Kothari, U. (2008). Global peddlers and local networks: Migrant cosmopolitanisms. *Environment and Planning D: Society and Space, 26,* 500–516.

Kraidy, M. (2002). Hybridity in cultural globalization. *Communication Theory, 12*(3), 316–339.

Kraidy, M. (2005). *Hybridity, or the cultural logic of globalization.* Philadelphia, PA: Temple University Press.

Kraidy, M., & Murphy, P. (2008). Shifting Geertz: Towards a theory of translocalism in global communication studies. *Communication Theory, 18,* 335–355.

Krishna, S. (2009). *Globalization and postcolonialism: Hegemony and resistance in the twenty-first century.* Lanham, MD: Rowman & Littlefield Publishers, Inc.

Kristeva, J. (1991). *Strangers to ourselves.* London: Harvester Wheatsheaf.

Kurusawa, F. (2011). Critical cosmopolitanism. In M. Rovisco & M. Nowicka (Eds.), *The Ashgate research companion to cosmopolitanism* (pp. 279–293). Burlington, VT: Ashgate Publishing Company.

Laclau, E. (1990). *New reflections on the revolution of our times.* London: Verso.

Laclau, E. (1992). Universalism, particularism and the question of identity. *October, 61,* 83–90.

Lammers, C. J. (1974). Localism, cosmopolitanism, and faculty response. *Sociology of Education, 47*, 129–158.

Lamont, M., & Aksartova, S. (2002). Ordinary cosmopolitanisms: Strategies for bridging racial boundaries among working-class men. *Theory, Culture & Society, 19*(4), 1–25.

Langsdorf, L. (2008). The reasonableness of bias. In K. Glenister Roberts & R. Arnett (Eds.), *Communication ethics: Between cosmopolitanism and provinciality* (pp. 241–261). New York: Peter Lang.

Leeds-Hurwitz, W. (1990). Notes in the history of intercultural communication: The foreign service institute and the mandate for intercultural training. *Quarterly Journal of Speech, 76*, 262–281.

Leeds-Hurwitz, W. (2010). Writing the intellectual history of intercultural communication. In T. K. Nakayama & R. T. Halualani (Eds.), *Handbook of critical intercultural communication* (pp. 21–33). Malden, MA: Blackwell.

Lingis, A. (1994). *The community of those who have nothing in common.* Bloomington, IN: Indiana University Press.

Lorde, A. (2007). *Sister outsider: Essays and speeches by Audre Lorde.* Berkeley, CA: Crossing Press. (Original work published 1984)

Lu, C. (2000). The one and many faces of cosmopolitanism. *The Journal of Political Philosophy, 8*(2), 244–267.

Malcomson, S. (1998). The varieties of cosmopolitan experience. In P. Cheah & B. Robbins (Eds.), *Cosmopolitics: Thinking and feeling beyond the nation* (pp. 233–245). Minneapolis, MN: University of Minnesota Press.

Malhotra, S., & Pérez, K. (2005). Belonging, bridges, and bodies. *NWSA Journal, 17*(2), 47–68.

Marcus, G. E. (1995). Ethnography in/of the world system: The emergence of multi-sited ethnography. *Annual Review of Anthropology, 24*, 95–117.

Martin, J. N., & Nakayama, T. K. (1999). Thinking dialectically about culture and communication. *Communication Theory, 9*(1), 1–25.

Martin, J. N., & Nakayama, T. K. (2010). Intercultural communication and dialectics revisited. In R. T. Halualani & T. K. Nakayama (Eds.), *Handbook of critical intercultural communication* (pp. 51–83). Malden, MA: Blackwell Publishing.

Martin, J. N., & Nakayama, T. K. (2012). *Intercultural communication in contexts* (6th ed.). New York: McGraw-Hill.

Matsunaga, M., & Torigoe, C. (2008). Looking at the Japan-Residing Korean identities through the eyes of the 'outsiders within:' Application and extension of co-cultural theory. *Western Journal of Communication, 72*(4), 349–373.

Mau, S., Mewes, J., & Zimmerman, A. (2008). Cosmopolitan attitudes through transnational social practices? *Global Networks, 8*(1), 1–24.

McConnell, M. (1996). Don't neglect the little platoons. In J. Cohen (Ed.), *For love of country: debating the limits of patriotism* (pp. 78–84). Boston, MA: Beacon Press.

McEwan, B., & Sobré-Denton, M. S. (2011). Virtual third cultures: Social media, cultural capital, and the creation of cultural spaces. *Intercultural New Media Forum: Journal of International and Intercultural Communication, 4*, 252–258.

Mendieta, E. (2009). From imperial to dialogical cosmopolitanism. *Ethics and Global Politics, 2*(3), 241–258.

Mendoza, S. L., Halualani, R. T., & Drzewiecka, J. A. (2002). Moving the discourse on identities in intercultural communication: Structure, culture, and resignifications. *Communication Quarterly, 50*(3 & 4), 312–327.

Meredith, P. (1998, July). *Hybridity in the third space: Rethinking bi-cultural politics in Aotearoa/New Zealand.* Paper presented at the Te Oru Rangahau Maori Research and Development Conference, Palmerston North, NZ.

Mignolo, W. (2000). *Local histories/global designs: Coloniality, subaltern knowledges, and border thinking*. Princeton, NJ: Princeton University Press.

Mignolo, W. (2002). The many faces of cosmo-polis: Border thinking and critical cosmopolitanism. In C. Breckenridge, H. Bhabha, S. Pollock, & D. Chakrabarty (Eds.), *Cosmopolitanism* (pp. 157–187). Durham, NC: Duke University Press.

Mignolo, W. (2010). Cosmopolitanism and the de-colonial option. *Studies in the Philosophy of Education, 29*, 111–127.

Mignolo, W. (2011). Border thinking, decolonial cosmopolitanism, and dialogues. In M. Rovisco & M. Nowicka (Eds.), *The Ashgate research companion to cosmopolitanism* (pp. 329–347). Burlington, VT: Ashgate Publishing Company.

Miike, Y. (2003). Beyond Eurocentrism in the intercultural field: Searching for an Asiacentric paradigm. In W. J. Starosta & G.-M. Chen (Eds.), *Ferment in the intercultural field: Axiology/value/praxis, International and Intercultural Communication Annual, XXVI* (pp. 243–276). Thousand Oaks, CA: Sage Publications.

Mitra, R. (2011). Outlining a dialogic framework of difference: How do Sri Lankan Tamil refugees in India constitute and negotiate difference? *Journal of International and Intercultural Communication, 4*(3), 181–200.

Moon, D. G. (1996). Concepts of 'culture': Implications for intercultural communication research. *Communication Quarterly, 44*, 70–84.

Moreman, S. T. (2011). Qualitative interviews of racial fluctuations: The 'how' of Latina/o–White hybrid identity. *Communication Theory, 21*(2), 197–216.

Morris, L. (2009). An emergent cosmopolitan paradigm? Asylum, welfare, and human rights. *British Journal of Sociology, 60*(2), 215–235.

Mota, A. (2012). Cosmopolitanism in Latin America. In G. Delanty (Ed.), *Routledge handbook of cosmopolitanism studies* (pp. 491–503). Abingdon, Oxon: Routledge.

Mumby, D. (1993). Critical organizational communication studies: The next ten years. *Communication Monographs, 60*(1), 18–25.

Muñoz, J. E. (1999). *Disidentifications*. Minneapolis, MN: University of Minnesota Press.

Nakayama, T. K., & Halualani, R. (2010). Conclusion. In T. K. Nakayama & R. T. Halualani (Eds.), *The handbook of critical intercultural communication* (pp. 595–600). Malden, MA: Wiley-Blackwell.

Nakayama, T. K., & Krizek, R. (1995). Whiteness: A strategic rhetoric. *Quarterly Journal of Speech, 81*, 291–309.

Nava, M. (2007). *Visceral cosmopolitanism: Gender, culture and the normalization of difference*. New York: Berg.

NBC's edit of Olympic opening ceremony draws ire. (2012, July 30). *National Public Radio, All things Considered*. Retrieved August 4, 2012, from http://www.npr.org/2012/07/30/157613411/nbcs-edit-of-olympics-opening-ceremony-draws-ire

Nederveen Pieterse, J. (2006). Emancipatory cosmopolitanism: Towards an agenda. *Development and Change, 37*(6), 1247–1257.

Nederveen Pieterse, J. (2009). *Globalization and culture: Global mélange*. Lanham, MD: Rowman & Littlefield Publishers, Inc.

Norton, B. (2001). Non-participation, imagined communities and the language classroom. In M. Breen (Ed.), *Learner contributions to language learning* (pp. 25–43). London: Longman.

Nowicka, M., & Rovisco, M. (2009). Introduction: Making sense of cosmopolitanism. In M. Nowicka & M. Rovisco (Eds.), *Cosmopolitanism in practice* (pp. 1–16). Surrey, UK: Ashgate Publishing.

Nussbaum, M. (1994). Patriotism and cosmopolitanism. *Boston Review, 19*(5), 3–34.

Nussbaum, M. (1996). Patriotism and cosmopolitanism. In J. Cohen (Ed.), *For love of country: Debating the limits of patriotism* (pp. 2–17). Boston, MA: Beacon Press.

Nussbaum, M. (2002). Kant and Stoic cosmopolitanism. *Journal of Political Philosophy*, 5(1), 1–25.

Ong, A. (1999). *Flexible citizenship: The cultural logics of transnationality*. Durham, NC: Duke University Publishing.

Ono, K. (1998). Problematizing 'nation' in intercultural communication research. In D. Tanno & A. González (Eds.), *Communication and identity across cultures, International and Intercultural Communication Annual, XXI* (pp. 193–202). Thousand Oaks, CA: Sage Publications.

Ono, K. (2010). Reflections on 'Problematizing "nation" in intercultural communication research.' In T. K. Nakayama & R. T. Halualani (Eds.), *The handbook of critical intercultural communication* (pp. 84–97). Malden, MA: Wiley-Blackwell.

Orbe, M. P. (1998). *Constructing co-cultural theory: An explication of culture, power, and communication*. Thousand Oaks, CA: Sage Publications.

Ossewaarde, M. (2007). Cosmopolitanism and the society of strangers. *Current Sociology*, 55(3), 367–388.

Papastephanou, M. (2002). Arrows not yet fired: Cultivating cosmopolitanism through education. *Journal of Philosophy of Education*, 36(1), 69–86.

Parker, D. (2003). Diaspora, dissidence and the dangers of cosmopolitanism. *Asian Studies Review*, 27(2), 155–179.

Parry, J. (2008). Cosmopolitan values in a central Indian steel town. In P. Werbner (Ed.), *Anthropology and the new cosmopolitanism: Rooted, feminist, and vernacular perspectives* (pp. 325–343). New York: Berg.

Pearson-Evans, A., & Leahy, A. (2007). Introduction. In A. Pearson-Evans & A. Leahy (Eds.), *Intercultural spaces: Language, culture, identity* (pp. xv–xx). New York: Peter Lang.

Pérez, K., & Goltz, D. B. (2010). Treading across Lines in the Sand: Performing bodies in coalitional subjectivity. *Text and Performance Quarterly*, 30(3), 247–268.

Peters, J. D. (1999). *Speaking into the air: A history of the idea of communication*. Chicago: University of Chicago Press.

Peterson, M. (2012). *Sound, space and the city: Civic performance in downtown Los Angeles*. Philadelphia, PA: University of Pennsylvania Press.

Petre, J. (2010, April). *Cosmopolitanism and 'the space of communicative praxis.'* Paper presented at Central States Communication Association Conference, Cincinnati, OH.

Pichler, F. (2008). How real is cosmopolitanism in Europe? *Sociology, 42*, 1107–1126.

Pollock, S. (2002). Cosmopolitan and vernacular in history. In C. Breckenridge, H. Bhabha, S. Pollock, & D. Chakrabarty (Eds.), *Cosmopolitanism* (pp. 15–53). Durham, NC: Duke University Press.

Pollock, S., Bhabha, H., Breckenridge, C., & Chakrabarty, D. (2002). Cosmopolitanisms. In C. Breckenridge, H. Bhabha, S. Pollock, & D. Chakrabarty (Eds.), *Cosmopolitanism* (pp. 1–14). Durham, NC: Duke University Press.

Poston, W. S. C. (1990). The biracial identity development model: A needed addition. *Journal of Counseling and Development*, 69, 152–155.

Prato, G. (2009). Introduction—beyond multiculturalism: Anthropology at the intersections between the local, the national, and the global. In G. Prato (Ed.), *Beyond multiculturalism: Views from anthropology* (pp. 1–19). Burlington, VT: Ashgate Publishing Company.

Pratt, M. L. (1992). *Imperial eyes: Travel writing and transculturation*. London: Routledge.

Putnam, L., Jahn, J., & Baker, J. (2011). Intersecting difference: A dialectical perspective. In D. Mumby (Ed.), *Reframing difference in organizational communication studies: Research, pedagogy, practice* (pp. 31–53). Los Angeles: Sage Publications.

Rapport, N. (2007). An outline for cosmopolitan study: Reclaiming the human through introspection. *Current Anthropology, 48*(2), 257–283.

Reardon, B. A., & Snauwaert, D. T. (2011). Reflective pedagogy, cosmopolitanism, and critical peace education for political efficacy: A discussion of Betty A. Reardon's assessment of the field. *Journal of Peace Education and Social Justice, 5*(1), 1–14.

Reimers, F. (2010). Learning for global competency. In J. E. Cohen & M. B. Malin (Eds.), *International perspectives on the goals of universal basic and secondary education* (pp. 183–202). New York: Routledge

Ritzer, G. (2007). Introduction. In G. Ritzer (Ed.), *The Blackwell companion to globalization* (pp. 1–13). Malden, MA: Blackwell Publishing.

Robbins, B. (1998). Introduction Part I: Actually existing cosmopolitanism. In P. Cheah & B. Robbins (Eds.), *Cosmopolitics: Thinking and feeling beyond the nation* (pp. 1–19). Minneapolis, MN: University of Minnesota Press.

Roberts, K. G., & Arnett, R. C. (Eds.). (2008). *Communication ethics: Between cosmopolitanism and provinciality.* New York: Peter Lang.

Robertson, R., & Khondker, H. H. (1998). Discourses of globalization: Preliminary considerations. *International Sociology, 13*(1), 25–40.

Robinson, K. (2008). Islamic cosmopolitics, human rights and anti-violence strategies in Indonesia. In P. Werbner (Ed.), *Anthropology and the new cosmopolitanism: Rooted, feminist, and vernacular perspectives* (pp. 111–133). New York: Berg.

Rodriguez, A. (2006). A story from somewhere: Cathedrals, communication, and the search for possibility. In M. P. Orbe, B. J. Allen, & L. A. Flores (Eds.), *The same and different: Acknowledging the diversity within and between cultural groups, International and Intercultural Communication Annual, XXIX* (pp. 4–21). Washington, DC: National Communication Association.

Rodriguez, A., & Chawla, D. (2010). *Intercultural communication: An ecological approach.* Dubuque, IA: Kendall Hunt.

Rogers, E. (1999). Georg Simmel's concept of the stranger and intercultural communication research. *Communication Theory, 9*(1), 58–74.

Rosenau, J. (2004). Emergent space, new places, and old faces: Proliferating identities in a globalizing world. In J. Friedman & S. Randeria (Eds.), *Worlds on the move: Globalization, migration, and cultural security* (pp. 23–62). New York and London: I. B. Tauris in association with the Toda Institute for Global Peace and Policy Research.

Roudometof, V. (2005). Transnationalism, cosmopolitanism, and glocalization. *Current Sociology, 53*(1), 113–135.

Rovisco, M., & Nowicka, M. (2011). Introduction. In M. Rovisco & M. Nowicka (Eds.), *The Ashgate research companion to cosmopolitanism* (pp. 1–14). Farnham, UK: Ashgate Publishing Limited.

Ruiz, A. (1990). Ethnic identity: Crisis and resolution. *Journal of Multicultural Counseling, 18*, 29–40.

Rumford, C. (2012). Bordering and connectivity: Cosmopolitan opportunities. In G. Delanty (Ed.), *Routledge handbook of cosmopolitanism studies* (pp. 245–253). Abingdon, Oxon: Routledge.

Said, E. (1978). *Orientalism.* London: Routledge and Kegan Paul.

Said, E. (1994). *Culture and imperialism.* New York: Vintage Books.

Sampson, D., & Smith, H. (1957). A scale to measure world-minded attitudes. *Journal of Social Psychology, 45*, 99–106.

Sánchez-Flores, M. J. (2010). *Cosmopolitan liberalism: Expanding the boundaries of the individual.* New York: Palgrave Macmillan

Sandoval, C. (2000). *Methodology of the oppressed*. Minneapolis, MN: University of Minnesota Press.

Sarup, M. (1996). *Identity, culture and the postmodern world*. Edinburgh: Edinburgh University Press.

Schattle, H. (2008). Education for global citizenship: Illustrations of ideological pluralism and adaptation. *Journal of Political Ideologies*, 13(1), 73–94.

Schuetz, A. (1944). The stranger: An essay in social psychology. *The American Journal of Sociology*, 49(6), 499–507.

Sen, A. (1996). Humanity and citizenship. In J. Cohen (Ed.), *For love of country: Debating the limits of patriotism* (pp. 111–118). Boston, MA: Beacon Press.

Sheller, M., & Urry, J. (2006). The new mobilities paradigm. *Environment and Planning A*, 38, 207–226.

Shepherd, G. (2006). Transcendence. In G. Shepherd, J. St. John, & T. Striphas (Eds.), *Communication as . . . Perspectives on theory* (pp. 22–30). Thousand Oaks, CA: Sage Publications.

Shin, C., & Jackson II, R. L. (2003). A review of identity research in communication theory. In W. Starosta & G.-M. Chen (Eds.), *Ferment in the intercultural field: Axiology/value/praxis, International and Intercultural Communication Annual, XXVI* (pp. 211–240). Thousand Oaks, CA: Sage Publications.

Shome, R. (2003). Space matters: The power and practice of space. *Communication Theory*, 13, 39–56.

Shome, R. (2010). Internationalizing critical race communication studies: Transnationality, space and affect. In T. K. Nakayama & R. T. Halualani (Eds.), *The handbook of critical intercultural communication* (pp. 149–170). Malden, MA: Wiley-Blackwell.

Shome, R., & Hegde, R. S. (2002). Postcolonial approaches to communication: Charting the terrain, engaging the intersections. *Communication Theory*, 12(3), 249–270.

Skrbis, Z., & Woodward, I. (2011). Cosmopolitan openness. In M. Rovisco & M. Nowicka (Eds.), *The Ashgate research companion to cosmopolitanism* (pp. 52–68). Farnham, UK: Ashgate Publishing Limited.

Sobré-Denton, M. S. (2011). The emergence of cosmopolitan group cultures and its implications for cultural transition: A case study of an international student support group. *International Journal of Intercultural Relations*, 35(1), 79–91.

Sorrells, K. (2013). *Intercultural communication: Globalization and social justice*. Los Angeles: Sage Publications.

Sparrow, L. M. (2008). Beyond multicultural man: Complexities of identity. In M. K. Asante, Y. Miike, & J. Yin (Eds.), *The global intercultural communication reader* (pp. 239–261). New York: Routledge.

Stade, R. (2007). Cosmopolitans and cosmopolitanism in anthropology. *Social Anthropology*, 15(2), 226–229.

Starkey, H. (2007). Language education, identities and citizenship: Developing cosmopolitan perspectives. *Language and Intercultural Communication*, 7(1), 56–71.

Starosta, W. (1991, May). *Third culture building: Chronological development and the role of third parties*. Paper presented at the annual meeting of the International Communication Association, Chicago, IL.

Stewart, J. (2008). Cosmopolitan communication ethics understanding and action. In K. Glenister Roberts & R. Arnett (Eds.), *Communication ethics: Between cosmopolitanism and provinciality* (pp. 105–119). New York: Peter Lang.

Stråth, B. (2012). World history and cosmopolitanism. In G. Delanty (Ed.), *Routledge handbook of cosmopolitanism studies* (pp. 72–84). Abingdon, Oxon: Routledge.

Strathern, A., & Stewart, P. J. (2010). Shifting centres, tense peripheries: Indigenous cosmopolitanism. In D. Theodossopoulos & E. Kirtsoglou (Eds.), *United in discontent: Local responses to cosmopolitanism and globalization* (pp. 20–44). New York: Berghahn Books.

Szerszynski, B., & Urry, J. (2002). Cultures of cosmopolitanism. *Sociological Review, 50*(4), 461–481.

Szerszynski, B., & Urry, J. (2006). Visuality, mobility and the cosmopolitan: Inhabiting the world from afar. *British Journal of Sociology, 57*(1), 113–131.

Tanno, D. V., & Jandt, F. E. (1993). Redefining the 'other' in multicultural research. *Howard Journal of Communications, 5*, 378–384.

Taylor, C. (1996). Why democracy needs patriotism. In J. Cohen (Ed.), *For love of country: Debating the limits of patriotism* (pp. 119–121). Boston, MA: Beacon Press.

Tervalon, M., & Murray-García, J. (1997). Cultural humility versus cultural competence: A critical distinction in defining physician training outcomes in multicultural education. *Journal of Health Care for the Poor and Underserved, 9*(2), 117–125.

Theodossopoulos, D. (2010). Introduction. In D. Theodossopoulos & E. Kirtsoglou (Eds.), *United in discontent: Local responses to cosmopolitanism and globalization* (pp. 1–19). New York: Berghahn Books.

Theodossopoulos, D., & Kirtsoglou, E. (Eds.). (2010). *United in discontent: Local responses to cosmopolitanism and globalization.* New York: Berghahn Books.

Thomas, N. (1992). The inversion of tradition. *American Ethnologist, 19*(2), 213–232.

Ting-Toomey, S. (1993). Communicative resourcefulness: An identity negotiation perspective. In R. Wiseman & J. Koester (Eds.), *Intercultural communication competence* (pp. 21–111). Newbury Park, CA: Sage Publications.

Ting-Toomey, S. (1999). *Communicating across cultures.* New York: Guilford.

Ting-Toomey, S. (2005). Identity negotiation theory: Crossing cultural boundaries. In W. B. Gudykunst (Ed.), *Theorizing about intercultural communication* (pp. 211–234). Thousand Oaks, CA: Sage Publications.

Tomlinson, J. (1999). *Globalization and culture.* Chicago: University of Chicago Press.

Tomlinson, J. (2007). Cultural globalization. In G. Ritzer (Ed.), *The Blackwell companion to globalization* (pp. 352–366). Malden, MA: Blackwell Publishing.

Toyosaki, S. (2012). Practice-oriented autoethnography: Performing critical selfhood. In N. Bardhan & M. P. Orbe (Eds.), *Identity research in intercultural communication: Reflections and future directions* (pp. 239–251). Lanham, MD: Lexington Books.

Useem, J., Donoghue, J. D., & Useem, R. H. (1963). Men in the middle of the third-culture. *Human Organization, 22*(33), 129–144.

Useem, R. H., & Downie, R. D. (1976). Third-culture kids. *Today's Education: The Journal of the National Education Association, 65*(3), 103–105.

Valls, A. T. I. (2010). Escaping the 'modern' excesses of Japanese life: Critical voices in Japanese rural cosmopolitanism. In D. Theodossopoulos & E. Kirtsoglou (Eds.), *United in discontent: Local responses to cosmopolitanism and globalization* (pp. 103–123). New York: Berghahn Books.

van Hooft, S. (2009). *Cosmopolitanism: A philosophy for global ethics.* Montreal & Kingston: McGill-Queen's University Press.

Vertovec, S., & Cohen, R. (2002). Introduction. In S. Vertovec & R. Cohen (Eds.), *Conceiving cosmopolitanism* (pp. 1–22). Oxford: Oxford University Press.

Waks, L. J. (2009). Reason and culture in cosmopolitan education. *Educational Theory, 59*, 589–605.

Walsh, J. (1973). *Intercultural education in the communication of man.* Honolulu, HI: The University of Hawaii Press.

Wardle, H. (2000). *An ethnography of cosmopolitanism in Kingston, Jamaica.* London: Edward Millen Press.

Warren, J. T. (2003). *Performing purity: Whiteness, pedagogy, and the reconstitution of power.* New York: Peter Lang.

Warren, J. T. (2008). Performing difference: Repetition in context. *Journal of International and Intercultural Communication, 1*(4), 290–308.

Werbner, P. (2008). Introduction. In P. Werbner (Ed.), *Anthropology and the new cosmopolitanism: Rooted, feminist, and vernacular perspectives* (pp. 1–29). New York: Berg.

Werbner, P. (2012). Anthropology and the new ethical cosmopolitanism. In G. Delanty (Ed.), *Routledge handbook of cosmopolitanism studies* (pp. 153–164). Abingdon, Oxon: Routledge.

Wilson, R. (1998). A new cosmopolitanism is in the air: Some dialectical twists and turns. In P. Cheah & B. Robbins (Eds.), *Cosmopolitics: Thinking and feeling beyond the nation* (pp. 351–361). Minneapolis, MN: University of Minnesota Press.

Witteborn, S. (2007). The situated expression of Arab collective identities in the United States. *Journal of Communication, 57,* 556–575.

Wolff, K. H. (Trans. & Ed.). (1950). *The sociology of Georg Simmel.* Glencoe, IL: The Free Press.

Wood, A. (1998). Kant's project for perpetual peace. In P. Cheah & B. Robbins (Eds.), *Cosmopolitics: Thinking and feeling beyond the nation* (pp. 59–76). Minneapolis, MN: University of Minnesota Press.

Woodin, J. (2010). Key themes in intercultural communication pedagogy. *Language Teaching, 43*(2), 232–235.

Woodward, I., Skrbis, Z., & Bean, C. (2008). Attitudes towards globalization and cosmopolitanism: Cultural diversity, personal consumption and the national economy. *The British Journal of Sociology, 59*(2), 207–226.

Yep, G. (2002). My three cultures. In J. N. Martin, T. K. Nakayama, & L. Flores (Eds.), *Readings in intercultural communication* (2nd ed.; pp. 60–66). Boston: McGraw Hill.

Yoshida, T. (1981). The stranger as god: The place of the outsider in Japanese folk religion. *Ethnology, 20*(2), 87–99.

Young, R. J. C. (1995). *Colonial desire: Hybridity in theory, culture and race.* London: Routledge.

Yum, J. O. (1988). The impact of Confucianism on interpersonal relationships and communication patterns in East Asia. *Communication Monographs, 55,* 374–388.

Index